Tales of a Western Mountaineer

Tales of a Western Mountaineer

C.E. RUSK

With a Portrait of C. E. Rusk

BY DARRYL LLOYD

THE MOUNTAINEERS
Seattle

THE MOUNTAINEERS . . . Organized 1906 " . . . to explore, study, preserve and enjoy the natural beauty of Northwest America . . . "

Published simultaneously in Canada by Mountain Craft, P.O. Box 5232,
Vancouver, B.C. V6B 4B3

Printed in the United States of America

Library of Congress No. 78-54427
ISBN No. 0-916890-62-7

Photo overlays by Gary Rands

PUBLISHER'S NOTE

BECAUSE they are such dominant landmarks, visible as they are from both sides of the Cascade Range in Washington and Oregon, the volcanic cones of Adams, St. Helens, Hood, Rainier, Glacier and Baker have been a source of fascination and superstition to man for several centuries. Born too late to be the first to set foot on these summits, Claude Ewing Rusk nonetheless made a significant contribution to their exploration and history. He was among the earliest to respond to their challenges, in the same way as today's climbers . . . climbing not just to reach the summit, but to do so by untried routes of unknown difficulties. Rusk's first-hand account of his early ascents, *Tales of a Western Mountaineer*, provided both information and inspiration to generations of climbers following its original publication in 1924. With tens of thousands now climbing these peaks each year, it is our hope that by again making these *Tales* available, their spirit will inspire climbers and mountain watchers of today and tomorrow.

In preparing this edition, we are grateful for the assistance of the following: The several climbers who suggested *Tales* as deserving of reprinting. Darryl Lloyd, who has collected a wealth of material about Rusk and literally followed in his footsteps, and who spent hours tracking down old photos and correspondence to provide a far more complete perspective of the author than Rusk himself chose to reveal. Rusk's only son, Rodney, now living in retirement in California, who sent family photos and correspondence. Maurice Barnes, a nonagenarian now living in Portland, who provided prints of many of the photos used in the original edition. Jack Whitnall, Yakima, who enhanced the photos with his processing expertise. Austin Post of the U.S. Geological Survey, Tacoma, who provided aerial photographs, and Gary Rands, whose artwork shows Rusk's routes on the various mountains. Dee Molenaar, whose two original maps locate the action. Ray Smutek, who contributed his considerable knowledge of Rusk. Susan Sommerman, Connie Pious, Donna DeShazo and others of The Mountaineers' Literary Fund Committee who brought the pieces together.

The publishers plan to continue to make such historic books more widely available. Suggestions are welcome at The Mountaineers, 719 Pike St., Seattle, WA 98101.

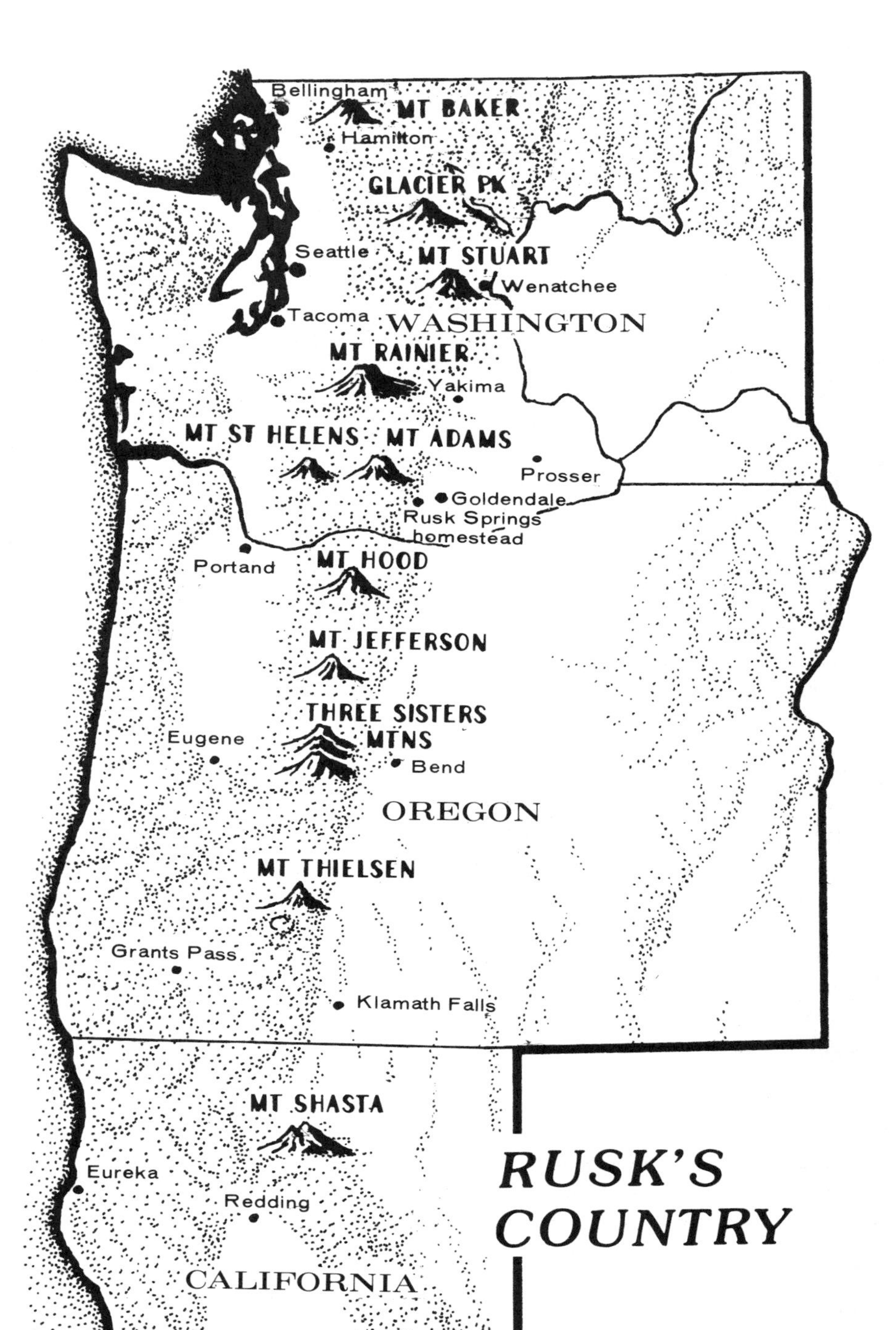

Bellingham
MT BAKER
Hamilton
GLACIER PK
Seattle
MT STUART
Wenatchee
Tacoma
WASHINGTON
MT RAINIER
Yakima
MT ST HELENS
MT ADAMS
Prosser
Goldendale
Rusk Springs
homestead
Portand
MT HOOD
MT JEFFERSON
THREE SISTERS
MTNS
Eugene
Bend
OREGON
MT THIELSEN
Grants Pass
Klamath Falls
MT SHASTA
Eureka
Redding
CALIFORNIA
RUSK'S
COUNTRY

A PORTRAIT OF C. E. RUSK

CLAUDE Ewing Rusk was a legend in his own time. He was a remarkably gifted, one of a kind mountain man. He was born with a passion for mountain exploration, and he developed a keen sense of perspective while mastering the art of writing. It was a rare mixture, and the result is a solid imprint on the history of Northwest mountaineering; C.E. Rusk will long be remembered for it.

Tales of a Western Mountaineer spans nearly half a century, from 1874 to 1923. The narrative is both a chronicle of an era and an autobiography of sorts. We follow C.E. Rusk from the time he was a boy pioneering the wilds of untamed territory to his years as a "humble but persistent" gentleman caught up in the age of "aerial flight." He led a rich and adventurous life, and much of it was devoted to one mountain: his loyalty to Mount Adams and the love story he writes are perhaps unmatched in mountaineering literature.

Not all of Rusk's mountaineering experiences are included in these *Tales*, although most of his favorite stories are here. He records events and the people involved, sometimes dutifully, but he carefully avoids telling us about his life and times away from the mountains. The truth is that Rusk occupied himself with an amazing variety of pursuits, and he seemed to be constantly on the move. At one time or another, he was a school teacher, newspaper editor, lawyer, gold miner, conservationist, justice of the peace, and an author of considerable talent and output.

Claude Rusk was born in Illinois in 1871. His parents, James A. and Josie (Maxwell) Rusk, moved to the Washington Territory in the fall of 1874, and settled in eastern Klickitat County, at a place known then as "Wood Gulch." There his sister Leah was born, and a few years later his father built the "Happy Home" stage station near what is now the community of Warwick, at the foot of the Columbia hills.

In 1887, when young Claude was 15, the family homesteaded in a log cabin on the wild Klickitat River. The site, called Wetemis Soda Springs, became known as Rusk Springs, where the family established a primitive summer resort. Today a modern logging road violates this beautiful sanctuary, and erases any trace of the original homestead.

Rusk's school teaching career began in the Camas Prairie (Glenwood) when he was 17. Later he taught at the Crossroads School outside of Goldendale, Washington. But the urge to write soon led him into newspaper work, and in 1892, at 21 years of age, he became editor of the Goldendale Courier. He continued that for only a year, then switched back to teaching; at the same time he studied law in the office of Brooks and Snover. He also fell in love with a beautiful Miss Rachel Gilmore, daughter of pioneer residents, and was married on October 30, 1898.

In 1902, Rusk became a founding member of the prestigious American Alpine Club. The same year he was admitted to the Washington State Bar. By then everyone knew that Rusk was the greatest living authority on Mount Adams. But he had climbed on few other mountains, and he obviously was eager for new scenery. So, in 1903, another vast mountain range became a part of Rusk's life. He and his plucky wife moved to Hamilton, on the Skagit River in northern Washington, and Mount Baker, a short distance away, became his first new challenge in 14 years.

The Rusks packed up all their belongings a year or so later, and rode their horses across the Cascade Range to Lake Chelan. This must have been quite a trip, but we know little about it. They bought a place on the lake, which could be reached only by horse or steamer, and in 1905 their only son, Rodney, was born. C.E. Rusk practiced law in the town of Chelan until his departure for Mount McKinley in 1910.

By then Rusk had gained the reputation of being "one of the most expert and daring mountaineers in the West."[1] In newspaper articles, he was described as " . . . in his prime, thirty-eight years of age, with his best work still before him. In build he is tough and wiry, light in weight, with firm, well-trained muscles. In all his mountaineering he has never encountered a difficulty that he did not conquer."[2] Asahel Curtis, at the time a celebrated climber-photographer from Seattle, declared that "Rusk has no superior as a mountaineer."[3]

Perhaps it should be pointed out that during this so-called "heroic age," climbers of the likes of Rusk were few and far between. Even so, there is little doubt that he was a climber of a different mold. Why and how so? Certainly, his self-reliant pioneering background set him apart from the large numbers of city dwellers who were discovering the "sport." Although Rusk did take part (in a leadership role) in a few herd assaults on the standard "safe" routes, he was usually at his best when he climbed alone, or with one strong campanion. We shall

1. Gertrude Metcalfe, *Pacific Monthly,* Sept. 1910, p. 259.
2. *Portland Oregonian,* April 24, 1910.
3. From Associated Press Dispatch, July 28, 1910.

see later how truly "alone" he was on his Alaskan ventures.

Rusk was among the first, I think, to break from the traditional "no risk" attitude towards climbing. He not only recognized that risk was inherent, but that it was *essential* to the sport. As a perfect illustration, Rusk writes of an incident where rockfall was imminent, " . . . a danger that no skill could avoid, a peril that must be met by the mountaineer if he would accomplish things worthwhile in mountaineering."

The thought of a first ascent on a difficult route delighted Rusk, yet he was extremely cautious at times, and often turned back with companions of lesser ability or lacking in the necessary fortitude. On one such occasion, Rusk confides in his *Tales*: "I was reluctant to lead any man into danger he did not fully understand."

Besides being a fulfillment of a 20-year dream, Rusk's "conquest of the Great East Side" of Mount Adams was one of the most significant climbs of the era. According to Fred Beckey, it was "an outstanding achievement in courage," and that says a lot. The ascent was long regarded as "impossible," and were it not for Rusk's persistence and perseverance, it is quite likely that the east side would not have been climbed for at least another quarter of a century. Tenacity of purpose was definitely one of Rusk's stronger traits.

Still, we know little about his personal character. Readers of *Tales of a Western Mountaineer* may be left wondering: just what sort of fellow was C.E. Rusk, really? I think he firmly believed that "the best proof of a man's good character is the fact that people do not talk about him." (Rusk wrote this about a cantankerous horse: he preferred horses to be quiet and well-behaved!)

Maurice Barnes, who remembers him mainly from a 1921 outing, recalls that Rusk was "a hard man to become close to. He was rather reserved, a little distant. I don't even know his first name. We always called him 'C.E.'"[4] Others who knew Rusk have related similar impressions. He was very much a solitary individual, quiet, thoughtful, and not inclined toward frivolous friendships. He was kind and generous, and he loved his family dearly.

His son, Rodney L. Rusk, who lives today in San Diego, had this to say about his father: "My father was the most honest man I've ever known. He always did what was ethical, rather than what could make him the most money. He was poor most of his life, you know. Gave much of his money to his folks. And he had a lot of guts, [was] a real

4. Maurice H. Barnes, personal communication, Feb. 22, 1978.

fighter for what he believed was right, especially in his later years."[5]

In his writings, Rusk demonstrates that while he may have been a bit stiff and formal at times, he also had a good sense of humor (remember Miss Blank?). And alone with his thoughts at the "Camp of the Stars," Rusk expresses a powerful feeling of humility:

> Here was I, alone and helpless, a mere atom, surrounded by the tremendous forces of nature . . . and compared with the life of the mountain my life was but a snuff of a candle — compared with the bulk of the mountain my frame was but a microscopic molecule.

C.E. Rusk became nationally known in 1910, when he led a Mazama expedition to Mount McKinley. It was a time when the highest point in North America was the subject of furious controversy and speculation. One objective of the expedition, therefore, besides a bid for the top, was to seek the truth about the various first ascent claims. While Rusk was forced to turn back well short of his goal, he determined independently and without a doubt that the famous Dr. Frederick Cook's claim was fraudulent.[6]

Rusk's effort is well documented, appearing as a lengthy series of articles he wrote for journals and newspapers from Portland to New York. What has never appeared publicly, however, is a sad and near-tragic story about the personalities involved. The story should be told now because it gives dramatic testimony to Rusk's quiet courage and unfailing resolve.

Rusk's small party consisted of only three other men besides himself, and two were hardly what you'd call mountaineers. Even before the real work began, on the boat trip to Talkeetna, a serious rift was developing in Rusk's team.[7] Moreover, another party was attempting the same route, and a feeling of competition existed, whether it was admitted or not.

The long march up Ruth Glacier took incredible work. A ton of supplies had to be hauled, which meant five miles of traveling for every mile of advance. The split deepened between Rusk and the three other men, and eventually, somewhere on the glacier, an attempt was made on Rusk's life! The exact details will probably never be known, but a letter written years later by Mrs. Rachel Rusk documents a

5. Rodney L. Rusk, personal communication, March 23, 1978.
6. C.E. Rusk, "On the Trail of Dr. Cook," *Pacific Monthly*, Oct. 1910, also in *Mazama*, December, 1945, pp. 8-31.
7. C.H. Sholes, personal letter to C.E. Rusk, June 20, 1910.

version of the incident:[8]

> . . . when you look at the photo of Mr. Rusk in a hole beside a big rock, know that in another such situation one member of his party, at the instigation of the other members, struck his head with a snow shoe. He was only stunned and the man, who was no *killer*, lacked what it took to strike him again. He fell upon his knees and implored pardon for the act. The other members of that unsuccessful expedition had tried in vain to persuade Mr. Rusk to leave the mountain and hunt for big game until time for their return to the outside. Of course they continued on and Mr. Rusk excused the *scoundrelly* act by saying they actually *feared the silence*. . . . It was two or three years after it happened that my husband told me. I have always greatly admired the courage required to continue the trip with men who would act with such purpose.

Rodney Rusk, who was only five years old at the time, recalls his father talking about the incident long after it happened. Rodney's version goes something like this:[9]

> One of the party shoved my father into a crevasse, and left him there to die. But he got out somehow, and the fellow begged him for forgiveness. Another reached into his sleeping bag one night while he was sleeping, attempting to steal the gold coins (expedition funds), but my father woke up and caught him. The three were pretty crooked guys. They stayed with my father because they didn't know how to get out on their own.

C.E. Rusk, of course, would not have wanted this unfortunate story to leak out. Mount McKinley did not need another scandal! In any event, the party continued on, despite the problems. After a month on Ruth Glacier, it became evident that supplies would be insufficient for the ascent, so one member headed back to Base Camp. Several more weeks of climbing, and "hunger stared us in the face," as Rusk wrote. Rusk was forced to turn homeward having reached only the foot of the great mountain he so desperately wanted to climb.

Following his return from Mount McKinley, Rusk helped his parents on their gold mine in Grants Pass, Oregon. The "Lucky Spot" mine was operated in the summer and fall, and the income it brought was barely enough to last the family through the winter.

In 1912, Rusk moved to the Yakima Valley and became editor of the Benton Independent, published in Prosser. Once again, however, the newspaper business was shortlived. The following year Rusk resumed the practice of law, and in 1915 he was appointed to a

8. Rachel Rusk, personal letter to Donald Onthank, Sept. 26, 1950.
9. Rodney L. Rusk, personal communication, Feb. 22, 1978.

four-year term as receiver of the U.S. Land Office in Yakima.

"Mr. Rusk gives his political allegiance to the Democratic party," wrote Professor W.D. Lyman in 1919, "but he has never been a politician in the sense of seeking office."[10] (In a county full of Republicans, Rusk might very well have been the first to admit that he was a Democrat!)

During these years, Rusk became a vocal conservationist. He was a great admirer of Teddy Roosevelt, and he appealed for the preservation of the mountain he loved most. Rusk felt that it was high time for Mount Adams, "so long neglected, to be accorded the recognition it deserves." He was distressed by the fact that the alpine meadows and forests were being ravaged by sheep, cattle, and fire. So he headed a local campaign to set aside the mountain as a National Park, to be called the "Yakima National Park." Rusk's own efforts on this behalf culminated in 1919 when he wrote a 26-page booklet entitled, *Mount Adams – Towering Sentinel of the Lower Columbia Basin.*[11]

So that "the mountain's grandeur could be accessible to the world," a branch road was proposed to Avalanche Valley, Rusk's "veritable mountain paradise." Fortunately, though, the road was never built. That lovely valley today is almost as remote as it was in Rusk's time, and is delightfully free of human hordes.

In 1920, Rusk became co-founder and first president of the Cascadians, a mountaineering club still thriving in Yakima. His closest friendships were formed during these years with fellow members of the club. Rusk generated an enthusiasm for making difficult climbs, and the tradition has carried on to this day amongst the young and very active climbers in the area.

In the year that his father died, 1923, C.E. Rusk moved back to Grants Pass, Oregon. There he set up his own law practice, and wrote *Tales of a Western Mountaineer.*

Rusk was eventually appointed justice of the peace of Josephine County. According to friends in Grants Pass, he was known to be "pretty stern." Kenn Carrell remembers Rusk well: "He was one hell of a prohibitionist! If someone got caught bootlegging and was guilty of it, he got the whole rap. Once the remains of a still were found on Rusk's property (on Olympia Creek), but Rusk never did find out who

10. W.D. Lyman, *History of the Yakima Valley of Washington,* Vol II, S.J. Clarke Publ. Co., 1919 p. 741.
11. C.E. Rusk, *Mount Adams – Towering Sentinel of the Lower Columbia Basin* — Reasons for its Preservation & Maintenance as a National Park, Yakima Commercial Club, 1919, 26 p.

it belonged to."[12]

Following publication of *Tales*, Rusk wrote another book entitled *Timberline Campfires*, a collection of essays and short stories. Except for one chapter, which appeared in the 1946 *American Alpine Journal* ("The Wonderful Story of Abe Lincoln"), the manuscript was never published.[13] At this writing, a search is underway for the missing manuscript, last seen in Grants Pass about 1950.

On many a weekend, Rusk would walk 14 miles from his home in Grants Pass to his father's "Lucky Spot" mine, spend Sundays doing assessment work, and then walk 14 miles back home. Occasionally, he would make a climb of one of the local mountains, such as Mount Thielsen. Foremost on his mind, however, was Alaska. He tried to promote another expedition to Mount McKinley, but could not get the necessary financial backing.

Instead, he planned a trip to 18,000-foot Mount St. Elias. Certain members of the Mazamas and Cascadians had promised to go along, but for one reason or another, everyone backed out. In the summer of 1930, at the age of 58, Rusk headed *alone* for once-climbed Mount St. Elias! When he got to Yakutat, he hired a local native boy to go with him. And he arranged a launch to take the two of them to the head of the bay, where the mountain could be approached.

Bad luck again plagued Rusk. Not long after they were dropped off, he discovered that they were surrounded by deep glacial meltwaters. He and the boy were, in fact, stuck on an island, with no hope of continuing their journey. They had no choice but to wait for the return of the launch, which was due to pick them up weeks later. It must have been a very demoralizing experience. During the many days of waiting, Rusk developed a bad cough. When he returned home, he told his family that the cough "strained his heart," that he would not last long.

C.E. Rusk died in his home on February 2, 1931. In a letter to the Cascadians, Mrs. Rusk wrote: "Your friend passed away last night. His last moments of agony, thank God, were short. He died of heart disease caused by the lingering cold contracted on his way north last summer."

Only two months earlier, Rusk had left instructions to the Cascadians, which read (in part):

> Whenever some party of that club is making the ascent of the east side of

12. Kenneth C. Carrell, personal communication, Feb. 28, 1978.
13. C.E. Rusk, "The Wonderful Story of Abe Lincoln," AAJ VI, 1946, pp. 48 - 53. (from unpublished manuscript entitled *Timberline Campfires*)

> Mount Adams I want (my) ashes placed in a rock cairn on top of the "Castle" and there left in a permanent resting place; providing this can be done without too much danger to the members of the party. In case it is found dangerous to attempt to place the ashes on top of the "Castle", I would like to have them dropped into one of the big crevasses on the east side of Mount Adams.

And so his old Cascadian friends, Truitt and Starcher, on July 27, 1931, carried out Rusk's last request. The urn containing his remains, along with a small plaque, can be found today on top of The Castle, one of the most splendid promontories in all of the Cascades. Often I cross a route pioneered by Rusk, or a ridge named by him, or a glacier that he explored. I am sobered and inspired by the memories of this wonderful man.

DARRYL LLOYD

Flying L Ranch
Glenwood, Washington
April 14, 1978

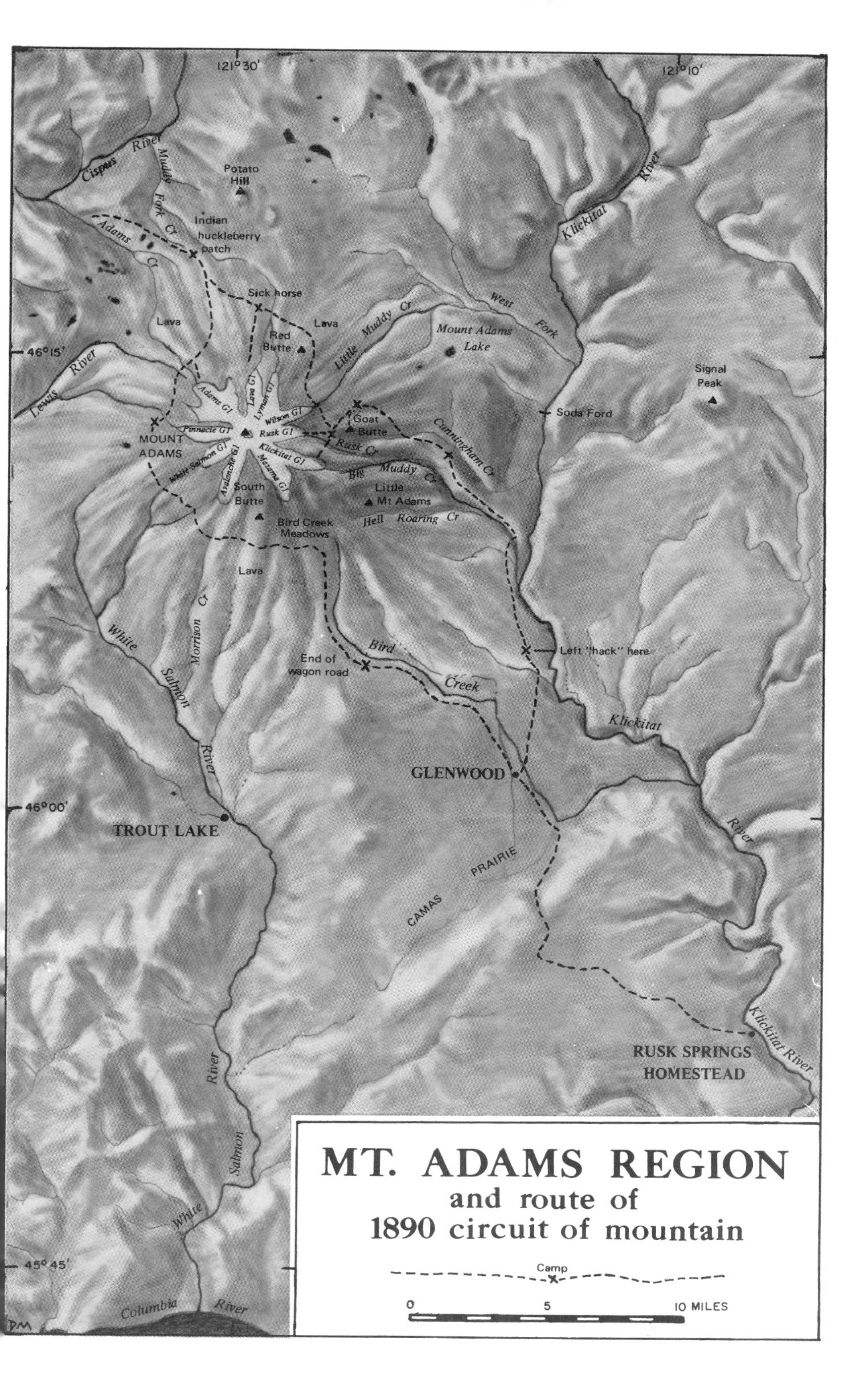

MT. ADAMS REGION
and route of
1890 circuit of mountain
Camp
0
5
10 MILES
121°30'
121°10'
46°15'
46°00'
45°45'
Cispus River
Muddy Fork Cr
Potato Hill
Indian huckleberry patch
Adams Cr
Sick horse
Lava
Red Butte
Lava
Little Muddy Cr
West Fork
Klickitat River
Mount Adams Lake
Signal Peak
Lewis River
Adams Gl
Lava Gl
Lyman Gl
Wilson Gl
Pinnacle Gl
Rusk Gl
Goat Butte
Soda Ford
MOUNT ADAMS
Klickitat Gl
Rusk Cr
Cunningham Cr
White Salmon Gl
Avalanche Gl
Mazama Gl
Big Muddy Cr
South Butte
Little Mt Adams
Hell Roaring Cr
Bird Creek Meadows
Lava
Morrison Cr
White Salmon River
Bird Creek
End of wagon road
Left "hack" here
Klickitat
GLENWOOD
TROUT LAKE
River
PRAIRIE
CAMAS
RUSK SPRINGS HOMESTEAD
Klickitat River
River
White Salmon
White
Columbia River
DM

Cascadians on top of Mt. Stuart, Sept. 5, 1920. Left to right: Harold Carey, Vern Mason, Mrs. Alice Whitnall, Mrs. Fern Richardson, Rolfe Whitnall, Clarence Truitt, C.E. Rusk, Wayne E. Richardson (in front). (Joseph Vincent photo)

Marriage photo of C.E. Rusk and wife Rachel. (October 30, 1898)

C.E. Rusk, probably about 1895, school teacher and student of law.

C.E. Rusk, at the age of 32, taken on the shoulder of Mt. Baker, September 1903.

C.E. Rusk on the summit of Mt. Baker, September, 1903. (Note hatchet in rucksack.)

C.E. Rusk with his mother, Josie. Also in photo are his wife, Rachel and son Rodney. Photo must have been taken about 1907.

C.E. Rusk, presumably at age 40 (1912), when he edited the Benton Independent, published in Prosser, Washington.

C.E. Rusk (right), next to Edgar Courson and Roland Whitmore, August 1921, in Avalanche Valley, prior to climb of east face of Mt. Adams. (Joseph Vincent photo)

Rusk on summit of Mt. Adams, August 1921. U.S.F.S. lookout (under construction) in background. (Joseph Vincent photo)

Mount Adams, Washington, from the southeast. The upper half of the usual southern route of ascent is shown at left. Marked with an "X" is the uppermost point of the Ridge of Wonders, in Rusk's words "one of the earth's sublimest viewpoints." (Chap. V) Rusk climbed to the summit of Mount Adams at least 10 times between 1889-1921. (Austin Post, U.S.G.S.)

The "Great East Side" of Mount Adams, as viewed from the air nearly directly over the top of Goat Butte. First ascent route of August 1921 is shown almost in its entirety. The "Camp of the Stars" is marked, where Rusk spent a night alone in August 1919. (Austin Post, U.S.G.S.)

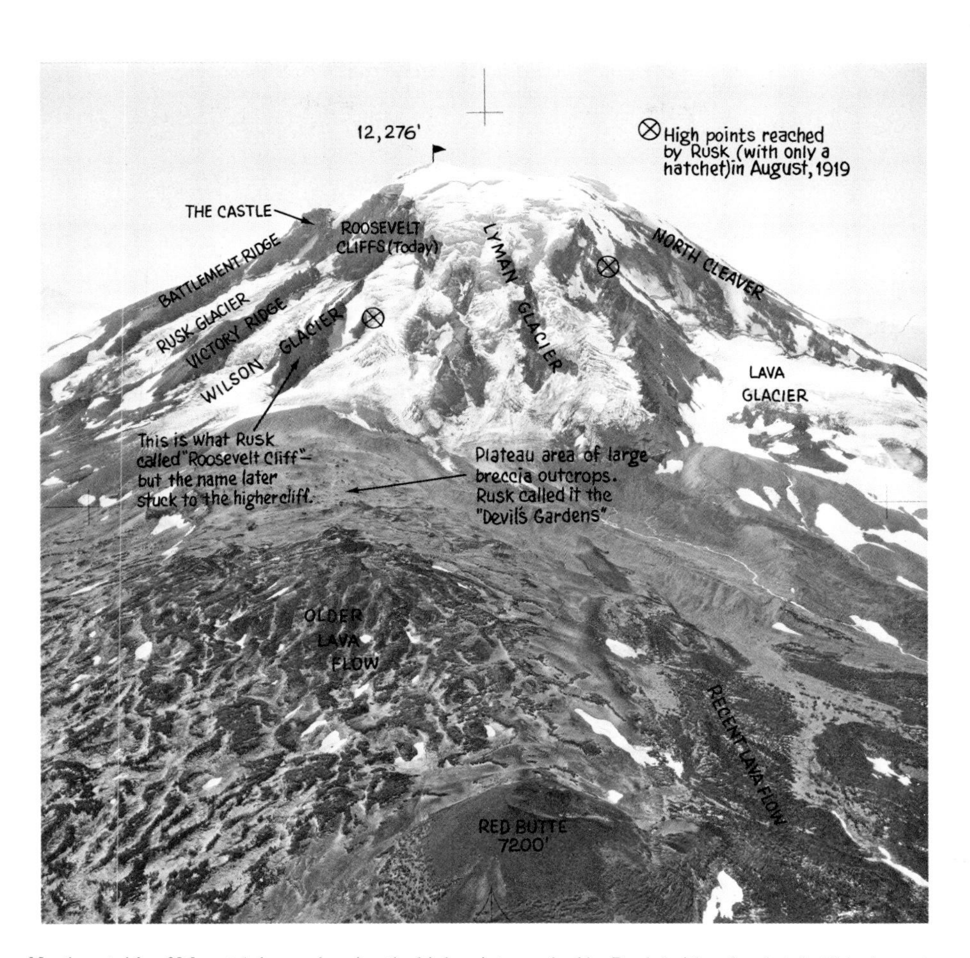

Northeast side of Mount Adams, showing the high points reached by Rusk (with only a hatchet!) in August 1919. The lava flows, both old and new, presented problems for the horseback crossings in 1890 and 1901. Compare this photo with the one taken by Professor Reid in 1901. The glaciers had considerably more ice at the turn of the century. (Austin Post, U.S.G.S.)

East side of Mount Baker, Washington (or "Kulshan" in Chap. VIII). The route taken by Rusk and Cantwell in September 1903, is now called Boulder Ridge. It is curious why Rusk claimed a first ascent over terrain that Joe Morovits called his own. (Austin Post, U.S.G.S.)

The south side of Mount Rainier, Washington. Shown are the July 1905 climbs described in Chap. IX. Rusk's attempt of the west side with Kiser probably went up the Kautz Cleaver, since a glacier crossing was described. (Austin Post, U.S.G.S.)

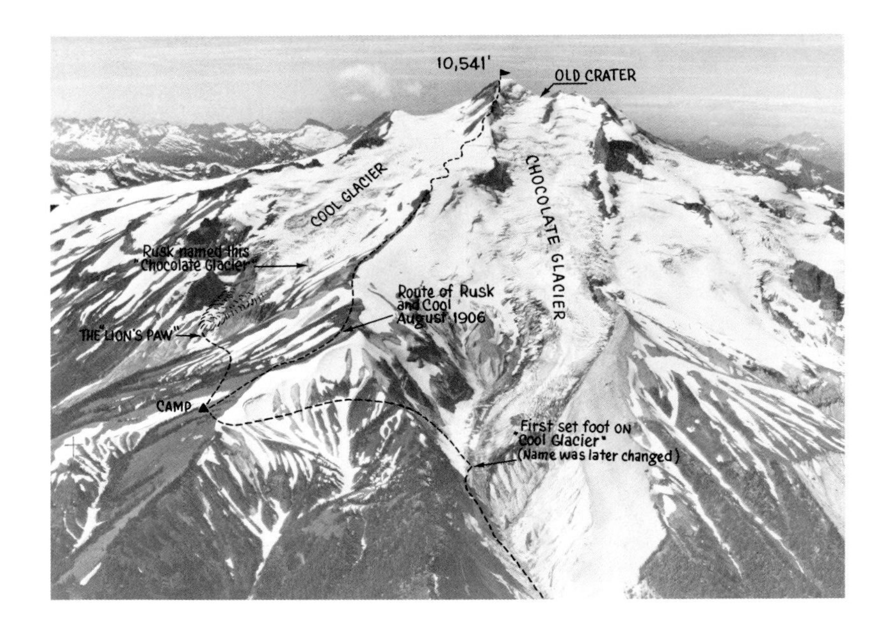

Glacier Peak, Washington, east side. The exploratory routes taken by Rusk and Cool in August 1906 are shown. A cartographic error switched the names of the glaciers from what Rusk intended. The ''lion's paw'' was some distance down valley from today's glacier snout. Their horse trip back to Lake Chelan has likely never been repeated. (Chap. X) (Austin Post, U.S.G.S.)

Mount Stuart, Washington, ''the mountain of thrills.'' (Chap. XII). Rusk climbed this a number of times in the early 1920s. (Wallace Guy, U.S.F.S.)

The northeast side of Mount Hood, Oregon. The entire "Coopers Spur" route, from timberline to summit, is shown. Rusk climbed this alone in August 1922, and had a close call on the steep icy slope below "the chimmney." (Chap. XIV) (Austin Post, U.S.G.S.)

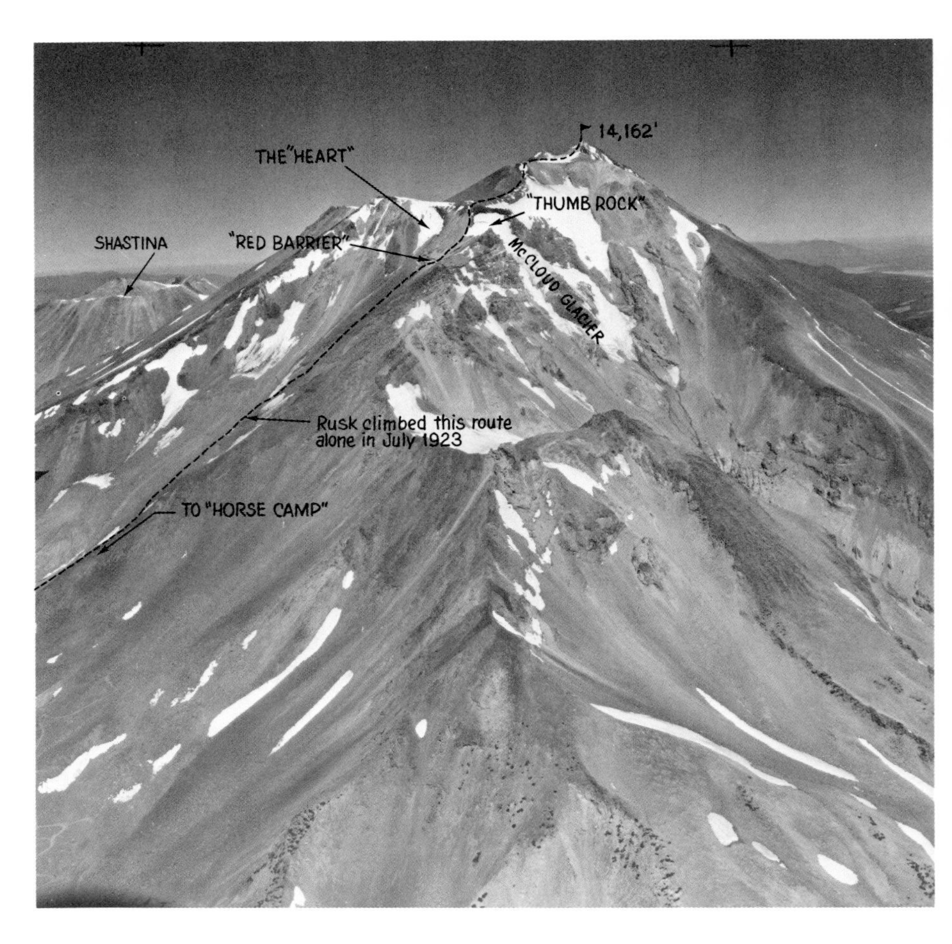

Mount Shasta, California, showing the southeast side in late summer. The mountain had much more snow on it when Rusk climbed in 1922, and when he went alone to the summit in July 1923. (Chap. XV) (Austin Post, U.S.G.S.)

TALES OF A WESTERN MOUNTAINEER

MT. STUART FROM TURNPIKE CREEK PASS,
WENATCHEE RANGE

TALES OF A WESTERN MOUNTAINEER

A RECORD OF MOUNTAIN EXPERIENCES ON THE PACIFIC COAST

By

C. E. RUSK

With Illustrations

BOSTON AND NEW YORK

HOUGHTON MIFFLIN COMPANY

The Riverside Press Cambridge

1924

The Riverside Press
CAMBRIDGE · MASSACHUSETTS
PRINTED IN THE U.S.A.

TO ALL THE TRUE-HEARTED MOUNTAINEERS
WITH WHOM IT HAS BEEN MY PRIVILEGE
TO SCALE THE ICE-CROWNED HEIGHTS
THIS WORK
IS SINCERELY DEDICATED

CONTENTS

ILLUSTRATIONS

Except where otherwise indicated the illustrations are from photographs by the author.

TALES OF A
WESTERN MOUNTAINEER

TALES OF A WESTERN MOUNTAINEER

I

THE MOUNTAIN OF DAYDREAMS

THEODORE WINTHROP saw the great mountains of the Pacific Northwest with the soul of a poet and the eye of an artist.

He saw them in their primal purity, when they were new to the world, and before the inroads of man had marred the beauty of their surroundings.

For a few short weeks he reveled in their grandeur; in the brief time that they were his he came to love them and to feel the thrill that must come to all true lovers of the sublime from an intimate contact with "Nature's noblemen"; then he set his face toward the east and rode back across the trackless miles, to civilization, leaving his new-found friends behind.

For days, at first, as he rode, he could look backward to the west and still see those snowy mountains, glistening in the sunlight; but they grew smaller and smaller, as he advanced, until, at last, came a day when he must write in his journal, "Mt. Adams and Mt. Hood are on the horizon, old friends to bid adieu to."

In the years that followed, before Theodore Winthrop rendered the "last full measure of devotion" to his country, we may not know how often came back to him the memory of those noble peaks as he last saw them on the horizon. How often must have recurred to him that sunset vision; how many daydreams may have centered 'round those distant friends that he was fated to see never again. Perhaps, just before his light went out forever, upon the field of battle, there came to him one swift moment when the mountains stood clear-cut upon the horizon in the sunset of his memory.

Happy is the man who can go through life with two such noble visions always upon his horizon.

Mount Adams first came to me through the medium of half-realized childhood impressions. It is among the earliest of my memories. Dim and misty, in the beginning, its image appeared far down the corridors of the nearly forgotten past. Gradually it took form and entity as my understanding grew. The years added to its distinctness. As I came physically nearer to it, it became more of a reality—a splendid and unusual reality, it is true. And at last we became friends and companions. Friends and companions I hope we shall always remain.

I cannot remember my first sight of the mountain. But I can remember, as a little child, seeing it, sixty miles away, something very vague, something very mysterious—and something of absorbing interest to the childish fancy. Cold and white and lone it was, more like a cloud than a part of the solid earth, guarding the domain of an empire yet unborn. And this was less than a quarter of a century after Winthrop bade adieu to it. It was then still the same as it was the day he saw it last; and the same it has been all the years I have known it—"noble enough to be the pride of a continent."

We had come, my parents and I, to pioneer the West. It was still in the third quarter of the nineteenth century. Our little log cabin had been built on the banks of a small stream in eastern Klickitat County in what was then Washington Territory. At that time I had little to say in the planning of affairs. My plans were generally laid out for me by others. But this lack of initiative did not keep me from taking a lively interest in everything pertaining to this strange, new life.

And there were many things to claim the attention of a child as well as of an adult. Our nearest white neighbors were seven miles away. For months at a time my mother did not see another white woman, and I did not see another white child. But there were the Indians, both big and little, and we were not always sure whether these were friends or foes. There were the hundreds of wild cattle roaming the fenceless hills—and of them I was much afraid. There were also the horses and the sheep, grazing over vast areas, filling the transitory period before the coming of the plough. There, too, were the coyotes, gaunt musicians of the night, that shattered the silence before dawn with their wild, unearthly noises. And there were the pine-trees, standing like tall, distant sentinels; there were the wide-spreading bunch-grass prairies; the tiny waterfalls; the moss-covered rocks, and the birds. And always on the horizon was the great white mountain, ever calling to the boy that would go to it some day "when he got to be a big man."

Occasionally there was an hour's play with an Indian boy; frequently we were favored by visits from the stolid red men; often a settler from some far-off ranch would drop in upon us; and sometimes the stockmen would stop in their rides across the range. But the day that I saw another white child was a red-letter day, indeed.

Once, I remember, my father brought home two sacks of apples from the young orchard of one of our distant neighbors. What a wonderful thing an apple can be sometimes! Another time, two squaws stopped at our cabin for a brief stay. One of them had a kitten some one had given her. I was allowed to play with it, and when they were ready to leave I clung to the little animal and cried bitterly at having to give it up. So much for a child's longing for a playmate.

But the most curious experience of my pioneer childhood occurred when I was about four years old. One day while I was playing alone near the cabin, a ruffed grouse, commonly called pheasant by the old settlers, came slyly out of the bushes, and made advances in friendship. It was evidently as lonely as I. We soon became the best of friends, and many were the hours we spent together. The bird became so tame that it would follow me around like a dog, and fly upon my shoulder. I named it "Winners," and I could go out at any time and call it to me. At first it would fly away when an older person approached; but it finally let my mother catch it and carry it into the house.

While we were playing, one day, some chickens came near. Winners immediately ruffled the feathers around his neck until they stood out in a broad, stiff collar like the frills of a mediæval grandee. The chickens squawked and fled in terror. In my childish ignorance I imagined that the bird had turned into some strange animal, and I ran screaming to the house.

Naturally the story of this strange friendship between the lonely boy and the equally lonely bird spread among the few settlers of the region, and some of these rugged men rode for miles to see for themselves if this thing could be true. Occasionally Winners would disappear for a time; but he would always reappear and our intimacy would be resumed. Our friendship continued until our family moved from our first cabin to one about three miles away. When we were ready to move, Winners could not be found, and I never saw him again. But I grieved long over his loss.

Later, when my sister was born, I rejoiced that I at last had a playmate. But it was long before she could run and play, and we had left the region ere she was old enough to join in my outdoor activities.

But this is the story of a mountaineer, and I must hurry on to the mountain. I may not even take space to tell in detail of the Indian scares of the late "seventies" when we fled to the settlements to escape dangers—some of which were real and others that were imaginary. We left the first home, and I came nearer to the mountain.

The second epoch of my daydreams began with that nearer residence to the great peak. But it was still far away—forty miles or more. And yet, living but forty miles from a grand old volcanic veteran is to be almost near neighbor to it.

At times it did, indeed, seem very near. When the air was clear and the sun was bright, the glistening snow-fields seemed right at hand, and the frowning precipices looked but a step away. And the boy of eight could dream far bigger dreams than the boy of four. So the dreams grew as the boy grew, and the desire to go to the mountain became more fixed as the years went by.

Our second place of residence was at the foot of the Columbia hills in the lower Klickitat Valley, almost directly south of the mountain. There were more settlers there than there were where we had first lived; but, even at that, neighbors were still few, and the herds of cattle and horses and sheep still roamed over the unfenced prairies. The cowboys often camped near us while they grazed their bands close by to give them the finishing degree of fatness before driving them across to market at The Dalles on the opposite side of the Columbia River. It was before the coming of the railroads, and long caravans of freight wagons daily passed on their way northward, bound for the Yakima Valley which had not yet felt the magic influence of irrigation.

Here, too, Indians were plentiful, and half a mile from

our house was the beginning of a long, level race-course. At certain times of the year hundreds of the red brothers and their families would congregate there to test the speed of their favorite race-horses, and much betting and great excitement was the result.

Possibly I became more self-reliant than would have been the case had I lived in a more thickly settled community. I often made little trips alone over the near-by country, to visit our distant neighbors, either on foot or upon my Cayuse pony. My parents were never alarmed for my safety, and I never met with accident.

From the top of the Columbia hills, at this point, a grand mountain panorama can be seen. Upon a clear day, more than half of the dominant snow-peaks of the Cascade Range are in sight, while the tortuous gorge of the Columbia River winds its rugged course beneath. The hoary old volcanoes form a regal line; each of them showing some individual glory not seen in the others, yet all so like in general character as to prove their splendid kinship. Near at hand, upon the north, the monstrous form of Adams bursts upon the startled vision. Farther away, great Rainier looms across the intervening folds of the range, while in the west the perfect cone of Saint Helens charms the eye. Just to the south, seemingly so close that you might touch it with your hand, the symmetrical beauty of Hood enchants the view. Then far down the range the white form of Jefferson appears, while farther still, so far away that one must look closely to see them, are the Three Sisters. The intervening spaces between the mighty snow-clads are filled with the great forested ridges of the Cascade Range. Here is the border-land between the forest region and the rolling, treeless stretches of the Inland Empire. The panorama is a grand one, and to see it once is to remember it forever.

For seven or eight years, from this as my homeland, I

knew the mountain. In all of that time it was an alluring mystery to long for and to center daydreams about. But to it I came no nearer.

Finally came another change. When I was fifteen we moved to the wilds of the Klickitat River, and took up our abode in a little log cabin on the banks of that rushing stream. We were following the wilderness back. No neighbors were here.

The Klickitat finds its way to the Columbia, from the heart of the Cascades, through a great canyon, a thousand feet deep at the place where we established our new home. Our only means of access was by Indian trails. There was no road. Everything had to be packed into the canyon upon horses or by hand. Even the flooring for the cabin had been carried down with the aid of Indians, and the transportation of a cookstove, later, taxed the strength and ingenuity of several strong men.

We moved to our new home on horseback, on a mild day in January when the streams were swollen from the thawing of a recent heavy snow. We had to cross the Little Klickitat, a tributary of the Klickitat River. It was bank-full, and there was no bridge. We rode into it with many misgivings; but we reached the opposite shore in safety and went on our way in triumph. We arrived at our primitive abode in the late afternoon without accident. The balance of the winter we knew the joy of pioneer life in a log cabin, before a huge rock fireplace that never knew the lack of wood.

Game was fairly plentiful in those days along the Klickitat. Bears of every shade were quite numerous in spring, summer, and fall. Deer there were also; and grouse, squirrels, raccoons, and other small denizens enlivened the woods. Many beavers were in the river. Then, too, the Klickitat was second to none as a trout stream, and many were the fine catches we made.

And only twenty-five miles away was the mountain! I could not see it from the cabin; but from the brow of the canyon it loomed tremendously and sent to me its everlasting challenge. But still two long years were to elapse before my dream was realized.

Others did not share my mountain enthusiasm. Those to whom I broached my desire to climb the great peak were but mildly interested, if interested at all. Mount Adams, perhaps, was all right in its way; but it didn't "weigh very much." Of course, being a local institution, it could not be of much importance. It takes distance, you know, to lend enchantment to the view. And Adams, being only a few miles away—how could it be enchanting? The idea that it was one of the great mountains of the world, how absurd!

And the geographies and the reference books—how they maligned it! Whenever they mentioned it at all, they gave its height at 9570 feet. And some of the books, even to this day, perpetuate the old slander, and persist in reiterating the stereotyped figures. I have often wondered how this libel against the mountain's true altitude originated.

However much others might hold my mountain in contempt, my loyalty never wavered. I felt that some day, in some way, it would come into its own, and take its true place among the great mountains of the world. And I patiently waited the time when I might go to it and know it as it really was.

My first near view of the mountain came in the fall of 1888, in the course of my first real mountain trip. During the delightful autumn weather of that year, my father, mother, and I undertook, what was then to me a wonderful fifty-mile journey, on horseback, to the headwaters of the Klickitat River, "the upper country," as we called it. We had long planned to go, and, finally, one memorable afternoon, we set forth, each upon a horse, while a fourth was heavily packed with our provisions and our equipment.

Our first night's camp was made a few miles above our home, where the wagon-road crossed the Klickitat on a wooden bridge that has long since gone the way of all wooden bridges. There was a family living at this place, and after supper we were invited into the house, where a part of our entertainment consisted in looking at some stereoscopic views of scenery in different parts of the world. While we were looking at these, some one remarked, "We have no such scenery as that in this country!" I was later to learn that some of the scenery I saw in the next two days compares favorably in grandeur with the finest to be found on the globe. But here again crept in the truth of the old adage that "distance lends enchantment to the view."

During our second day's travel we caught fitful glimpses of Mount Adams, through the trees, looming ever bigger as we advanced; but we got no unobstructed view of it. When we camped that night, it was only a few miles away. The vast snow-fields of the summit dome were plainly visible through the evergreens. Morning brought a glorious sunrise, and the dome was turned to gold. The great shoulders of the peak and the sparkling crown were thrown into one glowing mass of splendid, incomparable beauty, thrilling and sublime.

We were early on our way. A few miles brought us to the rude and precarious sheep-bridge across the Big Muddy which came plunging down from the mountain in its mad career. We crossed, and climbed the great ridge that forms the northern wall of the Muddy's canyon.

And there, before us, only three miles away, were the stupendous precipices and the tortured ice-falls of the mountain's eastern face. At last I was close to my mountain! But even then, after years of waiting, perhaps I did not comprehend its true bigness. Perhaps I do not, even now, comprehend its bigness, after all the thirty-odd years it has been growing upon me.

For a great mountain is like a great poem. At first acquaintance our minds have not the power to grasp its full magnificence. But as we know it day by day and year by year new beauties unfold, new grandeurs appear, as our senses develop new powers to understand and to measure, until, at last, if our minds be great enough to comprehend, it finally stands forth in all its sublimity.

Like an irresistible magnet the mountain drew me. Now that I was near to it, at last, it seemed I could not turn away. But our plans led not to the mountain, and the season was late. So, after drinking in the marvelous panorama for a brief time, we set our faces once more to the northward and rode toward the Klickitat River again.

The Klickitat River swings past the eastern base of Mount Adams at a distance of some six or eight miles from the snow-line, and receives mighty tribute from the waters of the eastern glaciers. We soon found a trail leading down through the fragrant evergreens toward the river, and the mountain was lost to view.

Our journey took us up along the river, into the delightful meadows on the headwaters, and among the splendid peaks of the Goat Rocks group of mountains. Here I fairly reveled in the glorious mountain scenery of the high Cascades. But the autumn rains came on, in a day or two, and we were compelled to turn homeward.

On the way back I had another brief chance to pay homage to my mountain; but there was time only for a swift greeting, and then away I must hasten to once more bide my time.

Next year came my opportunity.

II

HOW A BOY CLIMBED THE MOUNTAIN

Mount Adams dominates the southern part of the State of Washington. It is the second highest of the grand old volcanoes of the Cascades. Its geological history has been a stormy and a thrilling one, and its story would make a volume of absorbing interest could it be written in all its vivid detail. But this can never be done, for there is much that must always remain hidden from the investigations of the keenest scientist, even though the geologist may, in a general way, step by step, build up a fairly accurate record of the manner in which the great peak came into existence and fought its battles, throughout the centuries, with its rival Titans, until the peace of modern times settled upon their hoary heads.

It is not the intention of the author to attempt a history of the mountain. This is to be chiefly the narrative of personal experiences. Yet I trust that those who have the patience to follow the story of my various trips to Adams will find therein a fairly accurate description of the more interesting features of the peak and the glaciers that surround it.

When I was little more than seventeen years of age, I began my career as a school teacher. Washington was still a Territory. I secured my first school on Camas Prairie, that beautiful, fertile little valley that nestles so picturesquely at the foot of Mount Adams. From my cabin home on the Klickitat it was only a few miles' ride along old Indian trails, through fragrant, evergreen forest.

On my first trip to the prairie to make application for the

school, I had an inspiring view of the mountain. Riding down the long grade on the timbered hill that bounds the valley on the south, I came suddenly face to face with the mighty peak. It was but a few miles away to the northward on the opposite side of the prairie. It was still early spring, and the giant was clad in vestments of purest white from crown to foot. It was a magnificent spectacle, and the scene sent the blood thrilling through my veins. I hastened on to find the school directors, eager to begin my work as a teacher, if a teacher I must be, in such glorious surroundings.

My youth did not seem to alarm the men who presided over the destinies of the backwoods district, and I was employed. A few weeks later I was installed in the little log schoolhouse—the most primitive imaginable. The floor was of split "puncheons" and had never known the influence of a level. One or two small windows admitted the only light. The desks and benches were made of huge slabs split from the logs of the forest. It was a pioneer schoolhouse of the first degree. But all around it were the fine evergreens, and occasionally the monotony of the everyday programme would be broken by a big bear that dashed through the woods in full view of the window. The pupils ranged in size from the first-termer to those that were far larger than their teacher.

I was fortunate in securing board in the family of Mrs. Jane Myers, one of the pioneers of the prairie. Her fine farm was on the southern border of the prairie, and, from the commodious farmhouse at the foot of the timbered hill, a beautiful meadow sloped gently down to Conboy Lake, a shallow sheet of water which at that time occupied the center of the valley. Successive years of draining have long since reduced this once beautiful little lake to insignificance.

From the opposite side of the valley, or prairie, as it was more commonly called, long wooded slopes led gradually up to the snow-line of the mountain, some fifteen miles away. From the Myers ranch to the summit it was probably twenty miles in an air-line. For more than ten thousand feet the superb mountain towered above the valley, with no intervening heights to mar the view, and the effect was one of indescribable grandeur.

A big glacier (afterwards named the Mazama) lay on the southeast slope, directly facing us. Often, in the long, balmy spring evenings, I would sit and feast my eyes upon the vast snow-fields and the rugged crags. As the sun dropped toward its setting, the eastern face of the peak would fall into gradual darkness, while the lengthening shadow crept across the wooded foothills toward the east. The end of the great glacier plunged down out of sight into the mysterious depths of Hell-Roaring Canyon. Occasionally, from the gentler slopes below the timber-line the dust could be seen rising where some flock of sheep was being driven to its bedding-ground for the night. Long after the eastern walls were wrapped in semi-darkness, the sunlight would play upon the western slopes, and when the sun had dropped to rest behind the somber ridges of the far Cascades, the wondrous afterglow would linger lovingly upon the summit dome. Finally the darkness would creep slowly upward toward the highest peak until the whole magnificent mountain was wrapped in the oblivion of the solemn night. Then out of the profound stillness would come the cricket's chirp to show there was still life upon the slumbering earth.

But the real glory of the peak came with the sunrise. First a faint glow upon the frozen summit, then the measureless flood of golden sunlight playing upon the scintillating snow of the topmost pinnacle. Followed a wonderful transformation, as the glowing heralds of the morning rushed down the icy slopes, waking the sleeping crags to life, and routing the shades of night from the depths of the gloomy gorges. Down, down flew the joyous messengers of warmth and light until even the forest glades responded, and the whole range from lowest shrub to highest spire stood forth in one accord to proclaim that Day in all his majesty had come.

And the daydreams had grown almost to the size of manhood's estate.

The pleasant springtime sped along. My surroundings were congenial and my work was apparently successful. The mountain was near at hand; but for the time being, there was no prospect of a closer acquaintance. Every Friday evening, I would ride through the sweet-smelling forest to the little cabin on the Klickitat to spend two days with the home-folk, and on Sunday evening I would ride back to the Myers farm from where the mountain loomed so grandly.

Long before my school was finished, an event occurred that brought the fulfillment of my hopes to hand.

My uncle, W. A. Maxwell, then a resident of the State of Iowa, decided to heed Horace Greeley's injunction and come West. He did so; and in due time landed with his family at our cabin on the Klickitat. Being himself a teacher, he soon sought employment in this line of work, and was hired to teach a summer school at Trout Lake. This was a number of miles west of Camas Prairie and about twelve miles southwest of Mount Adams. So he was to be nearer the mountain than I.

I quickly decided to interest him in my plans to climb the peak. He proved a very receptive candidate. It was not long before we had laid out a tentative programme.

Mr. Maxwell's first trip to Trout Lake was made on

horseback on the Sunday before his school began, and from the Klickitat as far as my boarding-place on Camas Prairie we rode together. He was then a veritable "tenderfoot," without a bit of experience in the mountains of the West. The balance of the journey, from the prairie to Trout Lake, he made alone. It was quite an undertaking for a man fresh from the prairie States; but he made it without mishap, and took up his duties the following morning.

A week or so later, Friday evening, instead of riding to the Klickitat, I turned the pony's head toward Trout Lake. The distinctive feature of a trip from Camas Prairie to Trout Lake is the crossing of a great ridge, heavily timbered with pine and fir. The soil is a loose, volcanic ash, and the dust is somewhat annoying. The ascent from either side is rather tedious. After the crest is reached, in going from the prairie to the lake, one drops rapidly down into the valley of the White Salmon River, an angry little stream, rushing white from the glaciers on the western slope of the mountain.

Along the White Salmon are level tracts of land that the enterprise of the settlers has converted into rich dairy farms. A mile or so west of the river lies Trout Lake, a small body of water that, in the days of which I write, was famous as the Mecca of trout fishermen.

I reached Trout Lake settlement without unusual incident, and here had my first view of the scarred western face of Mount Adams. It looked nearer and huger than it had from Camas Prairie; but, to my mind, not nearly so picturesque. My visit lasted only a day; but during it I added a new locality to my acquaintance and saw, for the first time, some of the remarkable lava caves that abound near the lake.

My school closed shortly after Maxwell's began. I then helped to move his family, consisting of his wife, Lois Maxwell, and his small son, Seth, to the lake where they all took up their abode in a part of the log schoolhouse. By this time our plans for climbing the mountain were complete.

On the morning of July 4, 1889, I left my home on the Klickitat River, bound for Trout Lake. This was not a very patriotic way to celebrate the national birthday; but I felt that my celebration could be postponed for a day or so, since I intended to make it the most memorable one I had ever indulged in. My sister had loaned me her little roan cayuse pony, Cricket, for the trip. The day soon became oppressively hot, and, out of consideration for the little horse, I rode slowly. The heat, for most of the distance, was tempered, to a certain degree, by the shade of the great firs and pines that overhung the trail or road for the greater part of the way. But, at best, it was warm. However, I was going to the realization of one of my greatest desires, and the thought of the cooling snows, in which I was so soon to revel, served to mitigate the severity of the blazing sun for me. But Cricket had no such alluring thought to cheer him. No doubt, poor fellow, he considered only the hardships of the journey, with none of the promise that it held. But there were succulent grass and crystal water awaiting him in the glades at the foot of Adams, if he had only known it.

When the afternoon shades were growing long, we reached Trout Lake schoolhouse, hot, tired, and dusty. The next day was Friday, so we must await the close of school, at the hour of four o'clock, before we could take up our march to the mountain. Maxwell had secured a saddle-horse, so we lost no time at the close of school, Friday evening. We took with us enough cooked provisions for a couple of days and blankets enough for a bed. Our only scientific equipment was a cheap Fahrenheit thermometer. The sim-

MOUNT ADAMS FROM TROUT LAKE

CREVASSES ON WILSON GLACIER, EAST SIDE OF MT. ADAMS

plicity of our outfit precluded the necessity of a pack-horse. We were "going light."

Unassumingly arrayed, we set forth at four o'clock with great expectations. It was to be a new experience for both of us. The spirit of adventure rose high within us. We had the advantage of a long summer afternoon and evening to help us to the snow-line.

Crossing the White Salmon on the wagon bridge above the lake, we turned abruptly to the left upon the trail leading up the eastern bank of that stream. In those days the trail to the mountain was not heavily traveled, and in places it was dim and hard to follow. In a general direction it followed the course of the White Salmon, sometimes quite near the river, at others farther away; but always bearing toward the great peak, and, on the whole, it might have been said to maintain a water-grade.

For the first few miles we rode through a magnificent forest of evergreens. Our horses' hoofs struck softly into the dust of the volcanic soil, and the sweet fragrance of the woods filled our nostrils. Occasionally troublesome thickets of mountain laurel hung across the trail and impeded our progress; but more frequently our way lay along pleasant wooded hillsides or upon the crest of open ridges. At times the roar of angry waters rose to us from the depths of the shaded gorges where the White Salmon rushed in its impetuous course on its way back to its parent ocean. It was all delightfully cool and pleasant and primeval, and anticipation lent zest to the ride.

Finally we became aware that we were gaining altitude. Backward glimpses through the trees showed that the country we had just left was falling far below us. The trees, too, were showing the effects of a higher region. They were now not the giants we had seen lower down. Gradually they were taking on an Alpine appearance. Views of the mountain, through the foliage, were becoming more frequent. It was looming tremendously near.

Long before the sun had dropped into the billowy ridges of the Cascades, we were riding through the stunted evergreens of the upper timbered regions, and soon we sprang from our horses in a little, grassy glade, by the side of a twinkling stream of ice-cold water, with the mountain shooting up to the very dome of Heaven, right at hand.

For the first time in my life I was at the very foot of a high snow-clad mountain with nothing between me and it to impede a closer acquaintance. From our camping-place the slopes sprang steeply toward the snow-fields just above. There were still grassy steeps that struggled eternally with the savage Arctic conditions that encroached from above, and a few stunted, gnarled evergreens precariously clung to the inhospitable hillsides above our camp; but their existence was one of miserable poverty, at best. Below us the dark green of the trackless forest stretched away into the mellowing miles. Above, all was desolate, savage grandeur.

Our camp was virtually at the southwest corner of the mountain. We "staked" our horses—or picketed them, if one prefers to put it in that way—so that they were free to crop the luscious, green grass to the limits of their long ropes. We made a cold supper from our little stock of provisions. After this was done, we still had a fringe of daylight left to us. We utilized it by a short climb up the steep slope above camp.

We were actually upon the mountain, at last. A stiff pull up a grassy incline brought us well above the camp, with nothing to mar the marvelous view to the west and the south.

Thirty miles to the westward, across the densely forested ridges of the Cascades, now darkening into the night, the beautiful cone of Mount Saint Helens stood in perfect silhouette against the evening sky. Fair guardian of the mysterious regions roundabout, it caught the lingering radiance of departing day, and flung back the golden rays of the setting sun. Far away to the south, the glowing needle of Mount Hood pierced the sky, like a glorified pinnacle of light, pointing the way to the heavens above. Long after the humbler forests had settled to their sleep, these favored spires reveled in the glory of the afterglow, while high above our own noble peak flamed with the splendor of the sunset.

Exalted, we marveled in the wondrous beauty of it all, until the deepening shades warned us we must hasten back to camp. Reluctantly, we hurried down, at last, and, wrapped in our blankets, were enfolded in the great, unfathomable night, such as one can know only on the slopes of a regal mountain.

Finally came slumber; and then the awakening for the great day.

The morning air came fresh and bracing, as morning air must always come at mountain altitudes. We watched the dawn creep over the monstrous sky-line and invade the shadows farther down. The mighty lava ridges were between us and the sunrise, and to us, this day, must be denied the glory of the first golden sunbeams as they tinged the summit with living light. But there was enough glory in this dawn—to us the first dawn upon the inspired heights.

The first light found us astir. Breakfast was a small problem, with our cooked provisions. Next came cold drink for our faithful horses; a change of grazing space, and they were ready for a day of luxurious ease. We were prepared for the great adventure.

It was five o'clock when we started—five o'clock on the morning of July 6, 1889. Mount Hood, Mount Saint Helens and the lesser spires of the Cascades had already caught the radiance of the new day. The soul of Nature was athrob with the joy of life.

Slowly we climbed the first steep slopes above our camp. Often we paused to look down upon our contented horses as they diminished in size the higher we rose. We had no alpenstocks; but we secured rude substitutes in the form of stout fir sticks broken from the stunted trees near camp.

Taken as a whole, Mount Adams might be described as a shapeless mass. From no two different sides does it look to be the same mountain. It may be properly called a monstrous ridge, running north and south, with three summits, the south, the middle, and the north. The middle is the highest, and, consequently, the true summit. The south is usually called the "first" summit. The north summit, being really on the northwest of the main massif and leaning against it, broadens the northern part of this great ridge, so that the contour of the mountain really forms a rude sort of triangle with the apex pointing south. Therefore, seen from the east or from the west, the great peak presents a tremendously broad face. The eastern face may be likened to a stupendous wall, almost perpendicular. It will be described in detail as this narrative proceeds. The western face is not nearly so abrupt as the eastern, yet it is, for all that, wonderfully steep and rugged. On the north, the mountain presents more of a dome-like appearance with an almost unbroken covering of snow from summit to base. Viewed directly from the south, it takes on more of a pyramidal shape, seemingly quite pointed at the top. But only when one has seen it from all sides does he realize that none of these apparent shapes conveys a true idea of the actual form of Adams; but that it is, as I have said, in reality, a shapeless mass, impossible of adequate description. Withal, each side has a separate individuality of its own that seems to make of it a separate mountain, grand as a whole, and interesting to the least detail. And this scarred old volcano, in its entirety—this shapeless mass—combines all the elements that go to make a scene of noble, rugged, untamed grandeur.

The south side has the most gradual slope. This is the usual route of ascent. Springing from the central massif of the peak, at an elevation of about nine thousand feet, a mighty lava ridge far down below timber-line. On its eastern side this ridge breaks sharply down, and beneath it lie two glaciers. The wall, in places, is perpendicular, and occasionally actually overhangs. Under the protecting lava cliffs the snow drifts to great depths and feeds the glaciers below. On the west side, however, the ridge has no such abrupt facing. Here it broadens fan-like as it descends and is divided into numerous subsidiary ridges that descend southwesterly to below the timber-line. Between the eight-thousand- and the nine-thousand-foot levels the slope of the main ridge is very gradual; it assumes almost the form of a rocky plateau, and is finally connected with the massif of the mountain by a sort of depression or "saddle."

The warm west winds of late spring and early summer sweep off the snows of the broad fan-like slopes on the western side of the ridge, leaving the sharp lava backbones completely bare, while the depressions and gullies are still filled with great snow-banks, many of which remain throughout the season.

From our camp we had been able to pick out a probable route to the summit. In accordance with our plan, our first objective was the crest of the great south ridge. Slowly we mounted step by step. Soon the grassy slopes were passed, and the last stunted trees were left behind. Our way now lay over the rough lava rocks. In places the lava had weathered but little; the flow appeared to be of comparatively recent date, and the jagged points tried our shoe-leather to the limit. The way was harassingly steep. The altitude was beginning to manifest itself, and we found that frequent rests were a necessity.

Our progress was slowly satisfactory. The steeper slopes of the lower ridge were gradually overcome, and we approached the less trying grades of the upper end. Occasionally the monotony of the lava rocks would be broken by diverting our route on to a snow-bank which we would follow until it became necessary to take to the rocks again. The country stretching away from the foot of the mountain had fallen far below us. Seemingly miles away, the meadow-lands around Trout Lake spread like tiny maps, set in the deeper green of the surrounding forests. To the southward the more extensive farmlands of Camas Prairie lay smiling in the golden sunlight. Beyond, to the eastward, the great canyon of the Klickitat cut the timbered highlands; while farther still, beyond the forest zone, the gray expanse of treeless hills and plains stretched away for countless miles until lost in the misty distance. To the west the billowy ridges of the Cascades swelled to the horizon with the snowy cone of Saint Helens as their dominant feature. Far to the south the sharp spire of Hood seemed to hang in the very center of the sky, white and lone. But in the north the mighty bulk of Adams filled the sky, the only thing that met the eye.

By mid-forenoon we had reached the "saddle" and faced the second stage of the ascent.

From the saddle to the first summit, a great, long, steep slope leads up. This is the narrow southern face of the massif. In the center is an almost unbroken snow-field bounded on either side by bare ridges strewn with tremendous boulders. The long slope is by no means uniform, being steeper in some parts than in others; but it is very steep at any place, and its conquest involves the most arduous part of the ascent. The amount of boulder-strewn area running parallel to the snow-field on each side varies, of course, with different parts of the summer and with different years. During a year when the amount of snow on the mountain is quite heavy, the field is broad and unbroken, throughout the summer, from the first summit to the saddle; but, in the late summer of a season of light snow, it may be broken by rocky islands and the boulder ridges may encroach upon it in many places.

In climbing from the saddle to the first summit the mountaineer may take his choice of a snow route or a boulder route, or he may vary his programme between the two. To change from one to the other is often a rest to tired legs, although some climbers prefer to stick to one or the other route the entire distance.

We chose the snow, possibly because it was to us more of a novelty than the rocks, and for the further reason that our ascent had to this point been mainly over the stony way.

From the saddle to the first summit one must climb twenty-five hundred feet in height. This may be called the middle part of the ascent. By the time it is begun one generally begins to feel the effect of the altitude to some degree, more or less, according to the physical constitution of the individual. We tackled the snow-slope slowly and deliberately. The sun had already softened the surface so that we sank into the snow several inches at each step. Early in the morning or on a cold day the snow may be frozen so hard that it is impossible to climb the steeper portions of this great slope without cutting steps.

Frequently we stopped to rest. After every short, hard pull it was necessary to pause and take on extra oxygen fuel for the lungs. It is astonishing, at high altitudes, how quickly the breath goes. Yet, after one has paused to rest, feeling completely exhausted, a few minutes serves fully to restore the strength, and the climber resumes his upward march, apparently as strong as ever.

Notwithstanding our numerous rests, our progress was satisfactorily skyward. But a chill wind was blowing, and the clouds were beginning to swirl around the mountain. And clouds are always a source of anxiety to the novice on a mountain, for he does not know with what degree of safety he can venture into them. But it soon became a certainty that we must risk the clouds if we were to reach the summit. And I had waited for this day too long to be easily balked in my desire. So onward and ever upward we went, while the clouds gathered around the great peak in rapidly increasing companies.

As we slowly approached the first summit, the impetuous clouds grew denser, and the air was filled with flying frost. Never having been over the route before, we bore too far to the east, and soon found ourselves near the abrupt slopes. In an endeavor to bear back toward the safer southern slope, we were suddenly confronted by a small crevasse. In the later years of greater experience, I would have laughed at such an obstacle; but to us then it was formidable. We soon discovered that its lower end was bridged by an ample thickness of snow. Nevertheless, on hands and knees, we crept across with great caution, and heaved mighty sighs of relief when we were safely over.

Shortly after this little thrill, we reached the great point of boulders that marks the first summit. The climb from the saddle had been a long, steep, exhausting one, and we stopped to rest and to try to locate our position in the whirling clouds. We began to discuss our probable distance from the top.

Suddenly Maxwell exclaimed: "I can show you the summit!"

True enough! The clouds had quickly shifted, and the mighty summit dome stood revealed. Huge and forbidding it was, and we looked at it almost in awe.

Many a man has toiled up the heart-breaking slope from the saddle, and has eagerly craned his neck over the point of the first summit, under the pleasant illusion that he was almost on top, only to fall down in dismay as the menacing bulk of the summit dome burst upon his sight. And more than one has here turned back, discouraged and exhausted.

When the mountain is seen from a distance, the summit dome looks like a small butte perched at the top of the mighty bulk. I have asked men who had never been close to the peak how high they thought the summit dome to be. The answer would often be, "Oh, forty or fifty feet, probably." And it actually looms eight hundred feet above the first summit!

From the point where the first summit is reached, a crescent-shaped snow-ridge leads a distance of about half a mile to the foot of the summit dome. From its crest, the slope toward the west is very gradual for quite a way until it breaks off into the steep western slope of the mountain. This gradual slope, with its crescent shape, forms a considerable amphitheater. On the east, however, the ridge breaks abruptly off over the great eastern precipices.

As soon as the parting clouds revealed the situation to us, we started for the summit dome. Again we made the mistake of bearing too far to the east. We had not gone a great distance when the snow gave way beneath one of my feet. My leg sank almost to the hip. My other foot seemed to be on a solid foundation, and I lost no time in pulling my leg from its precarious position. Looking down into the hole my foot had made, I saw I was standing directly over a blind crevasse.

Intuitively, we realized that we had approached too near

the precipitous eastern face of the mountain and that we were among the crevasses. Quickly and cautiously, we angled toward the west, and were soon on safer snow.

Often these blind crevasses give no warning of their presence. They may be completely hidden by a few inches of perfectly smooth snow, and the first intimation the luckless mountaineer has of their proximity may be a tumble into one. Long experience will teach one to know the regions where they are apt to be encountered. Prudent mountaineering requires the members of a party to be roped together wherever there is danger of hidden crevasses.

Shortly after the incident of the crevasse, we reached the foot of the summit dome, and were ready for the last, hard pull.

At times the whole southern slope of the summit dome may be covered with snow. At other times a single bare ridge may lead up toward the top, and often, in the late summer, the whole slope is completely bare. When the snow is completely gone from here, the climber must toil up through loose, ashy deposits and small stones into which the feet sink to the ankles.

On this day in early July, we found the narrow, bare ridge. As we started up it, the clouds closed around us more thickly than ever. It was a monotonous, hard grind up into the unknown region of the mists. Nothing occurred to break the weary sameness of that climb, and we were shut off from the view by the clouds. Finally our ridge terminated in a point of boulders. Here, protected from the elements by some of the larger rocks, we found an old sardine can containing the names of a number of former climbers, written on cards and scraps of paper. One of our predecessors had left the somewhat disquieting information that there were dangerous crevasses at and near the summit.

Years afterward, different mountain-climbing clubs put

more pretentious record-boxes at this spot, and in these accumulated the names and experiences of many climbers. At the time of our ascent there had been less than thirty recorded ascents of the mountain. Our climb was made entirely on our own resources, as neither of us had ever talked with any one who had climbed the peak.

From the record-box point it is but a short distance, up a very gradual snow-slope, to the extreme summit of the mountain. By the time this place is reached, however, many climbers find themselves at the verge of utter exhaustion, and the last few hundred yards prove almost beyond their strength. Maxwell and I were both young and strong, and a short rest at the box put us in fine trim again. To reach the top was but a matter of a few minutes. Soon we stood upon the broad expanse of the summit. We could see that we were on top; but the clouds were so thick that our range of vision extended but a few yards in either direction, and the magnificent view with which Adams usually rewards the climber's persistence was that day denied us. Not until a later ascent was I to discover the awful spectacle that must always haunt the memory of one who has seen it.

A chill wind was driving the clouds across the summit plateau. The frost clung to our hair and our clothing. Maxwell's mustache was soon hung with little icicles. The mercury stood at freezing. It was a few minutes past noon. The ascent had taken a little over seven hours.

There was neither comfort nor profit in remaining. We could see nothing but the snow beneath our feet and the clouds that swirled around us. Yet we took a few glorious, satisfying minutes to celebrate our triumph over the great peak. The moment I had looked forward to for years was at hand. Although the weather had robbed us of the crowning glory of the ascent, our experience in the mysterious realm of cloudland was unique, and we were content.

But we were chilling to the bone, and soon we set our faces toward the south and hurried downward through the clouds.

With leaping steps we ran down the bare ridge to the first summit. The loose, ashy covering gave beneath our feet and broke the shock of our descent. To cross the snow-field to the long south slope was the work of a few minutes. And then we tried our great experiment.

The snow was soft; but the slope was very steep. Would we dare to slide? Cautiously we essayed the hazard. With a firm grip on our primitive alpenstocks, we sat down and started. Soon we were whizzing through the clouds with alarming speed; but soon assurance came, for we found that we could control the rate at which we went.

Oh, it was exhilarating! The long hours of toiling ascent were forgotten, as we rushed down, in a few minutes, a distance that had taken us a large part of half a day to come up. Behind us, as we sped, two ever-lengthening grooves followed in the snow. They were the records of our descent, impressed upon the soft, white robe of the mountain—records that a few hours of bright sunshine on the following day would obliterate.

It was glorious, this wild glissade down through the clouds; but, in the nature of things, it could not last. So, ever, are our pleasures more fleeting than our toils. Soon, too soon, came the lessening slopes as we approached the saddle. Before long, it was not steep enough for gravity to furnish us with momentum for our going. Perforce we, at last, came to a standstill. Henceforth our four good feet must take us on our way. We stood, somewhat regretfully, looking backward at the two long grooves leading upward into the clouds. And, for the first time, we became aware of the discomfort that must pay for the long toboggan slide.

We were wet—at least a part of our anatomies were wet—to the skin.

And now came the descent of the great lava ridge. For some time it was without incident—merely a monotonous hurry over the sharp boulders, and quick slides down the snow-slopes.

And then came an adventure that served to impress upon us how easy it is to run into danger, when it is thought all danger is past, and how easily the novice may make a fatal mistake on even the safest of great mountains.

We had reached a very steep snow-field which ended about two hundred feet below us in a jumble of rough, big boulders. We were preparing to step out on to the snow for another glorious slide, when one of us happened to toss a rock. The lightning-like rapidity with which it bounded down the slope, and the sharp crack with which it struck the boulders, started us, and brought us to a sudden stop. We threw out more rocks. They all acted in precisely the same way. We were brought rudely to a realization of the fact that the slope was far steeper than we had at first supposed, and that to have attempted to slide down it, with the jagged boulders frowning below, woud have been suicide.

The ridge of rocks on which we were standing extended down into the snow-field for about half of the distance to the boulder-field below, thus dividing the upper portion of the snow-field into two parts, and leaving the lower portion as a less abrupt slope of snow leading down to the boulders. We decided to go down to the point of the ridge and slide the balance of the way. Otherwise we should have to make a wide détour to get around the snow-field.

But when we got to the lowest point of the ridge we found a little, rocky island in the snow-field, about twelve feet below us. Between us and it was a tremendously steep pitch of solid ice. However, the distance was so short that we slid quickly down, bringing up rather abruptly on the island. Fortunately, we had sense enough to examine the condition of the snow before attempting to slide the balance of the way. To our dismay, we found an inch or two of soft snow on top, and, beneath, solid ice! What we had taken to be a snow-field was, in reality, a small remnant-glacier with a very thin coating of snow. To attempt to slide meant destruction.

There was but one thing to do. That was to get back on to the ridge, climb up the way we had come, and make the détour we should have made in the first place. But when we tried to climb back up the ice to the ridge we found it was far too steep. It was impossible to get either foothold or handhold. Maxwell took out his pocket-knife and tried to thrust it into the ice. The blade made no impression on the flinty surface. We were trapped!

The situation was serious. We dared not slide down, and we could not climb up. There was not enough snow on the glacier below to furnish footholds. There seemed no way of escape.

We studied the matter carefully. We evolved a plan that promised solution. Planting his feet firmly in the rocks, Maxwell leaned against the ice and extended his arms far above his head, with his stick grasped firmly in his hands and reaching up its full length. I then climbed cautiously up over his body and carefully along the stick until I could thrust my arm into the crevice between the upper part of the ice and the lower point of the rock. Hanging thus, I grasped the stick while Maxwell drew himself up by it, climbed over my body and reached a secure place on the rocks. For him then to help me to a solid footing was but the work of a moment. We had gained a lot of experience in a short time, at the price of a great deal of toil and considerable danger.

We lost no more time in making the long-delayed détour. The balance of the descent was made without further adventure, and at five o'clock we were gladdened by the sight of our faithful horses which had spent the day peacefully and in evident contentment.

Now that the exhilaration of the climb was over, we began to feel the pangs of homesickness, and we decided to ride to Trout Lake that night, even though it meant many hours of traveling in the darkness. So we bade our friend, the great mountain, good-bye, with the glow of the sunset glorifying his regal crest, for the clouds of the day were dispersing with the coming of the night. As we rode away down the long, timbered slopes the darkness settled upon us. It was rather a weird ride through the solemn forest, a strange close to a wonderful day.

III

THE CIRCUIT OF THE MOUNTAIN

NEXT year came better acquaintance with Mount Adams. I persuaded my mother and my sister to join me in an attempt to circle the mountain. My sister, Leah, was but twelve years old; but our pioneer life had taught her self-reliance, and she had learned to ride quite well on her pony, Cricket. My mother was the most fearless person I ever knew, and, at that time, she was capable of enduring long trips, with apparent ease. She thoroughly enjoyed the wild life of the hills, and she undertook this journey without hesitation.

It was September when we started. This is usually the finest month of the year for a mountain jaunt, although there is some danger of storms. We started in our hack. It was well loaded with provisions and equipment for the trip. In the outfit was a pack-saddle for use when wheels could no longer convey us. Of course, the little roan pony, Cricket, went along, for he would have his burdens to bear when we reached the long mountain trails. Two wiry cayuses made up our team; black Tony, the pigeon-toed, and brown Doc. Tony was to be saddle-horse when wagon-roads had been left behind, and Doc was to serve his apprenticeship as a pack-animal. Tony was an old campaigner and was to be relied upon on all occasions; but Doc was rather young and had never been packed. We were somewhat doubtful as to how he would perform.

Rough, roundabout roads were our portion for the first part of the journey, and not until well along in the second day did we drive our hack into a clump of evergreens, out of sight of the beaten track, and cover it with boughs. We had come as far as it was prudent to venture with a wheeled vehicle.

Then came the experiment of putting a pack on Doc. We did the job very gingerly and carefully, fearing that at any moment the horse might bolt through the woods and scatter our impedimenta to the four winds. But Doc was naturally docile, and he seemed to feel that whatever we did to him must be all right, so when he was loaded he stepped off as quietly as though bearing a pack was his sole mission in life. Doc was surely rewarded for his placid disposition, for he lived to an extreme old age, and I have no doubt that somewhere in this vast Universe there is a horse heaven in which he has a comfortable nook.

We followed the plateau above the inner gorge of the Klickitat River, and crossed the turbulent Big Muddy on the shaky sheep-bridge; thus keeping, for a time, to the route which we had traveled two years before when my father, mother, and I visited the "upper country."

After crossing the Big Muddy we toilsomely climbed the great ridge which forms the northern wall of its canyon. Late in the afternoon, I found myself once more facing, at a few miles' distance, the tremendous eastern slope of the mighty peak which was destined, in the years to come, to give to me many thrilling hours of mountaineering. But our plans called for an immediate going to the north side of the mountain, which was then a land of mystery. So thitherward we turned.

A short distance down the north slope of the ridge we found a delightful little stream, fringed with groves of stately evergreens. This creek is now known as Cunningham Creek. Here we camped.

Next morning we set northward across the long, grassy ridges of the lower slopes of the mountain. The day was not a resultful one. There was trouble in finding the trail.

In fact we did not find any trail that would take us where we wanted to go, so our progress toward the Pole star was but a few unsatisfactory miles. But that evening we camped in a fine little valley where every prospect was pleasing and there was abundant grass for our horses.

That night the weather took a hand in our affairs. It snowed. Not a great deal, to be sure, but enough to make matters decidedly disagreeable. We had no tent; for tents have weight, and, where weight is of the essence of a journey, they are sometimes omitted to make transportation more felicitous for the commissary department.

In the morning the outlook was gloomy. The snow was too familiar. It was too wet and cold and sticky for comfort. It was not advisable to proceed to the remote regions north of the mountain until meteorlogical conditions were more certain. So we decided to do a little exploring on the east side while giving the weather a chance to make up its mind.

Leaving our camp, we rode southward. Conspicuous as one of the striking landmarks on the east side of Mount Adams is a high pointed butte—one of the several subsidiary, parasitic cones surrounding the base of the mountain. Its top has an elevation of about seventy-five hundred feet. Although but a foothill of the great peak, it is a thousand feet higher than any mountain east of the Mississippi River. The walls of the crater that once adorned its summit have long since disintegrated, leaving but remnants sticking up in places in the form of picturesque cliffs. Erosion has here worked with much enterprise; but a great deal remains for it to do.

In early days, this butte had many aliases. At the time of our visit it seemed to be known as "Sheepherders' Butte." Years later, when Mount Adams was first mapped, it was designated as "Rainbow Butte," because of the brilliant col-

THE CASTELLATED YELLOW CLIFFS ON THE SOUTH SLOPE OF GOAT BUTTE FROM THE CASCADIAN CAMP IN AVALANCHE VALLEY

SCENE IN AVALANCHE VALLEY, EAST SIDE OF MOUNT ADAMS

oring of its cliffs. Eventually, however, the name "Goat Butte" settled permanently upon it, and such is the name as it now appears on all official maps. Goat Butte, therefore, it will henceforth be called in this narrative.

Up the northwest slopes of Goat Butte it is possible to ride a horse easily. Thither we rode that autumn forenoon, in the ninth decade of the nineteenth century, while we were awaiting the whim of the weather. From that great eminence we viewed with wonder the awe-compelling majesty of the east side of Mount Adams. The tremendous panorama of ice-fall and precipice sank into our consciousness and left there pictures that could never be effaced. The bigness and the splendor of it all grew upon us until we knew that we could not go to the north of the mountain until we had known more intimately the greater glory that was close at hand.

A thousand feet below us lay emerald, Alpine meadows. Beautiful gems they were, set in the park-like expanse of the valley that stretched from the foot of the butte to the ice-fields of the glacier. Their verdure, fresh as that of a well-kept lawn, drew life from the crystal streams that meandered down from the hill above. Here was the Elysian land, a veritable mountain paradise. The subdued roar of glacial torrents was borne to us on the clear air, and it spoke to us of the tremendous forces of nature at work in this sublime scene. Dominant peace was there, yet underneath that peace waged the everlasting conflict of the elements.

The many remarkable features of the great east side of Mount Adams will be described in fuller detail later on. A volume might be devoted to them alone. From our lofty point of observation we had seen enough marvels to convince us that we must know more of them. We must camp in the wonderful valley in the midst of those beautiful meadows.

Meanwhile the weather had assumed a more genial mood. The snow flurry had been but a bluff, after all. But it had changed the course of our plans, and we were well pleased. We returned to our camp of the night before; and when the shadows of the giant cliffs were lengthening in the peaceful afternoon we rode through the pass between Goat Butte and the main slope of the mountain, and pitched our camp in a grove of white-bark pines, with a natural lawn spreading out before and the savage wall of the great east side towering a mile above us. A quarter of a mile away frowned the ice-cliffs of a glacier's end.

This was the camp ideal. Abundance of dry wood and pure water; shade for the heat of the day; plenty of luscious grass for the horses; scenery beyond compare. The two-hundred-foot snow-wall that overhangs the terrific eastern precipices seemed but a stone's throw away; yet we knew it was three miles in an air-line.

The sun sank behind the monstrous bulk of the mountain, and the great shadow started on its eastward way across countless miles of earth-fold and forest. The chilling shades deepened into night. We made our beds in the shelter of the pines and sought repose.

Midnight came. We were wrapped in profound slumber. The distant drone of glacial torrents seemed only to add to the intensity of the silence. The white dome of the mountain lay cold and dim under the scintillation of the frosty stars. The peace of an unfathomable loneliness hung over the vast scene.

Suddenly the stillness was shattered by a wild, shrieking roar. We were instantly brought to startled consciousness. The whole valley seemed vibrating with the impact of mighty forces. The demons of gravity had been let loose. The shuddering air bore to our little camp the tale of a frozen cataclysm.

We knew what had happened. A tremendous mass of snow had broken from the two-hundred-foot wall on the brink of the awful precipice, a mile in vertical height above us, and the great avanlanche was now hurtling down the dizzy cliffs, a sheer two thousand feet, to the surface of the glacier below. For perhaps a minute we could hear the grinding rush as the white flood pressed down the rough surface of the rocky wall; then came the subdued swish of the broken, snowy masses as they poured on down the steep slope of the upper glacier, while the echoes reverberated from crag to crag. Gradually the Titanic uproar subsided to comparative silence; but long after the avalanche had spent its force came the sound of rolling stones loosed by the terrific concussion.

In awe, we lay and marveled, as we thought of the countless ages through which this Titanic war of the elements had been waging on the slopes of the mighty peak. The whole span of human history was but an hour in comparison with the cycles of the mountain's life.

And when morning came we knew that this must be known as "Avalanche Valley."

Good weather seemed to have returned for an indefinite stay. After breakfast, we left our horses to enjoy the bounteous provision Nature had made for them in this lovely vale, while we set out to explore. The earlier hours of the day were given to short journeys near camp; but in the afternoon we bent our steps southward, crossed numerous gullies that had been cut by the intermittent streams from our near-by glacier, made our way somewhat precariously across the larger permanent torrent that thundered down from the ice-wall; strolled leisurely over a mile or so of wooded ridges, and came to where the great Klickitat Glacier debouches into the broad upper canyon of the Big Muddy. Here was a scene of grand desolation.

The Big Muddy, one of the most remarkable streams in America, springs, a full-grown river, from the ice-caverns at the snout of Klickitat Glacier. White as cream, and almost as thick, it leaps forth from its frigid prison and plunges down over a bed of immense boulders, with a roar that makes the earth tremble. The grinding and rolling of big rocks in its fretful bed can be always heard. At the point where it emerges from the ice, no living thing could stand against its impetuous flood. It falls three thousand feet in six miles; fifteen hundred feet in the first two miles of its course. Eight miles from the parent glacier, it joins the Klickitat River.

I was curious to see the source of the Big Muddy. Ben Morgan, an old squaw-man who had spent years of his life with the Indians and was supposed to have traveled over all this region, had once explained to me the reason why the Klickitat River was so milky-white in the hot summer months. That was before I had begun to study the habits of glaciers. Morgan said that the Klickitat got its white complexion from "Milk Creek," a stream that came out of a claybank on Mount Adams, and was so "thick that it rolled." He had never realized that his "claybank" was a great wall of débris-covered ice and, if he knew there was such a thing as a glacier, he did not suspect the existence of one on Mount Adams. So much for the accuracy of the man who has neither acquired knowledge nor the power of correct observation.

At the time of our visit, in the fall of 1890, the Klickitat Glacier ended close against the great south wall of the canyon, and here was the source of the Big Muddy. The mighty ice-stream approached the canyon wall obliquely, and there was little space between the glacier's snout and the steep, thousand-foot slope of the gorge.

Just above the snout of the glacier, the canyon wall retreated southward in a grand, broad curve that formed a beautiful amphitheater with slopes of marvelous green, interspersed with long lines of talus, glistening snow-fields and beetling crags. The western arc of the amphitheater swept back to the glacier, and the upper end of the canyon wall overhung the ice-stream in a terrific precipice.

Old moraines gave evidence that the glacier had once extended much farther down the canyon than it did at this time. The ice of the lower end did not now have a very great thickness—perhaps it was not over forty or fifty feet deep near the snout. Farther up it seemed to increase in depth to two or three hundred feet.

I was destined to keep this great glacier under observation for more than thirty years. During that time it retreated at least a quarter of a mile. When I last saw it in 1921 the Big Muddy was that much longer than it was in 1890, and, instead of emerging from a forty-foot wall of ice near the south wall of the canyon, it came out, far back from the wall, from beneath a tremendous ice-cliff a hundred and fifty or two hundred feet in height.

The lower end of Klickitat Glacier is much broken, and covered by débris. The great ice ridges are deeply coated with gravel, and many immense boulders are borne down upon their crests. An examination of this detritus will give one an accurate idea of the material of which the mountain is built, for the waste matter has been brought down by the ice-stream from the towering cliffs that form the very core of the giant peak. The retreat of the ice has deposited the gravel and boulders as morainal refuse in great, uneven beds extending far below the present lower limits of the glacier. Young evergreens have taken root and are slowly following the ice, each year, farther and farther up the canyon.

The wonderful upper reaches of Klickitat Glacier were not for us this trip. Later we were to know more of them; but the time was not yet.

This was our first concrete lesson in glaciology, and we remained as long as time would let us. The advancing afternoon finally warned us that we must return to camp. The way back seemed long and tedious. The hills were surely steeper than when we had the urge of expectancy to aid us in the outward journey. But supper and rest were to be had at camp, and we reached there at last.

The sun had dropped behind the dome of the great mountain, and Avalanche Valley lay in shadow. The whole eastern slope of Adams was wrapped in evening shade; but league upon league the country roundabout was bathed in a rich flood of golden sunlight. Suddenly directly over the summit crest a brilliant star appeared. For some time it hung there, an unusual sight, slowly dipping toward the lofty horizon; finally it touched the snowy sky-line, blinked for a moment, and disappeared. The shadow of the mountain was still creeping eastward across the distant woodlands. It was yet some time until sunset.

Next day we continued our glacial exploration. Going up the grass-covered ridges and through the groves of stunted, timber-line pines, in a quarter or a half mile's travel we reached the lower end of the glacier nearest camp. Working our way carefully up the débris-covered ice-hummocks we finally stood well out upon the surface of the glacier and viewed that scene of wild grandeur.

As this narrative progresses there will be much more to say of this wonderful ice-stream which is now known as "Rusk Glacier." We were undoubtedly the first white persons to stand upon its surface. We did not then attempt to extend our explorations far along its course. We were content to stand in awe for a few minutes in silent contemplation of its great crevasses and rugged seracs, and of the stupendous colored precipices that form its cirque.

How much credit we are entitled to for original investigation on the east side of Mount Adams, on this brief visit, I cannot say. I believe we were the first to stand upon Rusk Glacier and to know it as a glacier. Possibly we were the first to view the head of the Big Muddy at close range. Ben Morgan had seen the stream coming from a "claybank"; whether from a near-by point or from afar, I do not know. Sheepmen had ranged their bands on the lower slopes of the mountain, for years; but these generally went no farther than the grass, and, if they knew aught of glacier or streamhead, they left no record. I feel almost safe in saying that we, on this journey around the great peak, were the first to see all of its glaciers and to *know* them as glaciers.

After our return to camp from the glacier, we decided to move on toward the north side of the mountain. Our time was limited, and we must away if we were to make the circuit of the peak while the weather held good.

During our stay in Avalanche Valley, we had seen, in the distance, a dim trail crossing the crest of a high moraine on the northern sky-line. This explained our failure to find the route, on our previous attempt, just before the snowstorm. We had kept too far down the slope. It was now well along in the afternoon when we resumed our interrupted journey toward the north. Winding again through the pass between Goat Butte and the main slope of the mountain, we bade adieu to our wonderful valley.

We had little trouble in following the old Indian trail. Past the littered end of another glacier we went, and across its small but vigorous stream. The trail then led us up sharply to higher levels. Over a steeply slanting snowbank and on to the top of the old moraine it led us. Here was a scene of igneous ruin. Great waves of blackened, shattered lava rolled away to the northeast, until lost in the forest miles below. A one-time molten river it had been, sweeping all before it in its resistless, fiery flood. Here had Vulcan once set up his forge and wrought mightily in the building of a world.

The upper part of this vast lava-flow forms an uneven, irregular plateau, over which the old trail winds at an elevation exceeding seven thousand feet. In the depression, between the jagged points and ridges, gravel, sand, and soil have accumulated, and there are many patches of greensward and a profusion of summer flowers. But even the brave highland pines cannot stand the rigors of the winter climate at this great height, and it is a timberless region.

Our interest in this desolate but entertaining bit of country was temporarily diverted. From the great eastern precipice which we were gradually leaving in our rear came a faint roaring. Looking backward we saw a white stream pouring down a cleft in the giant wall. At first we thought we were looking upon a far-flung waterfall—a rival to Yosemite. But soon we saw that the crystal cataract was of powdered snow—another avalanche plunging down its two-thousand-foot course from the wall of the summit snow-cap to the shattered névé of the glacier. Presently the flow ceased entirely, leaving the gash in the face of the cliff empty.

A possible mile's travel, across the plateau, took us past the foot of another red, volcanic cone whose summit rose four or five hundred feet above our route. Then the trail began to drop.

We now sa v, with some concern, that we had hardly given ourselves enough time to reach a good camping-place before nightfall. The timber seemed miles away, and it was getting late. As the trail descended, the lava became more and more exposed, and soon there was scarcely any soil at all. The rocks grew jagged and rough. The trail was dim and hard to follow. At places only the scratches of old hoof-marks indicated its presence. Prolonged searches were necessary to determine its sinuous course. Whenever possible we hurried; but the lava-points were cruel to the horses' feet, and our progress was perforce slow. The evening shadows were lengthening at an alarming rate. It began to look as though we should have to pass the night on that desolate lava-bed, without feed for our horses or means of building a fire.

On we went, determined to utilize every minute of daylight in an effort to reach a more hospitable region. A new difficulty confronted us. A turbulent little glacial current tumbled across the trail. It was narrow enough for me to cross by jumping from rock to rock; but we knew that treacherous round boulders lay in its bed, and there was danger that a horse might step between them and snap a leg. But the trial must be made. The sagacious animals, wise in the ways of mountain torrents, stepped gingerly, feeling their way foot by foot, and bracing themselves against the rush of the water. Soon all, including little Cricket, were safely over, and we hastened onward.

Darkness fell while we were still on the desert of blackened, twisted lava. But the worst of the route was over, and the trail was easier to follow. At last a cluster of trees loomed through the night, and soon we came into a little, open expanse. Whether the space was covered with grass or a low-growing heather we could not tell; but we had no choice. We threw off the saddles and pack, and tied poor Tony to a tree so that he could seek food the length of his rope. We managed to start a fire, and, so, we made a dry, unsatisfactory camp.

Morning did not improve our opinion of our camping-place. It had been a makeshift, and that was the best that could be said for it. But "any port in a storm." We were thankful that we had not been obliged to pass the night on the lava-fields.

Our poor horses had fared badly, through dearth of grass. After a hasty breakfast we started on in search of a more congenial habitat. We now entered the delightful sub-Alpine timber belt. The sharp lava spires had given way to pleasant, springy soil which responded happily to the impact of bruised hoofs. The trail was easy to follow. We had not gone a mile when we came to a spot so entrancingly beautiful that we went into camp forthwith.

Down through a little valley, fringed with sub-Alpine evergreens, came a stream, crystal clear. On either side lay tiny, lawn-like meadows, with short lush grass,, a delight to equine eyes. The creek made its advent into the upper end of the valley by a plunge over a small cliff, forming a silvery waterfall that added a touch of animation to the otherwise quiet scene. The tinkle of the water was music to the ear. Looking down the slope, one saw long vistas through solemn, stately groves; looking upward, there was a gleam, through trees, of the eternal snows of the mountain.

Here we decided to spend at least a day. We staked Tony where he could find his fill of delicious grass, and left the other horses to graze near by. Then we started on our rambles for the balance of the day. Up past the little waterfall we went; on up the stream, through a succession of diminutive valleys; the trees grew smaller as we climbed; the way became wilder and more rocky and we came, at last, to where the poor, gnarled evergreens, borne down by the snows of countless winters and whipped by a thousand icy gales, could no longer hold their heads aloft, but sprawled along over the stony surface like great, grotesque vines.

And what a wonderful view of the mountain we had! The

northern face of the great peak is more heavily burdened with snow than any other side. Great ice-cascades tumble down from the summit ice-cap to feed the glaciers that reach far down between the rocky ridges. These ridges extend well up the steeper upper slope of the mountain, forming sharp cleavers by some of which the summit may be reached. The whole north side presents an aspect of stupendous Alpine grandeur.

We stood in a region of tangled masses of stunted evergreens; of long rocky ridges; of vast moraines; and of shining snow-fields stretching up to the precipitous slopes of the massif. The view to the south was filled with the huge, ice-clad bulk of Mount Adams; but to the north the eye swept a broad expanse. Sweeping downward from our feet, the long slopes fell away, through ever-increasing density of evergreen, to a wide plateau covered with forest, and gemmed with many picturesque lakes. Beyond lay the great earth-folds of the Cascade Range; the far sky-line on the right was dominated by the serrated pinnacles of Goat Rocks; farther away, to the left, loomed the majestic form of Rainier.

It was late when we returned. As we approached the camp we saw that something was wrong. Black Tony, he of the pigeon-toes, lay rolling on the ground in agony. I saw, at once, that he was terribly sick; but I had no means of knowing the cause. It occurred to me that he might have eaten some poisonous plant at our miserable camp of the night before.

Here, indeed, was a serious situation. It was very likely that our horse would die. We were miles from the nearest human habitation. We had not seen another human being for many days. The great lava-beds, in addition to twenty miles of rough mountain trail, were between us and our hack. And the loss of Tony would mean that we could not use our hack if we reached it; for Cricket was too small to hitch to a vehicle, besides being unbroken. Therefore, even if we could get to the hack, there would still be thirty miles between us and our home on the Klickitat. We were in one of the loneliest spots in the United States, with a dying horse upon our hands.

We had no medicine. It seemed that we could do nothing but stand by and see the poor animal die. We were all deeply attached to him, and I think his suffering made a far deeper appeal to us than did the contemplation of our own situation.

I could think of but one thing to do. With much difficulty we succeeded in getting the poor beast on to his feet. Then leading him by a short rope I began trotting him back and forth on the greensward. Up and down we trotted, stopping occasionally to rest. Up and down, up and down, ever up and down, we went; backward and forward; around and around; turning and turning, through time interminable, always on the trot.

It grew dark; but still we kept on. Presently I began to think that the horse was better; gradually this thought became a certainty. Yet far into the night, we kept up this intermittent, weary process, in the flicker of the campfire. When, at last, I felt free to go to bed, it was with the conviction that the crisis was past and that our dumb friend would live. Several times during the night I got up to see how my patient was doing; but each time his condition was reassuring, and when morning came he showed little trace of his recent indisposition. Our relief can be imagined by those who have faced a similar situation.

Another glorious day dawned for us, and we set forth again. The trail led over a succession of timbered ridges and across little valleys, similar to the one in which we had just camped. Presently we met two sheepmen—the first humans, besides ourselves, that we had seen on the mountain. Although thousands of sheep, each summer, with their herders, roam the lower slopes of Mount Adams, so vast is this great wilderness that one may often travel through it for days at a time without seeing another soul. This was especially true at the time of which I am now writing.

The men told us we should soon come to a trail bearing down the mountain-side to the right. This, in the course of two or three miles, would bring us to the big huckleberry patch where many Indians were encamped. Thither we decided to go. We found the trail without difficulty, and bore off down the slope.

In rounding a thicket in a bend in the trail, we came suddenly face to face with a small cavalcade of Indians. In front rode a young squaw. This maiden of the forest, as unstoical as some of her civilized white sisters, emitted a little shriek of surprised alarm.

"Mika quash? (Were you scared?)" asked my mother in her best Chinook.

"Yes," admitted the young lady, in perfect English, "I was a little frightened."

Thirty or forty years ago, the Chinook jargon was the almost universal medium of oral communication between the whites and the Indians of eastern Washington, although it has now generally fallen into disuse. At that period, even many Indians who understood English refused to talk it, insisting upon conversation in this picturesque lingo. It was therefore natural for an old-timer to address an Indian in Chinook when he met him. However, an assumption that all noble red men must be so approached sometimes led to embarrassing situations. A friend of mine once met a party of Indians on a mountain trail. At the head rode a young buck wrapped in a gaudy blanket. By way of opening the conversation, my friend asked in classic jargon:

"Mika kumtux Chinook wawa? (Do you understand the Chinook language?)"

"Yes," answered the Indian, in purest English accent, "I *can* talk it. Is that the only language you understand?"

He was a graduate of an Eastern college.

A number of young Indians had received good educations; some of them in Eastern schools. But many of these had reverted to the primitive ways of their tribes, and you might meet, on the summit of the Cascades, an aborigine who was better qualified to converse in one of the dead languages than in Chinook.

A short time after meeting the little party of Indians, we reached the encampment. It was situated well down the edge of the plateau, in a park-like region, by the side of a dry stream-course. My mother asked one of the squaws where they got their water. "Oh, by-an'-by, some come," was the answer.

Sure enough, about the middle of the afternoon, there was a sudden rush and a roar, and a fair-sized little glacial torrent was tumbling down over the course that but a few minutes before had been dry. The stream continued to run until some time during the night; but in the morning the bed was dry once more. We were told that this was a daily occurrence.

I have often regretted that I never made an opportunity to follow this intermittent stream to its source, to determine the cause of its strange behavior. Thirty years after our visit, L. V. McWhorter, of Yakima, Washington, a great friend of the Western Indians, informed me that some of his Indian friends had recently told him of the stream; but I have never seen any one who could explain its mystery.

We were now in a different watershed. A greater part of the water on the east side of Mount Adams drains into the Klickitat River and so reaches the Columbia in eastern

Washington. The water from the part of the mountain we were now on drains to the Cispus and the Lewis Rivers, and thus finds the great river in the western part of the State.

The huckleberry patches northwest of Mount Adams and along the slopes of the Cascade Range draw hundreds of Indians each summer. In the latter part of the nineteenth century, these people came from far and near on horseback, and many and picturesque were the berry caravans in those days. The camps were scenes of animation and bright colors. The squaws devoted their time assiduously to picking and drying the luscious berries; but their lords and masters spent most of their waking hours in gambling, horse-racing, and hunting. There are several species of the huckleberry, all of which are delicious, and we thought it a rare treat to spend a day or more in feasting on them. One may eat huckleberries until he is so full that he feels he can never again look a berry in the face; and five minutes later he will be eating as voraciously as ever.

In the afternoon I left my mother and sister to feast on the huckleberries which grew in abundance near camp. Mounting Cricket, I set out on a trail leading toward the northwest, in the hope that I might reach some mining prospects that a number of Klickitat people were trying to develop. I knew that this camp was at least ten or twelve miles away; but I hoped that I might make the trip during the afternoon, provided the trail were fairly good.

It was a pleasant ride through the cool, fragrant forest; but after going several miles I found that the trail led down into one of the immense canyons, several of which are to be seen to the west and northwest of Mount Adams. Knowing that the mine lay at least no nearer than the bottom of this canyon, and that I could not penetrate its depths and get back before dark, I decided to return. About this time, a young Indian, who had been out on a deer hunt, came riding along the trail on his way back to camp. Finding him disposed to sociability, I turned and rode with him. We were soon in friendly conversation.

Suddenly he broke out in a sort of wailing call: "O-o-o-h, I'be lost my dog—my good dog—my heap sabe dog!"

Then presently again: "O-o-o-h, how can I find my dog—my good dog—my heap sabe dog?"

And after another interval: "O-o-o-h, he's my good dog—he's a heap sabe dog—where can I find him?"

So on, until we reached camp, with his long-drawn, wailing cry, which seemed to me an admixture of lament for the vanished pup; of call to the lost animal; and of effort to apprise me of the missing canine's virtues. Whether or not he ever found his "heap sabe" dog I do not know.

Next morning we resumed our journey 'round the mountain. As soon as we reached the trail we had left the day before, the one leading westward, trouble began. This part of the route was little traveled, and it was hard to follow. It was frequently necessary to leave the horses to graze while we scouted for the lost trail. On one of these little excursions, I rambled a considerable distance up the mountain-side, and so came on to the moraines of the largest glacier on Mount Adams. At one place where the overlying gravel had slid away, I was surprised to see blue ice. Other than this, there was no indication of ice near, although I had an excellent view of the glacier itself.

All of the trails on Mount Adams, at that time, were Indian trails, and those portions not frequently traveled by the red men were soon made hard to find by the action of the elements, if they were not obliterated entirely. So we had much difficulty this day, which otherwise was rather uneventful, and we did not go so very far; but when we camped at night we were well on the west side of the moun-

WEST SIDE OF MT. ADAMS FROM NEAR TIMBER-LINE AT MORRISON CREEK CAMP-GROUNDS

The great slide of May, 1921, is seen on the left side of the mountain

STORM CAP ON MOUNT ADAMS FROM AVALANCHE VALLEY

tain. We had an excellent view of its western face, capped by the triple summit. On this side the parkland belt has not so long and gentle a slope as it has on the other sides, and, taken altogether, it is probably the least interesting side of the great peak. Nevertheless, it is well worth a visit, for it has three considerable glaciers, a remarkable ice-fall, some fine precipices, and quite recently it was the scene of a tremendous slide that attracted nation-wide attention.

Our interesting trip around Mount Adams was now drawing to a close, and we were homeward bound. Aside from an animated jig which unlucky Tony danced when he ran into a yellow-jackets' nest, there were no more very exciting incidents. We were approaching the better-known portions of the mountain. We passed over a succession of sparsely timbered, park-like ridges on the White Salmon watershed; along the front of tremendous moraines; by the place where Maxwell and I had camped the year before; and ascended a great ridge to the southern slopes of the mountain. Here we must cross another jagged lava-flow; not so broad or so long as the one on the northeast, but sufficiently large to cause an annoying bit of trail. Then we came to the border of the wonderful Bird Creek Meadows and found that the trail bore straight down the long slope toward Camas Prairie. A few miles along this trail brought us finally, through quaking-asp groves, to the little flat on Bird Creek where ended the primitive wagon-road, the outlying link between civilization and the wilderness.

We now had a road on which we could have used our hack; but we must follow it to Glenwood and then take the other road for several miles, before we could gain the means for easier transportation.

We camped that night on Bird Creek. Next day we went on and retrieved our hack, so having completed the entire circuit of the mountain. We had seen each side of the peak, and had looked upon every one of its glaciers.

I think there can be no doubt that my mother and sister were the first white womenkind to go around Mount Adams. Eleven years later I met a party, containing two or three women, making the circuit of the peak. On their return, in the newspaper accounts of their trip, they made the claim that these were the first white women to circle the mountain. But this was more than half a decade after mention of our journey had appeared in print.

IV

THE GREAT STORM ON THE MOUNTAIN

Mount Hood had been illuminated, and I wanted to illuminate Mount Adams. I had a fervent desire to burn red fire upon that lofty summit, so that the unique display could be seen throughout the entire surrounding country. The night of the Fourth of July seemed to me a propitious time for such an event.

My uncle, W. A. Maxwell, who had been with me on my first ascent of the mountain, had graduated from the school-teaching profession and was now editor of the "Goldendale Sentinel," published in the county seat of Klickitat County. He joined in my plans, at first, but, as matters turned out, he could not make the trip, although he aided materially in giving publicity to the undertaking.

The night of July 4, 1891, was the one selected for the illumination. Without much difficulty I got together a small party. It was composed of my father, J. A. Rusk—"Jim" Rusk as he was called by all the old-timers—Milt Gilbreath, John Keel, Frank and Harrison Thompson, and myself—all local residents. Most of these were but mildly interested in the enterprise.

Maxwell had undertaken to secure red fire from The Dalles. But when we met him at Blockhouse on the afternoon of July 1st, we were disappointed to learn that no red fire could be had at The Dalles. There was no chance to get it elsewhere. Klickitat County in those days was without railroads. The stage-coach was the most rapid means of transportation. Portland was the nearest point from which we could hope to obtain the much-wanted article, and getting it from Portland in time was now out of the question. After consultation with my father, we decided we would go and climb the mountain, anyhow. So Maxwell returned to Goldendale and we set our faces toward the great snow-clad peak.

Glenwood, the little hamlet on the north side of Camas Prairie from where the mountain looms so grandly, was reached next day. Here we consulted one of the storekeepers to see if he might not have something that could be used as a substitute for red fire. It was decided that cotton-batting soaked in turpentine would come as nearly filling the requirements as anything we could obtain. This would make sufficient blaze, although lacking in the desired red color. So we bought a quantity, as the best makeshift we could get, and resumed our journey.

We had our hack, with the old reliables, Doc and Tony, for a team, and there was a saddle-horse or two besides. We were heavily loaded, and the second was an extremely hot day. Consequently we went slowly, and we had not reached the end of the Bird Creek wagon-road when we went into camp that night.

Around the camp-fire one may often hear learned discussions coming from most unexpected sources. Some of the theories there advanced are startling, to say the least, and occasionally one is promulgated that is worthy of permanent record. On this particular evening one of the men said the idea that the earth is round is all foolishness. (Possibly he expressed it a little more forcibly than that.) The world is not round; he knew better than to accept any such silly notion. The world, he said, is flat; it floats in water; in the summertime it floats down south where it is warm; in the winter it floats up north where it is cold. He had given the matter much profound study. We were so impressed by the soundness of his reasoning that we did not attempt to take issue with him. One minor detail, however, he did not make very clear. He did not tell us what sustains the vast body of water in which the earth floats.

The following day we left our hack at the end of the wagon-road, on the little quaking-asp flat, packed our outfit on the horses, and proceeded up the trail to Bird Creek Meadows, along the route down which my mother, sister, and I had come the year before. We made camp at an elevation of about sixty-five hundred feet.

In some countries the drive up Bird Creek would be considered picturesque enough to call for enthusiastic praise; but in this region of superlative beauty it is often passed unnoticed. From Glenwood to the end of the old wagon-road the drive was up long slopes, through a fine open forest; first of stately pines which later mingled with other conifers, the whole green-robed brotherhood gradually assuming an Alpine character as the upper levels were reached. The ground was well covered by a waving carpet of pine-grass, while many patches of bright-hued flowers gave dashes of brilliant color to the scene.

But when one gets to Bird Creek Meadows he is apt to forget the beauty he has passed through lower down. These so-called meadows form a broad park-belt lying between the five-thousand-foot contour and snow-line, and extending from Hell-Roaring Canyon on the east to the great lava-flow on the west. The delightful clusters of vales and meadows, watered by the rivulets of upper Bird Creek, are divided here and there by low ridges ornamented with rows of beautiful sub-alpine evergreens. Nature has here laid out her lawns on a grand scale. The level glades, richly carpeted by luxuriant green grass; the many groves of thick-limbed firs; the abundance of wood; the pure, cold water; the wide panorama of forest, mountain, and plain, make this favored tract ideal for a few days' sojourn. It has also been called "Happy Valley," and happy, indeed, is the man who has the chance to camp here for a while.

The view of Adams from this side, however, is not nearly so imposing as it is from the other sides. One here looks against the narrow southern face of the mountain and consequently gets little idea of the bigness and majesty of the peak. Moreover, from the upper part of the meadows, the massif is hidden by the tremendous moraines of Mazama Glacier. These moraines appear as great, sharp ridges extending across the face of the mountain, at an elevation of about seventy-five hundred feet, from Hell-Roaring Canyon to South Butte. On a stormy day the clouds dragging across the tops of these moraines make one of the impressively thrilling sights of the mountain.

The afternoon we pitched our camp in the Meadows was a remarkably clear one. As the evening advanced, we had a wonderful view of the mighty expanse to the south, extending across the great Klickitat Valley and on to the vast plateaus of eastern Oregon. Forty or fifty miles away, cast against the background of the gray Columbia Hills, a farmhouse was distinctly visible. We knew it, for it was the home of one of our former neighbors, when we lived in that very neighborhood years before. I think most readers will agree with me that forty or fifty miles is a good distance to see a farmhouse with the naked eye.

The delicate beauty of Bird Creek Meadows, or Happy Valley, has suffered greatly from the ravages of sheep and fire. For half a century thousands of sheep have ranged across this land of delight. Their sharp hoofs have cut the velvet surface of the greensward and trampled the dainty flowers into the earth. Their bedding-grounds have been eloquent of their presence, and the aroma of the evergreens has been lost in the odors of the sheep-camp. Dozens of clumps of the marvelous sub-alpine trees have been swept by fire. The red destroyer has, time and again, stripped whole ranks of these noble trees of their exquisite foliage and left the gaunt trunks to bleach throughout the years; and there they stand, as mute accusers, like millions of their stricken fellows throughout the West, grimly awaiting the day when mankind shall awaken to a realization of the crimes that have been committed against the beauty of the hills.

Even on the evening of which I write occurred an example of this thoughtless vandalism. One of the men of our party, without our knowledge of his intentions, just after dark, slipped up and set fire to a magnificent cluster of trees. When we knew what had happened, it was too late to save the group. The flames immediately enveloped the beautiful mass of green, feathery branches, and leaped high into the air, a roaring, bright column of destruction. It was a thrilling, though sorrowful, spectacle. The whole region roundabout was lit by the glow, and it must have been visible for many miles. In a few minutes the noble clump was nothing but a few blackened snags from which the glory had departed forever.

The man who did this deed was of strange composition. He was an excellent fellow and, in other ways, a good citizen. Yet, like many another man in those days, he was obsessed with the idea that the utter destruction of all forests would be a highly desirable consummation for the benefit of mankind. Several years later I happened to be in a prospecting party including him and three others—five of us in all. When we were in a remote part of the Cascade Range, this man began to set fires as we passed along the trail. Of all the party, I alone remonstrated with him, but in vain. Finally I told him he was liable to get into trouble with the law if he did not desist. Whereupon another member of the party spoke up and said: "If he does, I guess there's enough of us here to swear him out of it!"

What could one nature-lover do in the face of such public opinion as this? At that time the man who fought for forest preservation generally fought alone. Perhaps eight out of every ten average men thought it would be a good thing to burn off the timber and get it out of the way! The United States Government had not yet undertaken the protection of the Western trees. True, there were State laws against the setting of fires; but I never knew of an instance where one was enforced. So the great conifers were almost friendless, especially those that were not readily available for lumbering. These noble patriarchs were helpless against the onslaughts of any thoughtless or worthless individual who happened to have a match in his pocket.

Of late years the United States Forest Service has done great work in the saving of our Western trees. Still its system is neither perfect nor entirely effective; and we are forced to the reluctant conclusion that incompetent and unscrupulous men often creep into it. We are justified in believing that some of these wink at, if they do not actually connive at, violations of the law and regulations.

It may be well to say here, that within the past five or six years the Forest Service has set aside a large area of the Bird Creek Meadows for public recreational grounds. There is still enough left of the natural beauty of the place to make it wonderfully attractive, and if an earnest effort is made to conserve and improve it, it will eventually regain a great part of its original glory.

Milt Gilbreath had voluntarily assumed the rôle of cook for the expedition, and very creditably did he perform his functions. We went to bed in good season, and we were early astir on the morning of the Fourth, ready for the arduous work of the day.

Our plan was for the entire party to climb the mountain, each helping to carry the illuminating material, some food, and extra clothing. The rest would return to camp in the afternoon, while my father and I would remain all night on the summit, setting off the fire at nine o'clock. How much of this plan was carried out I shall now proceed to tell.

Our little party was sufficiently picturesque, as we slowly wound our way up over the snow-fields, through the upper part of the meadows, in the crisp morning air of the Fourth. The weather for some days had been perfect, although exceedingly warm, and we had no reason to anticipate a change. The dawn was clear and bracing, and there was every promise of another perfect day.

An hour's time served to bring us up through the rapidly dwindling tree-clusters, the velvety, flower-strewn lawns, and the boulder-capped ridges of the parklands and put us face to face with the savager aspects of the great moraines. The snow was still hard; but we topped the moraine by the aid of a steeply inclined snow-field, and proceeded across the gentle slope of a small glacier toward the great lava ridge which forms the lower stairway for the southern ascent of the mountain.

As we crossed the glacier, sharp gusts of wind cut our faces. But the sky was still clear and we were not alarmed. We soon reached the ridge, and a stiff scramble brought us on to the jagged crest. Here the wind assailed us a little more fiercely, a sharper bite in its icy teeth. But there were no clouds, and on we went, unafraid.

Now began a long, monotonous grind up the great lava backbone. The wind seemed to be steadily increasing in strength. The rough, unworn boulders and the sharp lava-points were trying to the patience, and they sapped our strength. Occasionally we gained some relief by taking to a snow-field that filled a depression between minor ridges.

But for the most part our way was over the rocks. Before we were halfway to the saddle the wind had gained such violence that, in climbing over one of the lava blocks, a particularly strong gust caught me and whipped me off.

The two Thompsons forged ahead, followed at short intervals by Keel and Gilbreath, leaving my father and me in the rear. These men were good backwoodsmen; but they had never climbed high mountains, and they had not learned that to climb a big peak quickly one must do it slowly. I have always refused to be hurried on a long ascent, and, generally, being one of the rear ones at the beginning, I have had the satisfaction of being one of the first on top.

At some place along the great ridge we converged into the route followed by Maxwell and me, two years before. Maxwell and I had come up from the White Salmon slope, and our starting-point had been several miles from the Bird Creek Meadows camp we had left this morning. The routes of parties climbing from the White Salmon side and those climbing from the Bird Creek side generally come together, either upon the lava ridge or at the saddle. One comes up on to the ridge from the west, the other from the east. Since I described the ascent of the mounain from this point on, in considerable detail, in my account of the first climb, it will not be necessary to repeat it here.

By the time I reached the saddle the Thompsons were far in the lead. They were well advanced on the great snow-slope leading to the first summit. The others were scattered along between, my father being just ahead of me. The wind had attained the dignity of a gale.

As we crossed the snow-filled saddle we found thousands of dead grasshoppers and other insects, besides a humming-bird and a duck, each in its own little depression in the snow. On different occasions, while climbing Adams, I have found numbers of such birds and insects; and once my party found a dead mouse at an elevation of nearly twelve thousand feet. One often finds live spiders crawling over the snow at high altitudes, and, rarely, live butterflies and other insects are seen. I presume the dead birds and insects that one finds are carried on to the high snow-fields in gales; or in making high flights they strike the mountain, where the glare of the sun on the snow so bewilders them that they cannot escape, and they soon chill to death. It is barely possible that a hurricane might sweep a small animal like a mouse far up the slopes—either dead or alive—but I think it more probable that the one referred to got lost and wandered on to the lonely heights to die. Or, again, it might have been carried there and dropped by an eagle or a hawk, although I have never seen any bird flying above the summit ridge of Mount Adams.

In discussing animal and vegetable life on the high peaks of the Cascades, it must be remembered that the snow-line on the northern Oregon and the Washington mountains is a great deal lower than it is on the mountains of Colorado and California. The snow-line in Colorado and California (if we except such northerly giants as Shasta), is eleven or twelve thousand feet above sea-level, while in the northern Cascades it may vary from a little over five thousand feet to about seventy-five hundred. So, to meet the same Arctic conditions that prevail on a twelve-thousand-foot Washington mountain, a Colorado or a California peak would have to be at least sixteen or seventeen thousand feet high.

There is no such thing as a uniform snow-line on any great peak; there are too many conditions to vary it, not only on different mountains, but on different sides of the same mountain; yet, as a general proposition, it may be said that Mount Adams is well mantled with snow and ice for more than five thousand feet from its summit down.

As we began the ascent of the great snow-slope, the wind swept us with added fury. But as yet there were only a few scattered clouds swirling through the sky. My father and I were now close together. Gilbreath and Keel had slowed down perceptibly; but the Thompsons still maintained their long lead. Our packs were not very heavy, yet the few pounds they weighed added greatly to the difficulty of climbing in the thin air. The gale, too, was striking us at right angles and its pressure increased our troubles and required much strength for resistance that otherwise might have been used to overcome altitude. We each had overcoats which were put on when we found, to our surprise, that we could not keep warm even while climbing. The wind was cold and it cut like blades of ice.

Our course was roughly parallel to one of the long boulder ridges that lead up the great slope from the saddle to the first summit. We could not see to the west beyond this ridge. We had chosen the snow route. Presently detached clouds began to sweep past us, with frightful rapidity, so close that we could almost reach out and touch them.

And now we saw, in truth, that we were in for a tremendous battle with a storm of no mean magnitude. As the wind increased, and the clouds rushed by in ever-increasing numbers, we found it harder and harder to fight off the cold that pierced to our very bones. As we climbed we could not hold up our heads against the fierce blasts, and we had to keep our eyes upon the steep slope just before us. The booming of the gale upon the rocky ramparts was now incessant. The fearful speed of the flying clouds attested the frightful velocity of the wind.

Fortunately for us, the recent hot weather had left the snow in so soft a condition that we had no trouble in keeping our footing on the steep face of the mountain, although the hurricane was now trying to tear us from our tracks.

In spite of our slow progress, my father and I soon overtook Gilbreath and Keel—both chilled to the marrow and utterly discouraged. We cheered them as best we could; but there was little one could offer by way of encouragement in the face of the elemental fury that assailed us. Presently we came upon the Thompsons, huddled in the lee of the boulders, trying to get some relief from the onslaughts of the gale. We, too, dived beneath the rocks, and there we all crouched for a few minutes listening to the roar of the wind as it swept across the rocky barrier.

The rock-huddling process now became a habit. It is astonishing how friendly a boulder can be at times. We would climb for a short distance, braced against the pressure from the west. Yet, with our heavy coats and encumbering packs, and with all our strenuous exertions, we could scarcely keep from freezing. We deserted the snow and took to the rock stairway. Whenever we could bear the piercing needles of the wind no longer, we would crawl beneath the protecting lava blocks for another brief respite. And then we would try it again.

Gilbreath was the first to give up. He said his health had not been very good the summer before, and he "believed" he would go back. Keel said he "guessed" he would go back too. So we took a part of their packs and watched them disappear down the mountain-side in the swirling clouds.

For Gilbreath I must say that he was a good fellow; but one of the earth's unfortunates. Although intellectually above the average, he was never strong physically. A number of years later he became totally blind, and finally died after long suffering. So I did not blame him for being the first to quit in the teeth of that howling storm.

But one member of the party, not heretofore mentioned, seemed to be having the time of his life. This was a splendid, big, part Newfoundland dog, named Nero, belonging to Frank Thompson. He frisked about over the snow, utterly oblivious of the cold or the tempestuous giant that was striving to drive us back. He was evidently enjoying himself immensely.

Soon after Gilbreath and Keel had left us, the clouds closed around the mountain so thickly that we could see nothing that was not close at hand. Had I not been somewhat familiar with the route, because of my previous ascent, it would have been impossible for us to proceed at all. We were now clambering up and around the great boulders, and our exertions brought us almost to the limit of our endurance; yet we could not keep warm. If it had not been for the brief periods of rest and relief from the driving cold, which we so frequently took behind the rocks, we should have been forced to instant retreat.

It did not take much of this to more than satisfy the Thompsons. Gone was their morning enthusiasm; gone was their early desire for a swift dash to the summit. They decided to go back.

My father and I took a part of their packs. They turned their faces downward, and the clouds instantly swallowed them. Notwithstanding the ferocious gale and the wild turmoil of rushing clouds, no fresh snow had as yet fallen, and our newly made tracks could be easily followed down the mountain-side. There was little danger in going back; the danger was in going on.

My father and I now faced the wild fury of the storm alone. Owing to the density of the clouds, there was no way of correctly judging our position on the mountain—that is, we could not tell how high we were. Although the velocity of the wind had increased immeasurably since we left the saddle, we judged that the hurricane had become a general one and that the lower levels were receiving their proportional share.

With our augmented packs we continued the process of alternate climbing and ducking beneath the rocks. I have no means of knowing how long we kept on. If such a thing was possible, the wind was increasing in ferocity all the time. The clouds were driving across the face of the mountain so thickly that we could not now see a half-dozen steps in any direction. We had to keep close together to avoid losing one another. Only by the contour of the peak could we tell the direction in which we were going. Such a situation could not last long.

Possibly an hour after the Thompsons left us, we suddenly came off of the boulder ridge on to a little patch of level gravel. I did not recognize the place. It had doubtless been covered with snow on my first ascent. Not until four years later was I to learn that we had reached the first summit.

We started across the gravel. The wind caught us with indescribable fury. We were grasped in the arms of the tempest and forcibly shoved several steps sideways before we could stop ourselves. A few steps more and we should have been hurled over the great eastern precipice. We had to brace ourselves desperately to keep from being swept bodily from the mountain.

My hat flew off and shot straight out into the clouds. How far it went I could not guess. Probably it sailed on through that seething riot of mist, for many, many miles, finally to settle down through ten thousand feet of vertical space, and at last come to rest some place in the broad expanse of the Inland Empire. Its memory is stored away in the archives of my conjectures with that of a treasured cap lost in a mountain adventure thirty-one years after.

No words can describe the terrible majesty of that storm. The terrific impact of the gale against the rocky buttresses of the mountain produced a booming roar continuous in its intensity. The hurricane struck the western face of the peak with awful force and was flung up over the summit ridge with ever-increasing velocity. In the great void beneath the eastern precipices, no doubt, the wind was whirling in mighty gusts and eddies, while every crag was vibrating like the strings of a giant harp. The clouds swirled around and over and past us, driving their icy needles through our thick clothing and chilling the blood in our veins. There was nothing we could see but clouds, and we sensed the desperate turmoil about us only by the tear of the wind against our bodies and its boom upon the cliffs.

Holding the position we had gained, by supreme effort, and standing close together, we hurriedly discussed the situation. To persist was suicide. There was no shelter either on the first or the main summit. If a man were to survive the night, he must do it in the teeth of the hurricane, with no protection. Even if one could avoid being actually blown from the mountain, he must inevitably perish from the intense cold that was sure to prevail during the long hours of darkness. It would take the storm hours to subside after it once began to abate. And, if anything, it was still on the increase. A fire could never be started in such a gale, and, even if it could, our illumination could not be seen through that tumultuous rush of clouds. If we had had ourselves alone to think of, we might have been justified in taking such risks as we were willing to assume. But there were others to consider. There was but one thing to do. We must go back.

Turning cautiously, lest the wind catch us again and throw us over the eastern brink, we worked slowly back to the point of boulders. We were still reluctant to return, but we knew it must be done. Carefully we won our way downward; but we found no relief from the storm. We had the advantage now, however, of not having to stop for breath and there was no longer the exhaustion due to climbing efforts. When we reached the saddle, the gale was still so fierce that the boom of the wind around the lava cliffs was like the roar of a mighty waterfall.

We were hours in working our way down the great lava backbone and in getting to camp. We found the other men there, with a roaring fire in the shelter of a timbered ridge. Looking back to the mountain, there was nothing to be seen but the battling clouds. At camp the wind was mercilessly whipping the tree-tops.

Late in the evening the clouds cleared for a time, and the upper part of the peak stood clear and cold in the frosty air. But by the time darkness fell, low, dense clouds were again rushing up the western face and over the summit ridge with the speed of an express train.

In the morning the wind had died; but the mountain stood out white in a mantle of fresh snow, and this extended down the slopes far below our camp. Ice stood in the cooking utensils, and the thermometer, hanging within a few feet of the fire, registered the freezing point. It must have been well below zero on the summit.

We packed our effects, and hurried down through the newly fallen snow to more hospitable regions.

When we got back to civilization we found that the gale which had swept eastern Oregon and Washington on that memorable Fourth of July was the worst that had been known in many years. Imagination alone can picture its violence on the great mountain.

V

WHEN PEAK SPOKE TO PEAK

THE MAZAMAS, Oregon's great mountain-climbing club, was organized on the summit of Mount Hood, July 19, 1894. On that day one hundred and ninety-three persons reached the top of the wonderful peak, and an association was formed which was destined to give a mighty impetus to mountaineering in the Pacific Northwest.

Mount Adams was chosen for the second annual climb of the club. An ambitious programme was outlined, in addition to the ascent of the Washington mountain. The great chain of Cascades peaks was to be climbed by different parties, and an effort made to establish heliographic communication from British Columbia to California. Besides Adams, Mounts Baker, Rainier, Hood, Jefferson, and Diamond Peak were to be attempted by small parties, each carrying a heliograph.

The 10th of July, 1895, was the date set for these efforts; a time rather early in the season having been selected because of the greater likelihood of an absence of smoke from forest fires. As the great day approached I could not resist the temptation to join in the enterprise. I was then at my home on the Klickitat River, within a day's horseback ride of Bird Creek Meadows. Camping near our house, at the time, with his family, was M. F. Derting, a young Klickitat Valley farmer. He was a vigorous enthusiast in everything pertaining to outdoor sport, a tireless hunter and fisherman, and withal a man of remarkable physical energy. Although he had never done any high climbing, he gladly accepted my invitation to go along. We were without proper equipment for mountaineering but we decided to use such makeshifts as came to hand.

With blankets and provisions strapped to our saddles, we set forth the morning of July 8th, expecting to reach the Mazama camp the following day. The members of the club were to go up to the mountain, along the White Salmon River from the Columbia, by way of Trout Lake; a route that was then, and still is, a popular one. Their camp was to be on the White Salmon side, near the 1889 camp of Maxwell and me. Derting and I planned to reach this camp by way of the Bird Creek Meadows trail.

But when we reached Bird Creek Meadows we found vast quantities of snow covering the trail on the high ridges between the Meadows and the White Salmon camping-grounds. We could have worked our horses through this snow; but we felt that it would be too great a task—and a needless one—for the animals. So we camped in the Meadows, satisfied to climb the great lava ridge from this side and to meet the Mazama climbers at some place on the ascent. We appeared to be the only human beings on this part of the mountain.

The decision to camp at Bird Creek Meadows gave us an extra day before the ascent. This day—the 9th—was gloriously spent in a visit to two great glaciers. We rode eastward across the Meadows—the superb parklands—now pretty well filled with snow, to the tremendous south moraines of the vast, fan-shaped glacier that occupies the southeastern slope of Adams. This glacier had heretofore been known as "Hell-Roaring Glacier," being the one that descends into Hell-Roaring Canyon. During this 1895 outing, however, a party of thirteen Mazamas visited it and the Klickitat Glacier, and renamed the former "Mazama Glacier." Whether this visit was a day or so before, or after, the visit of Derting and myself, I do not know. Professor

W. D. Lyman, the well-known historian and mountaineer, had previously approached and examined the two glaciers from the south, and his fine descriptions of them were perhaps the first to appear in print. Of course, his approach to Klickitat Glacier was from an entirely different point than that of my mother, sister, and myself in 1890.

Derting and I crossed the sharp, mountainous south moraine of Mazama Glacier, after leaving our horses; traversed the snow-covered expanse of the ice-field, keeping well clear of the steep break into Hell-Roaring Canyon; climbed on to the upper point of the great ridge dividing the two glaciers; and looked out upon that scene, the terrible sublimity of which no pen can ever describe.

"My God!" cried Derting, after the first glance, "I wish my wife was here!"

We stood upon tremendous cliffs, looking down upon the frozen cataract of Klickitat Glacier. The mighty river of ice, flowing over its wild, uneven bed, bound on each side by beetling lava precipices, rolled, with the gathered force of untold ages, toward the valley far below. A mile to the north the fire-twisted crags of an immense ridge, yellow, purple, red, and black, towered to a serrated sky-line, the farther wall of this canyon of God-given majesty. The southern wall was beneath our feet. Rent by a thousand gashes, the tortured ice tumbled, in Titanic confusion, down this lawless gorge, to be finally lost in the morainal débris of the lower end.

But to the west the awful immensity appalled the eye. The three-thousand-foot eastern precipice was close at hand. From the summit ice-cap, between the richly colored cliffs, to the fearful chaos of the glacier's upper end, the tumultuous ice-falls bore their burden of massed and broken blocks. Here was the home of avalanche and storm. These wondrous crags had never known the tread of living feet. They were as remote and lone as though upon another planet. The beauty of their coloring was beyond the artist's power. No ruins of ancient glory could rival the alabaster charm of the frozen piles at the foot of the monster wall. Infinite in design, unique in execution, they were the masterpieces in the architecture of the gods. And over all hung the soul-charm, the aura of the great mountain.

We stood at an elevation of about eighty-five hundred feet, at the higher point of the great ridge, the upper part of which divides Klickitat and Mazama Glaciers and the lower portion of which separates Hell-Roaring Canyon and the canyon of the Big Muddy. In my description of the circuit of the mountain in 1890, I have told how this ridge forms the southern wall of Big Muddy Canyon, and how, just above the then-snout of Klickitat Glacier, it sweeps southward forming a beautiful amphitheater. The western wall of this amphitheater, bending like a great fish-hook back toward Klickitat Glacier, forms the upper end of the ridge. It is not connected with the massif of the mountain, as the common névé of Klickitat and Mazama Glaciers sweeps around its western terminus. A big moraine is piled against the upper point of the ridge; and, as this moraine marks the dividing of two ice-streams, I have chosen to call it a divisional moraine.

Two years after the visit of Derting and myself, this ridge, which will some day be world-famous as one of earth's sublimest viewpoints, received its name. In August, 1897, my mother, Josie A. Rusk, my sister, Leah (now Mrs. M. Braat), and I had made a laborious ascent of the mountain. The following day we rode over to a beautiful little bench-meadow on the slope of Hell-Roaring Canyon and camped. From this camp, on August 21st, my mother and I made a trip across Mazama Glacier to the upper point of the great ridge. As we stood looking out upon that incomparable scene, my mother murmured in awe-struck tones:

"Surely, surely, this should be called the Ridge of Wonders!"

And the Ridge of Wonders it is to-day.

A chill wind was sweeping the mountain on the morning of the 10th. The sky was clear of clouds; but the lower air was full of smoke. The forest fires had begun their work of devastation early in the season. Derting and I made good time from our camp to the moraines. So far we had not seen another soul on the mountain.

Derting expressed a desire to get back to camp early in the afternoon so that we might ride far enough down the slopes to find abundant grass for the horses that night. I thought the horses were doing well enough; but my companion, being used to the large bunch-grass of the Columbia hills, did not realize that the small, hardy grass that grew in Bird Creek Meadows was far more nutritious than the rank-growing pine-grass along the lower part of Bird Creek.

The ascent of the great lava ridge, which leads up to the nine-thousand-foot level, was uneventful. The miserable pall of smoke shut off the distant view. There was no sign of Adams's southern neighbor, Hood, nor the western neighbor, Saint Helens.

As we approached the saddle, looking to the west, we saw three men working up the ridge from the White Salmon side. We knew they were the advance guard of the Mazamas. They seemed to have the advantage of us in position. Our call brought a distant response. We were suddenly assailed by a desire to beat them to the summit.

Crossing the saddle, we took to the long snow-slope leading to the first summit. The Mazamas chose the stairway of broken lava blocks. Soon they appeared to be well in the lead.

MOUNT ADAMS AND LYMAN GLACIER FROM THE NORTHWEST

MOUNT ADAMS FROM THE RIDGE OF WONDERS
Showing Klickitat and Rusk Glaciers

MOUNT HOOD ACROSS RIDGE OF WONDERS FROM BATTLEMENT RIDGE

Débris-covered end of Klickitat Glacier beyond fringe of trees in lower center

And now Derting, with the enthusiasm of the inexperienced mountaineer, feeling that his boundless energy would never exhaust, began to crowd matters. He forged ahead, and kept urging me to hurry. Although the foremost Mazamas were, by this time, considerably in advance of us and apparently gaining, I refused to make the mistake of too much speed. I felt that I was already pushing myself as hard as prudence would permit. No doubt my pace seemed exasperatingly slow to Derting.

Meanwhile other miniature figures had appeared below us, straggling up the mountain, and we knew that we should have much company in time. However, we were chiefly concerned with the few in the van, for they were showing evidences of being excellent climbers.

I have already mentioned our lack of proper mountain equipment. Not having hobnails for our shoes, we had wrapped gunny-sacks around our feet, and we managed to do fairly well in the snow with these. Nevertheless, our unpreparedness put us under a considerable handicap.

Suddenly above the wall of smoke the spire of Hood appeared. Later the rounded dome of Saint Helens sprang into view. We had risen higher than the cumbering murk of the lower world.

Derting continued to urge me on. Just as persistently did I refuse to hurry. We had lost sight of the leading Mazamas, and I felt that the race was lost. I stopped and ate a few bites of the lunch I carried.

As we slowly approached the point of rocks that marks the first summit, a suspicion dawned upon us that no one was ahead. When we topped the last of the boulders and looked toward the great summit dome, the suspicion became a certainty. Not a man was in sight. We were leading, and if we could only maintain our pace we should be the first on top. But we could not be sure of keeping the advantage we had gained. There were still eight hundred feet of hard climbing between us and the summit, and much can happen in eight hundred feet of hard climbing.

As I stepped out on to a patch of level gravel at the first summit, I recognized it as the place where my father and I had turned back in that terrific storm four years before. But how different were the conditions! True, a cold, disagreeable wind blew the entire day of the Mazama ascent, and it has been described by some as a gale; but it was a gentle zephyr compared to the hurricane that assailed us on that other trial.

We lost little time on the first summit. We hurried across the snow-field to the foot of the summit dome. The long grind up the last, toilsome slope began to have an effect on Derting that was inevitable. He had used too much energy in crowding, below the first summit. Now he began to lag. On the other hand, I had conserved my strength and now felt stronger than at any other point during the climb. I knew we were within striking distance of the top, and I was determined to keep the lead we had gained. I continually urged Derting to hold on to his nerve a little longer, for victory was in sight.

We reached the last pile of rocks, where Maxwell and I had found the sardine-can-record-box six years before. Here was now a more pretentious box and we hurriedly inscribed our names. Derting seemed strongly inclined to rest. But I did not know at what moment a pursuing Mazama would stick his head up over the rocks, so vigorously urged resumption of our upward trend. The short, gradual snow-slope was all that lay between us and the goal. On we went, and soon we stood upon the topmost swell—alone.

We had been four and one half hours on the way from the moraines of Mazama Glacier. Undoubtedly, up to that time, this was the fastest climb that had ever been made.

Glancing to the north, we saw the tremendous bulk of Mount Rainier rising above the smoke. But three points of the earth's surface were visible—Hood on the south, Saint Helens on the west, Rainier on the north, like great white icebergs standing out of a purple sea.

Turning to the east, we walked a few steps to the brink of the snow-precipice. With one look downward, Derting grabbed my arm and shouted:

"Get back from there!"

To look, for the first time, down the eastern face of Adams is an experience that is apt to test the strongest nerves. The level snow-field of the summit breaks off suddenly and overhangs in a white ledge of several hundred feet. Immediately beneath, the snow is heaped in a wildly crevassed, steeply sloping mass which rests upon the brink of the eastern precipices. Tremendous gashes, veritable snow-canyons, here cut across the face of the mountain. The icy, two-hundred-foot wall, standing above the precipices, is divided near the center by a great, flat-topped, rocky turret which forms the culminating dome of the great ridge I have mentioned as the north wall of Klickitat Glacier. The glance, sweeping downward from the summit-ledge across the jagged snow-mass, falls to the surface of the glacier a mile beneath. All detail of the awful crag-face is hidden from the view; but the terrific contortions of ice- and snow-fall stand plainly out; and you shudder at a realization of the fearful height on which you cling.

The day before we had looked upward from the Ridge of Wonders at this stupendous scene; now we looked down from its point of culmination.

Maxwell and I had missed this view, because of the enveloping clouds. We well might have walked over the brink before we knew it was there. We must have been within a few steps of it, yet we turned down the mountain in ignorance of what was so close at hand.

A few minutes after Derting and I had looked over the edge, the foremost of the Mazamas reached the summit. For the first time I now met C. H. Sholes, that splendid mountaineer, who for so many years proved a help and an inspiration to the climbers of the Pacific Coast. Sholes, together with T. Brook White, secretary of the club, and W. A. Langille, Mount Hood guide, was in charge of the Mazama expedition. It appeared that the leaders, quite a distance below the first summit, had yielded to the temptation to seek shelter from the wind, behind the rocks, and had there dozed sufficiently long to permit Derting and me to gain the lead.

Soon others began to get to the top. For hours stragglers appeared, a few at a time. During the day about twenty-five attained the summit, and this was nearly as many as the entire number of people who had climbed the mountain previous to that time.

It was seen with alarm that the smoke was rising. Soon Saint Helens was blotted out. Mr. White quickly had his instruments trained on Hood and Rainier. The heliograph, I may explain, is simply a mirror mounted on a frame set on a tripod. A shutter enables the operator to divide the sun-flashes into dots and dashes; and these, arranged according to the Morse code, enable the distant observer to read the message sent.

Suddenly, like a tiny star, a point of light shot from the summit of Mount Hood. All was excitement in our little group. A few minutes more, and messages were flying back and forth between the two mountains. How we onlookers thrilled as White and his assistants spelled out the signals from the distant summit, and answered in kind. So far had victory perched on the banner of the Mazamas.

But the remorseless smoke was rising slowly. The operators worked with feverish haste. Gradually the splendid mountain to the south disappeared from view, and exasperated disappointment prevailed. All attention was now turned upon Rainier. The upper part of this great peak stood out clearly the entire day; and a party was upon its summit with their heliograph trained on Adams; but, for some inexplicable reason, not a spark was seen from one to the other.

It was afterwards learned that the parties on Jefferson and Diamond Peak made successful ascents; but the miserable smoke foiled all efforts to communicate with the other mountains. The Mount Baker party, owing to lack of trails, failed even to reach the peak. So the net result of heliographic ambitions was confined to the messages flashed between Adams and Hood; but this, in itself, was a "signal" triumph for the club.

The summer of 1895 was one of devastating forest fires in this region. Later in the season terrific conflagrations swept through the timbered sections north of Mount Adams. So fearful was the havoc that from points south of the mountain great clouds of smoke could be seen rolling far up above the summit dome.

During the stay of the Mazamas on the top of Mount Adams, two pairs of carrier pigeons, from Portland lofts, were released. The poor little birds seemed bewildered when let loose. After circling a few times near the surface, they dipped sharply downward and disappeared into the smoke over the western face of the mountain. They were never seen again.

But the most important result of this important expedition

was in the determination of the approximate altitude of Mount Adams. To me it was a gratifying victory. I have previously told how the great peak's height had been persistently slandered. On this occasion W. A. Gilmore, of Vancouver, Washington, made many readings with a boiling-point thermometer. Professor Edgar McClure, of Eugene, Oregon (who a year or so later met a tragic fate on Mount Rainier), took careful observations with an aneroid. When their data were worked out they gave an elevation well over twelve thousand feet above sea-level; and Mount Adams took its rightful place as second among the mighty peaks of the Cascade Range. Great was the surprise and consternation of our Oregon friends when it was found to be more than a thousand feet higher than Mount Hood.

Derting did not forget his desire to get down to good grass before nightfall. So we left the summit early. We reached camp in due season, and without accident; saddled our horses and set off in search of that equine nutriment. But the way was long, and darkness fell upon us before we had found a place to camp. The strenuous exertions of the day had been too much for even Derting's tireless energy. In Western parlance, he was "all in," and my condition did not vary from his in any great degree. At last we reached a little flat by the side of brawling Bird Creek. Derting crawled down, threw off his saddle, tied his horse to the nearest tree, and rolled into the blankets, without looking to see if the grass he had been talking about all day was there or not. I was not far behind him.

Next day came the lesson I was never to forget. This time there had been no clouds to protect from the sun's fierce glare upon the snow. Derting and I awoke to the agonies of snow-blindness. For long hours we rode, unable to hold our eyes open, taking a swift glance now and then to see if our horses kept the right road or trail. The penalty for going up the mountain without colored glasses was a severe one, and the excruciating pain was a constant reminder of our folly; but it was over at last, and we were back on the Klickitat once more, with the relief that comes from a judicious application of potato poultices.

VI

MAPPING THE MOUNTAIN

EVERY winter more snow falls on Mount Adams than can melt away in the summer. The great summit dome is completely surrounded and covered by an immense snow- and ice-cap whose depth no man can know. It is evident that unless Nature provided some method for disposing of these vast accumulations the burden would eventually become greater than the mountain could bear. The solution of the problem is found in the glacial system of the big peak. Consequently, we find radiating from the mountain a number of glaciers, each of which is a mile or more in length. There are, besides, several smaller glaciers or fragments.

The snow, pressing downward from the summit, hardens as it advances, under pressure of its own weight, until it finally becomes steely-blue ice which forms great ice-streams that melt as they go and end well down the mountain. From the lower end, or snout, of each of these ice-streams, one or more small rivers of milk-white water spring, full-grown, and rush with mighty roar over boulder-strewn beds.

Some of the glaciers are fed directly from the summit-cap by means of great ice-cascades plunging down frightfully steep slopes; others receive their supply of snow through the medium of avalanches that thunder over tremendous precipices; while a few, that have their origin lower down, are fed by the snow which falls directly on their upper surfaces.

The study of glaciers is a fascinating one. They are the greatest of all landscape-makers; and mighty is their influence in shaping the destiny of continents.

I had had a number of interesting mountain experiences in the last quarter of the nineteenth century, and I was now to begin the twentieth century with a trip that was full of both interest and instruction.

Late in June or early in July, 1901, I received a letter from Professor Harry Fielding Reid, head of the geological department of Johns Hopkins University, conceded to be the leading glaciologist of the United States. Professor Reid was planning an extended Western trip to study the glaciers of the Cascade Range. He intended first to spend some time on Mount Hood with the Mazamas; then to put in a couple of weeks on Mount Adams; later going to Mount Rainier and Mount Baker. He asked me to make the arrangements for the Mount Adams journey and to accompany him on his visit to the mountain.

I was delighted with this opportunity. I lost no time in getting together a camp outfit and in securing horses.

I made my plans to meet Professor Reid at Trout Lake near the foot of the mountain. On my way thither from Goldendale, I reached Glenwood on July 27th. Here I had my first experience with the United States Forest Service. The Mount Adams country had just been included in one of the newly created forest reserves; and Ed. Snipes, an old-time Klickitater whom I had known from childhood, was the ranger in charge. We met at Glenwood. I told him where I was going.

"But," demanded Ed., "has he got a permit to go on the reserve?"

I explained that this was the first intimation I had had that such a permit was necessary.

"Well," said Snipes, "you tell Professor Reid not to go on that reserve without a permit from *me*."

Here was a serious dilemma. I was sure that no permit was necessary; but how was I to convince Ed. of that fact?

A bystander solved the question. He suggested that the new ranger write out a permit and give it to me to hand to Professor Reid. This procedure seemed to satisfy both the dignity and the authority of Uncle Sam's forest guardian. He took a pencil and promulgated a short document giving to Professor Reid and party the right to ramble over his domain. He handed the paper to me. This was the last sign I saw of a Government tree protector during the entire trip.

Late that evening I reached Trout Lake and met Professor Reid at the Guler Hotel. Next forenoon he visited some of the large lava caves near by, accompanied by Colonel L. L. Thomson, of Goldendale. Meanwhile there had also arrived from Goldendale Mr. N. B. Brooks and Dr. H. S. Goddard, friends of mine who wished to climb Mount Adams with us.

Professor Reid's equipment included a large tent, a large camera, an Eastman kodak, an aneroid, and the instruments for plane-table work. These things added to the provisions and camp outfit I had brought made a good load for the two pack-horses. At two-thirty on the afternoon of the 28th, we started for the mountain, accompanied by Mr. Brooks and Dr. Goddard. We followed the old White Salmon trail which I had traveled twelve years before when my first ascent was made. But the trail was dim and hard to keep, so we did not reach the snow that night.

The following morning, however, a short jaunt brought us well up to timber-line on the southwest slope, where we pitched camp. That afternoon we rode over the ridges; across the old south lava-flow; and through Bird Creek Meadows to Mazama Glacier. Professor Reid took a number of photographs, and did plane-table work as the beginning of his map of the great peak. We returned to camp in the evening.

On the next to the last day of July, Professor Reid, Mr. Brooks, Dr. Goddard, and I climbed the mountain by the usual southern route. The ascent was uneventful, aside from the scientific data secured.

Next day Mr. Brooks and Dr. Goddard went home, well pleased with their mountaineering experiences. Professor Reid and I returned to Mazama Glacier and established a station on the brink of Hell-Roaring Canyon. Here a white flag was left fluttering in the breeze in the hope that it would be visible from the Ridge of Wonders, across the great canyon, when we had completed the circuit of the mountain and had come once more into this part of the country.

We saw from the beginning that we were to be hampered by a vast amount of snow. There was more snow on Mount Adams in 1901 than in any other year in which I have visited the mountain. The broad expanse of the Mazama Glacier ice-field was well covered with snow, the bare ice appearing in but few places. At times when the ice is well exposed, this glacier, in common with one or two others on Mount Adams, presents some fine examples of the ice-well. These beautiful cylindrical wells, varying from a few inches to a few feet in diameter, lead straight down through the solid ice—some of them so deep that the bottoms cannot be seen. They are so regular in formation that many look as though they had been bored by machinery, although there are frequent variations. Usually a small stream falls into the ice-well, and its hollow roar can be heard in the cavernous depths. Some of the wells are free of water; in others clear water may be seen standing far below the surface; while occasionally one may be filled to the very top.

I have heretofore spoken of the great south moraines of Mazama Glacier. These are undoubtedly the greatest moraines on the mountain, having been gouged out and piled up along the southern ice-front because the glacier has no confining walls on that side. In places they are several hundred feet high. Terminal moraines are great ridges of gravel and boulders ploughed up at the ends of glaciers by the ice in its advance or deposited by it in its retreat. Lateral moraines are similar to the terminal, except that they have been piled up along the sides of the glaciers instead of at the ends. Medial moraines are deposits of rock and gravel that are being carried down on the ice near the middle stretches of the glaciers. Frequently ice remains beneath the rock- and gravel débris of moraines for many years.

Of recent years the courts have held that the best proof of a man's good character is the fact that people do not talk about him. The theory is, of course, that so long as he leads a decent, upright life there is no occasion for his neighbors to discuss him; but that the moment he transgresses, and his transgressions become known, he becomes the subject of criticism and condemnation on the part of those who know him. I think the same is true of horses, and that the quiet, well-behaved animals get themselves talked about a great deal less than the cantankerous ones. On this trip our equine equipment was rather limited and uncertain. Owing to the fact that a great many of the horses of the Klickitat Valley had been sent to summer pasturage before I received Professor Reid's letter, the supply of available ones was not great and I had to take what I could get.

First, for saddle-animal, we had Dandy, a black-and-white cayuse that had formerly been my sister's riding-pony, a successor to the lamented Cricket that had some years before gone to the place where all good horses eventually go. Dandy was a very good, dependable little mountain fellow, perhaps more accurate than the average of his kind. He was often detailed to bear Professor Reid on his side-trips to occupy observation stations, while I worked the pack-train, limited, around the mountain-side toward the next camping-place. However, Professor Reid's desires and Dandy's desires did not always run in the same channel, resulting in frequent disagreements, as a consequence of which Professor Reid eventually decided that he preferred to make his side-trips on foot.

The two pack-animals I had hired from my friend M. S. Short, an old pioneer of Klickitat County. One of these, Dan, was a staid and sober gray. Being of good disposition and perfectly reliable, he need not be the subject of gossip. The other was a small bay mare. She was called "Leatherhead"; but the name really flattered her. Keeping in mind a wild afternoon's chase, over the sand dunes along the Columbia River, in company with Mr. Short's son Ariah, before Leatherhead could be finally corralled, I was always careful to see that she never escaped the restraining influence of a good, stout rope; and whenever she was put out to graze this rope was always attached to a substantial tree or a thick stake driven well into the ground. She often evinced a desire to scramble the pack; therefore, she was the object of more earnest solicitude on my part than both of the other horses and our camp equipment combined.

Moreover, Leatherhead possessed an enterprising colt. At first Professor Reid called this a "foal," which is an Eastern method of saying "colt." But feeling that the honor of the Pacific Coast was at stake, I persisted in the word "colt." Finally Professor Reid began to say "colt," too. Thus did Western perseverance win in the end.

My contests with Leatherhead's colt were the cause of much quiet amusement to Professor Reid. I am not naturally cruel-hearted; but I began to have hopes of what *might* happen to that little beast when we came to ford the Klickitat River at the latter end of the journey. Aside from being always in the way or tangled in his mother's gear, or continually getting lost and causing frantic expostulations on the part of his dam, the colt's chief offense was his chewing of ladigo-straps and other leather paraphernalia, at every opportunity. No amount of suasion—moral or otherwise—would induce him to desist. Long before the trip was over, everything about Leatherhead's equipment, that looked or tasted like leather, was in a sorry plight. I have since put in long years wondering why I didn't have sense enough to sprinkle those straps generously with pepper.

In those days, in that remote section, it was almost impossible to get foods prepared especially for mountain work. Flour, bacon, beans, dried fruits, and coffee were generally the staples for such a trip as ours, and I had not been able to depart far from the accustomed path in providing for the journey. I had some canned stuff for lunches, such as sardines and oysters. But Professor Reid, being from Baltimore, had no appetite for oysters. I never did shine lustrously as a cook, and poor Professor Reid fared badly. I could fully sympathize with his occasional wistful references to Cloud Cap Inn on Mount Hood, and I could also understand his frequent desire to try his own hand at the cooking.

"Well, Professor," I would say in the morning, "what shall we have for breakfast?"

Followed a few moments of deep study on the part of the geologist. Then would come the reply:

"Suppose we have some coffee, some bread, and some bacon."

Then as the noon-hour approached, I would ask:

"What shall we have for dinner, Professor?" (Mount Adams society, I may remark, calls the midday meal dinner.)

Profound thought by the eminent scientist. Answer:

"Suppose we have some bread, some bacon, and some coffee."

As the shades of evening began to envelop the lower levels, I would inquire:

"What shall it be for supper, Professor?"

Meditation on the part of the man from Baltimore.

"Suppose we have some bacon, some coffee, and some bread."

Thus did we vary our menu from meal to meal.

The first day of August found us ready to start toward the north side of Mount Adams. The 1890 circuit had been made from east to west; now we were going from west to east. The great quantities of snow, extending far below timber-line and covering the old Indian trail except on the bare ridges, made the traveling hard and uncertain. In many places the streams had hollowed out great tunnels or caverns beneath the packed surface of the snow, and extreme care had to be used to keep a heavily laden horse from breaking through into one of these cavities. The loss of an animal and the consequent crippling of the expedition might easily have occurred at almost any moment during this hazardous journey along the western slopes of the mountain. Then, too, man or animal might at any time plunge into a hole caused by the melting of the snow around a sunken rock or a fallen tree. It was impossible to go farther down the mountain-side and avoid the snow, for there the surface was too rough and broken and too much covered with forest and down timber. When the Indians, long ago, made these trails they followed the lines of least resistance, and it was not the part of wisdom to depart from their routes any farther than necessary.

As I worked the pack-horses along this uncertain highway, Professor Reid, with Dandy, made his side-trips farther up the mountain, photographing and doing plane-table work. He could always pick up my tracks in the snow, so there was no danger of our getting separated. During the first day he made observations on the Avalanche and the White Salmon Glaciers. The former glacier, terminating in huge moraines, receives a great part of its snow supply from the very steep slopes on the southwestern part of the mountain. It was swept by the great slide of 1921. The White Salmon Glacier is fed by an ice-cascade which sweeps downward from between the main summit and the north summit, the last-named eminence breaking off on the south side and overhanging the upper part of the ice-stream in a considerable vertical precipice. The White Salmon Glacier also received part of the rush of the 1921 avalanche.

We camped for the night on what is known as Stegman Ridge. Of the thirteen nights we spent on the mountain, perhaps no particular one stands out in my memory more prominently than the others. All of our camp-fires were a rare treat to me. Professor Reid, even at that time, was a world-traveler, as well as being a scientist of note. He was a member of the International Committee on Glaciers; he had spent many seasons studying the glaciers of the Alps; he had climbed a number of the world's famous mountains; he had visited Mount Ararat, the Mountain of the Ark, in company with a party of other well-known scientists, under the auspices and protection of the Russian Government; and he had made the first map of Glacier Bay, Alaska, a part of his work in that interesting region being contemporaneous with that of John Muir. His investigations dealt particularly with the variations of glaciers, in size, from year to year, and one of his principal objects in coming to the Pacific Coast was to determine whether our ice-streams were advancing or retreating. The experiences of such a man, when told in an interesting manner, could not fail to be intensely entertaining, and I considered myself fortunate, indeed, to have the privilege of being his listener. In addition to the knowledge of other places that he imparted to

MOUNT HOOD OVER LOST LAKE

MOUNT ADAMS AND ADAMS GLACIER FROM THE NORTHWEST

me, I learned much of our own mountain, by reason of my association with him, that I could have learned in no other way.

On the second day of August we moved onward to a camp in a natural park on the northwest slopes of the mountain. The traveling was very rough and uncertain. We crossed many deep snow-fields, with the ever-present danger of breaking through into the cavernous depths of a hidden watercourse. The lava ridges, too, that led down from the higher slopes were abrupter and more broken than those encountered the day before. On the way, Professor Reid took observations on a glacier lying north of the White Salmon Glacier and fed from the steep slopes of the north summit. It was considerably smaller than the two already observed, and he named it the Pinnacle Glacier.

Our camp lay immediately below a big glacier. The following morning we set out to explore this, and we soon came to the lower end of the largest ice-stream on the mountain, the moraines of which I had reached eleven years before.

A magnificent view is here presented. The broad northwestern face of the great peak towers upward like a mighty wall, draped in white and streaked with the black of sinister lava-ridges. The true summit is hidden beyond vast snowy swells; but the north summit looms close at hand. Between the north summit and the broad north shoulder of the mountain, a marvelous ice-cascade plunges down two thousand feet and spreads out in a wide, fan-shaped expanse on the gentler lower slopes to form Mount Adams's biggest glacier.

Unfortunately, the snow lay heavily upon its entire surface; the ice peeping through only here and there. Much of its beauty was lost to us. We went far up along its course and crossed it from west to east. We were in much danger of falling into hidden crevasses; but luck favored us and we got over without accident. On the moraines we saw tracks—either of mountain sheep or of goats. The big glacier lies in no gorge along its lower end. It spreads over much surface, restrained only here and there by low ridges or its own moraines. The waters from this part of the mountain flow to the Cispus and the Lewis Rivers.

The big glacier had no name. I wished to call it the "Reid Glacier." Professor Reid, in view of the fact that I had seen it years before, recognized my right to give it a name; but begged me not to exercise my prerogative in this way. He was making a map of the mountain and he modestly wished to refrain from placing his own name on the map. He said an Alaska glacier already bore his name, and that the Mazamas were trying to name a glacier on Mount Hood for him. I finally yielded to his wishes, and the big ice-stream went on the map as "Adams Glacier."

I have since talked with other mountaineers about the matter, and they also have expressed the opinion that it should be known as the "Reid Glacier." In recognition of Professor Reid's invaluable services in exploring Mount Adams, I hope that this name will eventually prevail.

We had some difficulty in crossing the stream from Adams Glacier when we moved camp the next morning. Like all other glacial rivers, it was turbulent and muddy. Just below the trail, we found a snow-bridge over which we could walk; but this was not strong enough to bear the horses. However, we got them over without accident; and even the obstreperous colt crossed with apparent unconcern. Although the Adams is the largest glacier on the mountain, being on the northern slopes, disintegration is not nearly so rapid on it as on some of the other glaciers, and its glacial river is not nearly so wild and large as that of the Klickitat Glacier.

We moved camp eastward two or three miles and Professor Reid occupied two stations, making observations on the Adams, and a new glacier which he named the "Lava." The lastnamed lies in a deep niche almost directly on the north face of the mountain. The upper part of it is a fearfully steep, smooth ice-slope leading down from the summit ice-cap and ending in a great Bergschrund which overhangs the central body of the glacier.

Then came a day of rough traveling. We crossed the great lava-beds which had given our little party an evening of anxiety in 1890. We missed the trail at the farther side and kept too far down the slopes. We got into the timber where the ridges were sharp and the gullies frequent. Late in the afternoon we were glad to work back up the ridges and find a camp in the parklands near timber-line, on the east side of the mountain. During the day we observed two more glaciers. One of these, fed by tremendous ice-falls from the summit ice-cap and flowing off to the northeast, I requested Professor Reid to name for Professor W. D. Lyman, for years Professor of History in Whitman College, Walla Walla, one of the earliest investigators of Mount Adams. The other was left unnamed.

Next day we back-tracked. From our camp we could easily see the high trail leading over the seven-thousand-foot sky-line toward the lava-fields we had crossed the day before. Riding Dandy and Dan, we passed up to this elevated plateau and climbed, on foot, to the top of the red volcanic butte which has been mentioned in the story of the 1890 trip. Here we found a well-defined crater whose fires had long been cold. I was curious to know why one side of the rim of this crater was lower than the other. Professor Reid explained that this was due to the direction of the prevailing winds during the formation of the crater. Here, too, we found fulgurite, a peculiar glass-like substance which is said to be formed by lightning's striking the rocks at high elevations and melting portions of the surface which harden and glaze.

The volcanic cone, which has an elevation slightly in excess of seven thousand feet, was named Red Butte. The view of the tremendous ice-falls on the northeastern slopes of the mountain is magnificent, and the great eastern precipice with its overcapping two-hundred-foot snow-wall is but little farther away.

Descending Red Butte, we left our horses and crossed the lower part of Lyman Glacier to a high, roof-like moraine of Lava Glacier. We estimated the height of this moraine to be about two hundred feet, and perched on its very top we found an immense glaciated boulder, some twelve by twenty feet in size.

We reached camp again at six o'clock that evening. That night we had our first threat of storm. So far, the weather had been perfect, and, after the first day or so, we had not put up the tent at all. This night, however, I was awakened by Professor Reid who asked if we had not better put up the tent. Angry-looking clouds were rolling across the summit of the mountain. After observing them closely for a few minutes, I said I did not believe they were storm-clouds, and my guess proved to be correct.

Next forenoon we had an example of the accuracy of the aneroid as a weather prognosticator. We had gone to the top of Goat Butte to establish an observation station for Professor Reid. Again angry clouds gathered over the mountain and cast themselves above our position. A storm seemed imminent. But the aneroid refused to be stampeded. It kept its equilibrium. We felt that it was showing its unreliability. Presently a few big drops of rain fell—and then the clouds dispersed. The aneroid was vindicated.

The splendor of Goat Butte as a viewpoint has already

ICE-SLOPE AND BERGSCHRUND OF LYMAN GLACIER
Showing curious effect of erosion on the cliffs

GREAT ICE-SLOPE OVERHANGING LAVA GLACIER

EAST SIDE OF MOUNT ADAMS FROM THE RIDGE OF WONDERS

Showing Klickitat Glacier, the Great Eastern Precipices, the Castle, and Battlement Ridge

been mentioned. As an observation station, for photography and plane-table work, it is equally efficient, and Professor Reid secured many data. This was Station 15, and there remained for us the occupation of but two more stations for the completion of the map. We returned to camp for dinner.

During the afternoon Professor Reid felt very unwell, yet we realized the necessity of moving camp over into Avalanche Valley so that we might be in easier reach of the last stations. Our time was growing short and we must now make the most of it. We packed up and defiled through the pass between Goat Butte and the slopes of the mountain. On the way we met a young sheepherder, the first person we had spoken to in nearly a week. I wished to pitch camp on the main stream coming down from Rusk Glacier, and I knew there were several very rough gulches between us and it. I made the mistake of following the sheepherder's advice as to the best route, instead of relying on my own judgment. He directed us to a roundabout way, far downstream, and we had a terrible time of it the rest of the afternoon. At last we worked up an interminable backbone, through brush and down timber, to the site of our proposed camp on the glacial stream. This stream, I was afterward to learn, Professor Reid placed on his map as "Rusk River," and its parent glacier went on record as "Rusk Glacier."

It was late when we arrived. We had scarcely pitched camp and put our horses out to grass, when we were surprised to see a horseman splashing through the stream from the south side. He proved to be an old acquaintance of mine, Ad Gilmore, a sheepman who had spent many seasons on the ranges of the mountain. He readily accepted our invitation to pass the night with us, and we joyously turned the bread-making over to him.

Ad had been over on the peninsula between Rusk River and the Big Muddy, a timbered, park-like region with an area of a few square miles. He showed us the claw of a large cougar he had killed there a few days before.

The following morning Professor Reid was feeling so unwell that he decided that it was best for him to stay in camp all day. Ad Gilmore told me that my father-in-law, James L. Gilmore, Sr., was encamped a few miles to the northward on the head of Cunningham Creek, where he had a band of sheep. Accordingly, I rode with Ad to Mr. Gilmore's camp where I had dinner and enjoyed a very pleasant visit. Upon my return in the evening, I found Professor Reid feeling considerably better.

For several days Professor Reid and I had been planning an attempt to ascend the east face of the mountain. This was a feat that had never been tried, and there was much doubt as to its possibility. The great eastern precipice surely offered a forbidding aspect. The almost constant fall of avalanches gave token of the fate that was sure to befall one who ventured beneath the giant crags; and, as Professor Reid expressed it, to set forth upon so foolhardy an undertaking would be courting death.

The key to the eastern ascent—if a key there were—appeared to be the immense lava backbone or cleaver, now known as Battlement Ridge. This tremendous ridge, the greatest on the mountain, leads down from an elevation of about 11,500 feet to timber-line, between Klickitat and Rusk Glaciers. Professor Reid says of it: "The great precipice is divided approximately in the middle by a long ridge, which begins near the top of the mountain and extends five or six kilometers almost due east. The head of this ridge is a massive pinnacle, which I have called Castle Rock; the stratification and double crest appearing at one point of the ridge suggest that it may have been the remains of a former lava-flow, which, hardening on the surface, allowed the liquid lava inside to flow out; and later the top broke in. There is a somewhat similar ridge on the eastern side of Mount Ararat; its well-marked double crest makes it fairly certain that its origin was similar to that suggested above."

The Rusk Glacier lies higher than the Klickitat Glacier and not in so deep a gorge as the latter. Consequently it is a greater vertical distance from the crest of Battlement Ridge to the surface of Klickitat Glacier than it is to the surface of Rusk Glacier. The lower half of the ridge is broad and doubly crested, as Professor Reid has said; but the upper portion where it merges into the Castle is narrow and shattered. Great rock avalanches frequently thunder down to one or the other of the glaciers. North of Rusk Glacier a shorter and less prominent ridge leads down from the great precipice. It has a striking red color and is rugged and broken. To the north of it we find a splendid ice-fall which makes a tributary of the glacier I have mentioned as not having been named.

And south of Klickitat Glacier looms the Ridge of Wonders, completing the trio of tremendous cleavers that mark the eastern face of the mountain.

We decided that the most feasible—if not the only feasible—route of ascent on the east side was by way of Battlement Ridge and the Castle. So we planned that after Professor Reid had occupied his last station, and all the necessary data for the map had been secured, we would make the attempt. To this end it was now only necessary to take a trip across Klickitat Glacier and to the top of the Ridge of Wonders. One more day would suffice for this.

The morning of the 9th was ushered in by a marvelous sunrise. The great ice-cap of the mountain was turned to gold under the magic alchemy of the dawn. The clear, pure air pulsed with the glow of life, and the colored crags stood vividly forth in their wondrous beauty.

On this day I was to witness an example of calm, patient fortitude, such as it has seldom been my lot to see.

We started at six-forty-five. We had some trouble in crossing the little river; but we got over without being very wet. Our first mile was across timbered ridges, clothed in Druid-like evergreens, interspersed with many natural lawns. The banks of the occasional rivulets were lined with a variety of brilliant-hued flowers that lent a dash of animation to the more sober aspect of the silent trees.

While on Mount Hood, Professor Reid had suffered a slight abrasion on one of his heels. This had given him little trouble during the first part of our circuit of Mount Adams. During the past few days, however, the place had begun to pain him a great deal. It seemed that an infection had occurred. The foot had swollen considerably, and blood-poisoning threatened. On this particular morning the pain became intense. The swelling had so increased by the time we reached Klickitat Glacier that Professor Reid could no longer keep his shoe on. Most men would have turned back under the circumstances. Not so with Professor Reid. He insisted on making that last station notwithstanding the agony he was in. He had a small pillow or cushion that he used in his pack-bag to keep his large camera from rubbing his back while climbing over the rough mountain ways.

Removing the shoe, we bound this little cushion with cloths around the foot. Then we made our way slowly across the rugged lower part of Klickitat Glacier. Every step was keen agony to Professor Reid. Yet he did not flinch. Painfu'ly, heroically, he persisted in his purpose. At last we won the far side of the glacier. Then came a thousand-foot climb up a precariously steep snow-slope and over rough boulders. It would have been a toilsome march under the most favorable conditions; in our plight it was inconceivable. But there was never a hint of return from my companion. Grimly, unwaveringly, he kept on. Measured in miles, the distance was not great. Measured in the suffering of this resolute man, it was interminable.

Finally, at the end of toilsome hours, we stood on top of the Ridge of Wonders, with the marvelous view around us. It would be useless to attempt once more to describe that wonderful scene which is, at all times, beyond the power of words. Those who have seen it can appreciate the futility of the effort; those who have not must see it for themselves or never realize its glory. Some day men will come from the farthest parts of the earth to look upon its splendor. Until then, mankind must take it on the faith of the few who have gazed upon its enthralling majesty.

Professor Reid made his first station on the brink of the ridge, looking down into the Big Muddy Canyon. On this side the slope is very abrupt and precipitous; but on the south side it swells gradually down into Hell-Roaring Canyon, generously dotted with sub-Alpine evergreens.

A short distance to the south of us, a parasitic cone rose from the southern slope of the ridge. Hither we made our tedious way, after Professor Reid had finished his observations at the station already mentioned. Under favorable conditions it is a short, sharp climb to the top of this cone; but we found it arduous enough up through the volcanic detritus. When we reached the top we perceived it to be an eminence similar to Red Butte on the northeastern part of the mountain, with a well-formed and well-preserved crater. These two seem to be the most characteristic of the parasitic cones on the great peak. They have not suffered so much from disintegration as the others, notably Goat Butte on the east and South Butte on the south. These parasitic cones are miniature mountains. The theory is,

I believe, that they are formed by side-vents from the main craters and make a final outlet for the expiring internal fires. They are a sort of by-product, as it were, in the construction of volcanoes.

Professor Reid established his seventeenth and last station on top of the cone and called the butte "Little Mount Adams." Through his powerful binoculars we could plainly see the little white flag we had left on the farthest brink of Hell-Roaring Canyon nine days before. His plane-table work and his photography had, therefore, covered the entire circuit of the mountain. The ten distinctive glaciers had been seen and their features transferred to paper. When the data were compiled, Mount Adams would no longer be an unrecorded peak.

Away down on the meadows at the bottom of Hell-Roaring Canyon, through the glasses, I could see a band of horses. So far below us were they that no sign of them could be seen with the naked eye.

On this part of the great ridge were many evidences of comparatively recent volcanic activity. On the slopes were many dikes, standing straight up from the surface like ruined walls. Many volcanic fragments were found, which looked like twisted, melted bits of iron that had just cooled after being subjected to tremendous heat. Professor Reid was of the opinion that some of this fusing might have occurred within the past one hundred years.

Professor Reid worked as rapidly as possible, but his work was thorough and it took considerable time. At last we were ready to start on the toilsome, painful journey back to camp.

We desc^nded the steep side of the Ridge of Wonders, working carefully down the long snow-slope, and finally reached once more the Klickitat Glacier. The condition of Professor Reid's foot did not improve. If there was any change, it grew worse. Again we were confronted by the necessity of crossing the boulder-strewn lower glacier. It was obvious that we could not go above it; we could not go below it because of the lawless flood of the Big Muddy.

Near the middle of the glacier we reached a place where the turbulent stream, already full-grown, thundered from beneath a high pinnacle of ice, tumbled over a rocky bed for a couple of hundred yards, and went under the ice again finally to emerge an eighth of a mile or so below at the snout of the glacier. As we could not cross the stream, we were compelled to go down to the ice in order to get over.

It was eight o'clock when we at last stumbled into camp. The agonizing six-mile journey had taken more than thirteen hours.

An immediate retreat to civilization was now imperative. Aside from the excruciating pain he was suffering, it was doubtful if Professor Reid would escape without serious consequences. His foot was in a terrible condition, and it would still be so long before it could receive medical attention that the outcome promised to the tragic. All thought of an attempt to scale the east side of the mountain was at an end.

With the utmost difficulty, next morning, we prepared for the start. When the horse had been packed, the task of getting Professor Reid into the saddle was slowly accomplished at the expense of great pain to him. Now the value of a gentle, reliable horse was manifest. With one less patient and considerate than Dandy, our plight would have been increased many fold.

The first stage of our homeward journey was a rough one. We had to cross a number of sharp-cut, rocky gullies that had been washed by previous floods from Rusk Glacier. Then we worked up on to the ridge that forms the northern wall of the Big Muddy Canyon, passing beneath the great castellated, yellow cliffs of Goat Butte, on the way. Next we descended the timber-strewn slope to Cunningham Creek and the camp of my father-in-law, Mr. Gilmore. Most of the distance was without trail, and it was perhaps almost as severe a test to Professor Reid as the foot-trip the day before had been.

At Mr. Gilmore's camp we enjoyed a dinner not of our own cooking. He said he had a horse he wished to send out to Glenwood, and he asked us to take it and leave it there to await his arrival in a few days. I have a strong suspicion that this was his tactful way of providing us with another riding-horse. Be that as it may, the addition to our caravan was a welcome one. At two o'clock in the afternoon we resumed our journey, each upon a horse and each leading a pack-animal. Just before beginning the descent of Cunningham Ridge toward the Big Muddy, the horse Professor Reid was riding kept its forward course while the one he was leading held back. Professor Reid was jerked to the ground. Fortunately, aside from the pain resulting to his foot, he escaped injury, although the little accident might well have had serious consequences.

I had hoped that when we reached the level trail and the wagon-road beyond the Big Muddy, we should be able to ride more rapidly and thus shorten the time required to get to some place where assistance could be obtained. But Professor Reid found that any attempt to ride faster than a walk caused unbearable pain in his foot, so we had to wear the weary miles slowly away.

It was half-past eight o'clock when we arrived at the hospitable home of Mr. and Mrs. H. M. Trenner at Glenwood. Professor Reid was unable to stand alone.

Next morning I secured a man with a hack to take him to White Salmon. Once on the Columbia River, he had no trouble in finding medical treatment, and the infected foot, which was verging on blood-poisoning, soon yielded to scientific care. When he got to Portland, Professor Reid received a telegram informing him of serious illness in his family. He immediately abandoned all plans for further glacial investigations in the Northwest, and hurried eastward. I have never seen him since; but I shall never forget the patient courage with which he bore the hardships and pain of that trip.

He secured a splendid series of photographs of Mount Adams, many of them taken from points that had never before known a camera. His maps and the names he bestowed were adopted by the United States Government. His observations upon the glaciers were important, and he has described his results in many published scientific articles. In short, it would be hard now to find any extended reference to or description of the mountain that does not bear the mark of his painstaking work.

Left alone after the departure of Professor Reid for White Salmon, I started for my old home on the Klickitat River, with my three horses. It was evening when I got there. The colt crossed the river with the utmost ease.

Two weeks later I was back on Mount Adams. A day or so after my return from the trip with Professor Reid, I attended the Klickitat County teachers' institute held at Goldendale. Superintendent C. L. Colburn had put me on the programme for a talk on the glaciers of Mount Adams. A number of the teachers became interested, and the result was that, at the close of the institute, a party was organized for an immediate visit to the great mountain. Fourteen of us, after an uneventful journey in various kinds of vehicles to the end of the road on Bird Creek and from there on foot, reached the flower-decked camp-grounds of Bird Creek Meadows. Our party was made up of the following members: Mr. and Mrs. C. L. Colburn, Mr. and Mrs. T. E. Wright, Miss Hattie Gunn, Miss Kate Moore, Miss Emma Clanton, Miss Lena Barker, Miss Janet Locy, Miss Mary Gilmore, Miss Orelle Chapman, Mrs. C. E. Rusk, Mr. G. H. Roush, and myself. On August 24th, the four men climbed the mountain. A day or so later, while a few of us were viewing the grandeur of the east side from the Ridge of Wonders, storm-clouds began to gather around the summit dome. This time I needed no barometer to tell me we were in for trouble. We hurried back to camp.

That night, gathered under the protecting branches of a big fir-tree, we weathered a continuous downpour of rain, in comparative comfort. Morning showed fresh snow on the mountain, with indications of several days of uncertain weather. We beat a retreat.

At Glenwood the party separated, the majority going home. Mrs. Rusk, Miss Gilmore, Miss Locy, and I took a team and hack and started for the east side of the mountain. We left our hack at the usual place before reaching the Big Muddy, intending to go to Mr. Gilmore's camp on Cunningham Creek; but, on the way, we got word that Mr. Gilmore had already taken his sheep across the Klickitat River, so we decided to turn up into Avalanche Valley for a few days' camp. We pitched our camp in the beautiful meadow-lawns at the foot of Goat Butte, feeling greatly disappointed to have missed Mr. Gilmore. Late that evening, we were surprised to see a horseman riding up the little valley toward our camp. To our delight it proved to be Mr. Gilmore himself. The report that he had crossed the Klickitat had been a mistake. He had started on a trip to Glenwood; on the road he met some one who had seen us and who told him we were on the way to the mountain. He turned back, and at the Muddy found our tracks pointing toward Avalanche Valley. He surmised our destination and followed.

Next morning we set forth for a mountain ramble with no particular objective in view. A half-mile's walk brought us to the north side of Rusk Glacier. We crossed the glacier to Battlement Ridge. On the way we passed a hummocky portion of the great ice-stream where curious cavern-like fissures led back toward the heart of the glacier. Here we saw a small bird which flew into the icy caves, going clear out of sight in the cold retreats.

On a snowy plateau near the southern side of the glacier we came upon some tremendous crevasses. The largest of these I estimated to be sixty feet in width and two hundred feet in depth, with walls that were sharp-cut and smooth. Following an impulse, we climbed up the very steep side of Battlement Ridge, over rough boulders. It was a long, hard climb; but at last we stood upon the broken crest of the ridge. Then came a tedious pull along the top of the sharp backbone toward the Castle. It was rough going, for the way was blocked by many shattered rock-masses and pinnacles that stood squarely across the top of the ridge. But the way led gradually upward. Finally the others decided they had had enough of such traveling. But the enthusiasm of the mountaineer was now in my veins, and I saw the long-looked-for opportunity of determining the feasibility of Battlement Ridge as the key to the ascent of the eastern precipices. Requesting the others to wait for me, I hurried upward along the ridge, the great wall becoming more precipitous and narrow as I advanced. At last I came to a sharp pinnacle, thirty or forty feet high, standing directly across the crest of the ridge. I believe they call such things "gendarmes" in the Alps. The south side was overhanging. Directly beneath was a very steep talus slope leading down for twenty or thirty feet and then a drop of fifteen hundred or two thousand feet to the surface of Klickitat Glacier. Getting down on my hands and knees, I crawled cautiously beneath the pinnacle, taking good care to hug the solid rock-face as closely as possible, meanwhile eyeing with considerable apprehension the steep slope of loose rocks below me.

I was trembling a little with excitement when I finally had passed the pinnacle and stood once more on top of the ridge. The consequences of a slip at this place were not alluring. A few steps more brought me to a point where the crest of the ridge narrowed to the width of a foot or two, with the apex covered by small loose stones. At every step many of these little rocks would bound away and go hurtling down on either side—some a thousand feet to the glacier on the north, others almost twice as far to the glacier on the south. Their rattle and their crash were almost continuous, and I began to fear that my people below, hearing the commotion, would tremble for my safety.

A short distance of this precarious going brought me to the end. The top of the great ridge was cut as squarely in two as though it had been cleft by a giant ax. I could not see over the edge to ascertain the depth of the chasm. But one thing was certain. The impossibility of Battlement Ridge as a way to ascend the east side of the mountain had been determined. I could see the Castle, not so very far away; but there was no means of reaching it from where I stood.

I had attained an altitude of perhaps ten thousand feet, and a point where no human being had ever stood before. The view of the tremendous precipices and the frowning glaciers was, from here, appalling. In awe-struck loneliness I looked for a time upon the wild grandeur of the scene and then turned backward. I rejoined my party without mishap, and we proceeded down the ridge.

VII

THE HUMAN TOBOGGAN

THE MAZAMAS came back to Mount Adams for their outing in the summer of 1902. A few days before they went into camp at Trout Lake, Mrs. Rusk's sister, Miss Mary Gilmore, and Mr. O. O. Carrell were married at Goldendale. Mount Adams was selected for the wedding trip. Mr. and Mrs. Carrell and Mrs. Rusk and I proceeded to Trout Lake in two buggies, taking two days for the journey. The evening of our arrival, while our three horses were in a pasture, somebody, either maliciously or accidentally, shot one of them with a small caliber rifle, inflicting a wound which rendered the poor animal useless and from which it eventually lost its life. This left us with but the two ponies of Mr. Carrell's team for pack-animals with which to reach the mountain.

We found the Mazamas in difficulties. Their packing contract had been let to an incompetent man. They were beginning to have doubts about the possibility of getting their large party to the camp-grounds at snow-line. They were very anxious to send an advance guard to Bird Creek Meadows, or Happy Valley, to establish camp for the main body of climbers. But their pack-train had not put in an appearance and they could get no word of it.

Accordingly, Mr. Carrell offered them the services of his two horses. It was decided that an advance party of six Mazamas, Mr. Carrell, and myself should start immediately for Bird Creek Meadows. The Mazamas of this party were: Rodney L. Glisan, A. S. Pattullo, W. L. Brewster, Gerald Beebe, and Miss Ella McBride of Portland, Miss Bessie

Merriam of New York, and W. D. Lyman of Walla Walla. We got away in the afternoon of the day after our arrival and proceeded without interruption to a camp well up the timbered slopes. Next morning we found snow extending far down into the timber and we had to cross many large fields of it before we finally reached the delightful camp-grounds in the Meadows.

Leaving the six Mazamas, Carrell and I at once started back to Trout Lake to bring up our own people. When a considerable part of the distance had been traversed, we met another small party of Mazamas on their way with the pack-train to the upper camp we had just left. The pack-train had at last got into action; but some of the packs, swinging beneath the horses instead of reposing on their backs, proclaimed the inefficiency of the packers. We felt that the party was in for trouble before it reached the high camp.

When we got to Trout Lake we found a number of other Klickitat people who had come to climb the mountain with us. The Mazamas were in a state of great uncertainty because of the incompetency of their pack-train. The success of the outing was threatened.

We gathered the Klickitat contingent together, proceeded a mile or two up the White Salmon, and camped for the night. Next morning we started early and made good progress. Just before we reached Bird Creek Meadows we met the Mazama pack-train which had had nearly twenty-four hours the start of us, leaving on the return to Trout Lake. We had almost made the round-trip while they were making it one way.

The Klickitat party numbered eighteen when we filed across the ridge into the camp-ground and joined the two Mazama contingents.

During their 1895 outing the permanent camp of the Mazamas had been on the White Salmon side. Those of

THE GREAT SLIDE OF MAY, 1921, ON WEST SIDE OF MOUNT ADAMS

Telephoto taken from Trout Lake, July 4, 1921

CRATER OF MOUNT BAKER ABOUT 1900, AS SEEN AND PHOTOGRAPHED BY JOHN A. LEE'S PARTY

them who knew of the beautiful Bird Creek Meadows were determined to have the main camp for this year at the spot where Carrell and I had left the advance party which had now been joined by the second advance party and the Klickitaters. Professor Lyman, who had long proclaimed the beauties of Happy Valley, as he called it, was a member of the advance guard, and he, above all others, wished to have all of the Mazamas see the glories of the mountain from this camp and to use it as a base for the ascent. Those now here began to prepare for the coming of the main body.

Imagine, then, the consternation that prevailed when, the next day, messengers arrived with instructions for the Mazamas at Bird Creek Meadows to pull up stakes and proceed westward to the old White Salmon camp-ground. The owner of the so-called pack-train had refused to make another trip over the snow-fields that were necessary to traverse to reach Bird Creek Meadows. So the main party had been dumped down at the White Salmon camp. To one who had, less than a year before, made nearly the entire circuit of the mountain with pack-horses, over vast snow-fields, such incompetence was exasperating, to say the least.

Obediently, but sadly, the two advance parties of Mazamas departed for the White Salmon side. Although the Klickitat party had intended to make the ascent with the Mazamas, we were under no obligation to do so, and we felt that we could not risk failure by leaving our established camp and going to another several miles away and thereby losing a day or so of good climbing weather. Our sympathies were with the departing mountaineers; but we could do them no good by going with them. We decided to climb the mountain next day.

We got an early start on the morning of July 19th. Our party now numbered nineteen, one Mazama, E. H. Loomis of Portland, having remained to make the ascent with us.

The weather was excellent. Our crowd was a mixed one containing five women and fourteen men. Aside from myself, only Mr. Loomis and Dr. Goddard, who had climbed the mountain with Professor Reid, Mr. Brooks and me, none of the party had ever made a complete ascent. Some of the men were not at all physically strong, and I had little hope of getting them all to the top. Nevertheless, we made slow but steady progress.

On the lower end of the great lava ridge we met four loggers who were out on a vacation and were climbing the mountain as a part of their programme. We had seen them on our way up from Trout Lake; but their camp had been made farther west than ours. They joined us for the rest of the climb, thus increasing our numbers to twenty-three. Our party included the Reverend J. K. Buchanan, who had performed the ceremony uniting Mr. and Mrs. Carrell, so we had the wedding party almost complete.

The climb may be said to have been uneventful, except that the number of participants made it a rather unusual one for this mountain; especially was this so from the fact that the individuals throughout the entire ascent kept in a well-ordered, compact line. The work proved very arduous to some of the men, and, at times, there were indications of several failures. Nevertheless, we finally reached the record-box and inscribed our names as those of the largest party that had ever reached the summit in a body. Although it had long been, and still is, a custom to consider a climb to the record-box a complete ascent (as a consequence of which many who get that far never gain the actual top and so miss a wonderful view), the fact remains that two or three hundred feet of actual elevation remain between the box and the apex. I, for one, have never been satisfied until the last foot of height has been overcome.

Therefore, when we had all written our names, we still

had the long, gradual snow-slope to surmount. By this time several of the party were bordering on exhaustion. I found it necessary to resort to expedients to get them all up. I lined them up abreast. We would take ten steps and rest; then proceed for another ten steps and rest again. During the process I would make all sorts of foolish remarks and comments, in this way endeavoring to divert the thoughts of the lagging ones and to cheer their failing spirits for the final effort. Whatever may be said of my performances from the standpoint of dignity, they were certainly successful from a mountaineering standpoint, for, at last, the entire twenty-three stood upon the very summit and we had made a hundred per cent climb. But it had taken us twelve long hours. One of my previous ascents had been made in considerably less than half that time.

The names of our party, except those of the four loggers, and another which I do not recall, were: H. S. Goddard, E. H. Loomis, W. P. Flanary, W. J. White, T. J. Devine, C. M. Ryman, O. B. Frisbie, Mr. and Mrs. O. O. Carrell, J. K. Buchanan, Lydia Crowe, Effie Byrkett, R. A. Byrkett, Fred Morer, Frank Egan, Mrs. Rachel N. Rusk, C. E. Rusk and Miss Blank.

Although, as I have said, the weather was excellent, a chilly wind was blowing across the summit, and many of the party who were not used to mountain altitudes began to feel the discomforts of their position. Mr. Flanary, the photographer, had us stand in a long row and the result was a picture of twenty-two shivering subjects. Then, of course, they were taken to the eastern edge and thrilled by the view down the great precipices. Here one amateur photographer grew so excited that he spoiled what would have been a splendid picture by leaving an alpenstock standing immediately in front of his camera.

And now we come to the incident which sets this ascent

apart and makes it different from all other climbs I have made. In the description of these events I have been rather undetermined whether or not to use the name of the actor who played the star part. However, since she, at the time, made vigorous demands that all publicity concerning the affair be suppressed as far as possible, I have finally decided not to reveal her real name and to refer to her in this story as Miss Blank.

Miss Blank, that summer, was on a visit to the Pacific Coast, although her home was some place east of the Rocky Mountains. She had once walked up Pike's Peak, and as Pike's Peak is about two thousand feet higher than Mount Adams, during the first part of our climb, she was somewhat inclined to speak sneeringly of our Washington mountain. I told her she might find before the day was over that climbing Mount Adams and walking up Pike's Peak were two different propositions. I hardly expected, at the time, however, that my position would be so dramatically vindicated, and Miss Blank refused to be convinced.

Nevertheless, Miss Blank appeared to make the climb and to arrive at the summit in much better shape than some of the men in the party. We had had our round of picture-taking and all had been duly impressed by the terrific view from the eastern brink. We were about ready to begin the descent when Miss Blank suddenly crumpled down and lay unconscious in the snow. Excitement instantly prevailed. Dr. Goddard, skillful physician though he was, tried in vain to revive the stricken woman.

The situation was serious. The afternoon was well advanced, and it was growing colder as the day waned. It was imperative that we get Miss Blank down the mountain before darkness set in, for to leave her on those frigid heights throughout the night would be to insure her chilling to death. But we were a mile in height above the nearest timber, and this meant that we must traverse more than four miles of broken lava and compact snow-fields before we could hope for enough fuel to kindle even the tiniest fire.

But we lost no time in inactivity. As soon as it was found that Miss Blank could not be restored to consciousness, we picked her up and carried her bodily down the gradual snow-slope to the record-box. From here to the vast snow-fields of the first summit, a vertical distance of about five hundred feet, the slope is very steep, and fortunately it was now well covered with soft snow.

When we reached the record-box, Mr. Loomis generously proposed that we use him as a human toboggan. This expedient had been used once before on Mount Hood and it has been used on that mountain several times since. No doubt it has been resorted to elsewhere. The human toboggan is brought into requisition only when the need is very great, and it is available only under peculiarly desperate conditions.

One or two of the other men, now that they understood the plan, volunteered to act as the toboggan; but since Mr. Loomis had been first to offer himself, to him was accorded the honor of the sacrifice.

He lay down on his back in the snow. We placed the form of the unconscious woman upon him and strapped their ankles together. With his arms he held her firmly to him, so there was no danger of her injury through contact with the frozen snow. We dragged them swiftly down the steep slope.

But when we reached the level stretch at the foot of the summit dome our troubles had but begun. There was now nearly half a mile to the point of the first summit over which we could not drag our toboggan. Taking two gunny-sacks, we stretched them on alpenstocks and thus made a rude litter. In this we carried Miss Blank. It was an extremely difficult task, for the snow was soft and the two-mile altitude made any extra exertion painful. But at last we got our burden to the point of the first summit, and were confronted by a tremendous slope leading down to the saddle twenty-five hundred feet beneath.

To get this far had been a relatively easy part of our problem. The job before us was Herculean. It was necessary now to make systematic plans for what we had to do.

Miss Blank was still unconscious. Dr. Goddard's repeated efforts at resuscitation had been without avail. The four loggers, although by reason of their outdoor labors probably in the best physical condition of any of the men in the party, made no offer to help. They went their way down the mountain and we saw them no more. The Klickitat men were willing to do all they could. Some of them, of course, were needed to help the other women get down. Others were scarcely able to look after themselves. The stronger ones stood staunchly by to do all that could be done.

Feeling the utmost confidence in Mrs. Rusk's ability to look after herself, I readily assented to her suggestion that she make her way back to camp unaided. She not only did this, but actually took charge of two or three of the exhausted men and led them safely down the mountain.

Standing at the upper point of the great snow slope which leads down from the 11,500- to the 9000-foot level, we faced the situation with many misgivings. The human toboggan was our only recourse, yet there was danger in the plan. If the two prostrate forms should once get beyond our control in the swift descent, tragedy would be inevitable. The way was flanked on either side by jagged rocks. In many places patches of hard ice lay beneath the soft upper layer of snow. But the chill of night was coming on apace, and we must get down.

The others had been started on the descent, but Goddard, White, Devine, Buchanan, and possibly one or two whom I do not now recall, remained to help Loomis and me. Loomis once more lay down in the snow, again we placed the unconscious woman upon him, and he clasped his arms around her to hold her firmly in place. I then strapped their ankles tightly together and tied a short rope just above their feet. A strap was fastened about each of Loomis's arms at the shoulder and a man detailed to come slightly behind on either side to act as a sort of guy to keep the toboggan in the proper course. Another man was sent a few yards ahead to scout for icy places beneath the snow. We were then ready.

Taking hold of the rope I started down the great slope dragging the man and woman after me. The day had been a reasonably warm one for that altitude and the snow was quite soft on top, although, as I have said before, there were occasional patches of ice just beneath the surface. Had the snow been hard on top what we did would have been impossible.

We were soon whizzing down the mountain-side. The rocks on either hand flew by, and a glance now and then backward at the point of the first summit showed it shooting higher and higher into the air. Had not our situation been so serious, it would have been exhilarating, this flying dash down the long slope of a great western snow-peak; but it was a race against night, with a human life as the prize. I was under much apprehension as to how it might be faring with poor Loomis; but we were making speed, and speed just then was very essential, so we dared not stop to find out.

We had soon found that there were sufficient men to control the strange toboggan and to keep it from gaining a dangerous speed. When we found this out, we no longer put a check upon the rate at which we were capable of going. We exerted ourselves to the limit of our capacity.

Down and down we plunged. The inhospitable summit rose farther and farther behind; the timbered foothills and safety drew nearer and nearer. We rushed in a few minutes over a distance that had ground from us interminable hours of toil on the ascent.

In the very nature of things, such vigorous measures must soon bring results. The work was exciting, but short. How long it took us I do not know. Our ascent was measured in hours; the descent was measured in minutes. Presently, to our unspeakable relief, the saddle appeared close at hand. This was made apparent by the lessening of the slope, and a consequent lessening of our speed. Ere long, instead of having to check the toboggan, I began to have to pull—then came a point at which we had to stop. From a perch 11,500 feet in the air, we had come in one swift rush to an elevation of only 9000 feet.

The decreasing altitude had somewhat revived Miss Blank. When we unstrapped her from her self-sacrificing toboggan, we soon succeeded in getting her on her feet. When Mr. Loomis rose from the snow, there was blood where his head had lain, for a bit of ice had cut a gash.

Miss Blank was soon able to walk supported by a man on either side. But the long, rough lava ridge had still to be traversed, and after that came a mile through the timbered parklands. Yet it is one of the strange things about mountaineering that one may be for a time in utter collapse and yet revive and regain almost full strength within a few minutes. Miss Blank continued to gain, the lower the altitude reached. Yet it was a long, long, weary way. Nevertheless, there was a fringe of daylight left when the last of the party stumbled into camp. By the following morning Miss Blank was apparently as strong and well as ever.

Next day, Mr. Loomis, apparently none the worse for his rough experience, departed for the Mazama camp. He had won the lasting admiration of our entire party by his quiet, unassuming courage, and his readiness to sacrifice his comfort and his safety for the rescue of one he had never seen before. All of the Klickitaters, except the Reverend Mr. Buchanan, Mr. and Mrs. Carrell, Mrs. Rusk, Miss Blank, and I, left for home at the same time.

We who had remained spent a leisurely day in the delightful meadows. Here one never tires of exploring the fairy dells, through which tinkle meandering, crystal streams over beds of shining sand cut deep in the greenest of green swards. Many tiny waterfalls enliven the scene and silvery cascades frequently charm the eye. Between the vales run long, low ridges covered with dense growths of Alpine evergreens overhanging feathery bowers fit for the abode of the Dryads. Tucked snugly away in hidden nooks are many tiny lakes, purest water gems set in emerald. Some of the shallower of these, and those that have been warmed by the sun, make the finest of bathing-pools. Here bloom the mountain flowers in wondrous profusion. Dainty blossoms of many colors lift their heads by the side of the summer snow-banks. The flash of the humming-bird is often seen, as it darts from place to place through this wonderland of plant life.

The flora of Mount Adams is rich in variety and beauty. It ranges from the delicate grass-blade beside the limpid pool to the stately evergreen that defies the storms of centuries. Its color scheme is complete to the minutest detail and embraces every tint and shade from those of the modest violet to those of the most gorgeous flower. Botanists have found that the plant life of Mount Adams contains practically all the species found on the other peaks of the Cascade Range, together with some of the species found in the Rocky Mountain flora. There are also present some of the species of the Sierra Nevada Mountains.

VIII

KULSHAN, THE GREAT WHITE WATCHER

EDMUND T. COLEMAN, an Englishman, spent five years of his life in an effort to be the first to reach the summit of Mount Baker, the mighty snow-clad mountain that stands far north in the State of Washington and overlooks the international boundary. At last he succeeded, in the summer of 1868. Since the mountain bears the name of an Englishman, perhaps it is altogether appropriate that he should have done this, especially as few Americans had at that time awakened to the delights of mountaineering, greatest of sports. Moreover, at that time, few Americans were aware that we had any mountains worth climbing, even as there are many of our citizens, at this late day, who do not know we have mountains that are worth traveling around the world to see.

Kulshan, the Great White Watcher, the Indians called it; and for ages their generations, in awe, had seen it, watching over the gateway to the Western Ocean, with its smoky banner waving across leagues of untracked forest.

In 1903, Mrs. Rusk and I lived for many months in the picturesque little town of Hamilton on the Skagit River. From near-by points, the great snowy dome of Kulshan could be seen looming high above the intervening timbered ridges, and it sent its challenge to me, even as Mount Adams had sent its challenge to the boy of long ago.

And the challenge was accepted, as that other challenge had been, and early in July Mrs. Rusk and I set forth, seeking the unknown, for Kulshan then was a little visited mountain and there had been but six recorded ascents. A branch of the Great Northern Railway led far up the Skagit River, through the land of big timber, and on this we went to the town of Baker at the mouth of Baker River. This town has since assumed considerable importance in the manufacture of Portland cement, and has changed its name to "Concrete"; but at that time it was only a village whose principal business seemed to center in the saloons. We did not linger there long after the train had put us down, but went on our way a mile or so up the Baker River and camped, glad to be away from the drinking brawlers that hung around the town.

From our camp we caught distant glimpses of Shuksan, Kulshan's smaller brother, and we could see that we were headed for a region of mountain delight. In the morning rain threatened; but we started at half-past six. I was carrying eighty-five pounds and Mrs. Rusk had twenty-five. We took it slowly, for the trail was very muddy and in places we sank to the ankles. We passed through magnificent forest, and some of the cedars were of enormous size. We crossed many gullies on horse-bridges, some of which were made from single logs hewed flat at the top, with pole railings on each side.

But we did not go far that day. In the evening we found a picturesque camp in a grove of small alders, on the bank of the boulder-fretted Baker River, with the magnificent dome of Kulshan looming over the forest-robed ridges.

We did not put up the tent, for the sand was dry beneath the alders. It was a wild spot, and when we went to bed, feeling there might be some danger from prowling animals, I laid my small axe where I could reach it handily. I was very tired, for the day had been a hard one. Some time during the night I either heard, or dreamed I heard, something come crashing through the bushes toward the camp.

When I awoke, I was sitting up in bed with the axe in my hand.

This little incident impressed forcibly on my mind the thought that it is often safer to have no weapon where it can be too easily reached. A man in a nightmare is not a responsible citizen, and he should have the opportunity of becoming thoroughly awake before he possesses the means of doing harm to others or himself. Since my very earliest trips I have never carried a gun of any kind, unless hunting for game. I have camped in some of the wildest spots in America, and never has any denizen of the wilderness offered to molest me or any of my companions.

The following day we reached the Government fish hatchery on Baker Lake, then in charge of Henry O'Mallery, who has since become nationally prominent in the conduct of Uncle Sam's piscatorial business. We were much interested in an inspection of the work being carried on; but our visit was a hurried one, for but a few miles away towered the mighty mountain with its glistening sides seamed by row upon row of yawning crevasses.

At the hatchery we found Mr. Gilbert B. Coleman, a forest ranger who had a station on the opposite side of the lake. Accepting his invitation to spend the night with him, we crossed in his dugout canoe.

Baker Lake is a veritable mountain gem, set in a circle of forest-clad mountains, with here and there a craggy, evergreen island standing clear-cut and serene above the blue surface of the water. In the unruffled calm of a summer's day the shimmering majesty of Kulshan is reflected in its peaceful depths, and the glint of the sun on the fleecy clouds is mirrored in its placid bosom.

After a night spent under the hospitable roof of Mr. Coleman, we started again for the mountain, accompanied for a short distance by him and John R. Smith and Mr.

Galbreath, two other Forest Service men.

We soon came to Swift Creek, a white glacial stream with a current like a mill-race. So wild and powerful is this creek that it is doubtful if one falling into it could ever get out, unless a very skilled swimmer, and it is scarcely probable that one from the shore could rescue another so unfortunate as to be caught in its flood. We were to cross by means of a small fir-tree which had been cut down to make a foot-log. The larger end of this log rested on the opposite bank, six or eight feet above the stream, and the log sloped downward until the smaller end rested on the gravelly beach on our side at the water's edge.

Taking most of my pack so that I should be free to assist Mrs. Rusk, the foresters crossed and sat down on the farther bank. Not dreaming that she would try to cross until I was ready, I lay down to get a drink. When I arose I saw with consternation that Mrs. Rusk had already reached the middle of the log. What was still more alarming, she seemed to have become dizzy and was slightly swaying back and forth, unable either to advance or retreat. It was evident that in a few seconds more she would plunge head-long into the seething water.

We all seemed to realize her danger at the same moment. Once in that hissing flood no power could save her. There was no time for fright. Action alone would avail. The three foresters sprang to their feet ready to go to her assistance. Feeling that her life hung upon a few brief seconds, I stepped upon the vibrating log, and, balancing myself with my alpenstock, came quickly up behind her, took hold of her arm, spoke reassuringly; and soon we were safely on the farther shore. It was only then that I had time to get scared. From that day to this I have always been uncertain on a foot-log.

It was but a short distance from this place to the cabin

of Joe Morovits on Park Creek, where we separated from our friends of the Forest Service. Morovits, a native of Switzerland, had here taken a ranch and established himself in an environment to remind him of his own loved Alps. For years he had hunted and prospected over the surrounding mountains until both his body and his constitution were like iron. Looking up Park Creek Canyon, between its great timbered walls, one could see at its head the monstrous form of Kulshan, ineffably grand and inspiring. The giant peak was not more than four or five miles away, its yawning crevasses and frowning sėracs seemingly within a ston's throw; but so far as means of transportation were concerned it might have been a hundred. There was neither road nor trail, and the only way of reaching snow-line was by an ascent of the tremendous forested ridge between Park Creek and Boulder Creek. This involved a climb of four thousand feet within four miles, through dense underbrush, between giant trees and over fallen logs of immense size.

The climb up that great ridge seemed interminable. Our way was beset by rocks and cliffs. In the thick undergrowth, the devil's-club with its poisonous spires clutched at our ankles. Sometimes the logs were too big to crawl over, so we had to go around them. Although the bottom of the gorge fell farther and farther below us, by looking upward we could see no top. From the far north wall of the canyon came the subdued roar of white torrents plunging toward the depths we had left.

Night caught us still upon that giant slope. We camped in a little depression at the foot of a towering tree. A drizzling rain began, and once, during the darkness, the odor of a near-by bear was plainly perceptible.

Morning brought a heavily overcast sky, and it rained intermittently throughout the day. Early in the forenoon we gained the crest of the ridge and followed it well toward the upper end to a point not far from the termination of the timber. Here we put up the tent, and prepared for a siege of weather. We and our effects were wet, so we built a good fire in front of the tent-door to dry out the interior as much as possible. Looking through the trees, to the south, we could see, close at hand, the banded ice-belts of Boulder Creek Glacier.

The rain continued throughout the following day. We could see little of the main mountain; but the grandeur of the storm impressed us. The rain-clouds dragging across the ice-fields; the columns of mist sweeping grandly up from the canyon's depths and across the ridges; the hide-and-seek play of lava-crag and fleecy vapor; the exhilarating breath of enfreshing air; the redolence of dripping evergreens; half-revealed vistas down steaming slopes; mysterious glimpses of fog-draped glaciers; all combined to make for us a memorable day.

Between showers, we made little excursions near camp. Through interstices of the shifting clouds we could occasionally see far down into the gorges, and, now and then, a gleam of snow high above. But we were wrapped in the battle of the elements and we could do little but wait until Nature smiled again. We saw that this was the home of the mountain goat, for white hair clung to many of the bushes. The rain could not put out our cheerful camp-fire, and its warm glow dispelled the encroaching gloom of the forest until late that evening.

The sun again beamed on us next morning. We moved our camp about a quarter of a mile farther up the ridge and pitched the tent under the last clump of little firs in a place from which we could throw a stone on to a glacier on either side. On this ridge the big trees grow almost up to "snow-line," which on Mount Baker cannot much exceed five thousand feet in elevation. That day we went beyond the farthest point of land and well up on to the snow, and gained an idea of the very rough character of the mountain.

Our trip had been a hard and exhausting one. Mrs. Rusk did not feel equal to an ascent of the mountain. I would not try the climb alone, because of the danger involved; not on account of the chance of accident to myself, but for the reason that if anything should happen to me she would be left in a position so terrible that no woman should ever have to face. For this mountain, at that time, was one of the loneliest and most inaccessible in the United States.

Next morning the weather threatened further complications, so we started home. The descent of the great timbered ridge was not so arduous as the ascent had been; but it was arduous enough. On the way down we came upon an enormous cedar-tree which we estimated to be twenty feet in diameter. It is doubtful if any other person had ever seen it.

At the Morovits ranch we were much interested in Mr. Morovits's account of an ascent he had made of Kulshan, two or three years before, as guide for a party of men. One member of this party was John A. Lee with whom I was to become intimately connected in an important mountaineering project several years later.

We were fortunate enough to secure a chance of sending our camp equipment out by a pack-train, so our journey back to the railroad was made much easier than the mountainward trip had been.

Shortly after our return to Hamilton, I heard of some people at Everett who planned to climb Kulshan that summer. I immediately entered into correspondence with them. At first it seemed there would be quite a party, but only one finally came; and so it happened that in the closing days of August I again got on the train at Hamilton and met George G. Cantwell for the first time.

Cantwell was an expert photographer. He had been at Dawson in the palmy Klondike days. His outdoor experiences—Alaskan and otherwise—had been extensive and varied. He was a light-weight, weighing at that time about one hundred and thirty pounds, yet he was one of the best men I have ever seen in the mountains. I have found in my third of a century of mountaineering that you cannot measure a man's efficiency in pounds, and that his value and reliability depend upon qualities which have no connection with avoirdupois.

Before we reached the town of Baker, Cantwell and I not only had become acquainted with each other, but had also scraped up an acquaintance with W. A. Alexander, a veteran of the Spanish-American War. Alexander had had no experience in mountain-climbing; but he was very anxious to join us, so we decided to stay over at Baker a day to give him time to gather some equipment for the trip.

While the hours were passing rather slowly in the little hamlet, I met an old prospector who, after the manner of old prospectors, asked my destination. I told him we were going to climb Mount Baker. He gave a snort of contempt. "Huh!" he said, "I climbed that thing last March, on snowshoes!"

My spirits immediately departed for the bottom of the Valley of Despair.

"But," I asked, and I tried hard not to let my hopelessness show in my voice, "were you clear to the top?"

"No," admitted Old Prospector, "I was not right on top; but I could have gone on to the top, from where I was, in ten minutes. I was up to the timber-line."

My spirits at once took the uphill trail.

A pack-train was leaving for the Morovits ranch with some equipment for a mine which Morovits had discovered and had sold to a company. The packers agreed to take our outfit as far as the ranch. We were thus left free to pursue our way unhampered. The trail was very muddy in places, for in this region of big timber there are many spots where the sun's rays seldom reach the ground, and even in summer a trail will not dry out, especially if it is traveled to any extent.

As we went along, I could see that Cantwell had something on his mind. It finally came out.

"I wonder," he said hesitatingly, "if you and Alexander care if I do the cooking on this trip? I like to cook, and if you don't mind rustling the wood, I will be glad to get the meals."

We shouted our joyous assent.

A little later, Cantwell confessed to me: "I was really afraid you boys might want to do the cooking."

We spent the night at the Morovits ranch, and the next morning started up the great ridge along practically the same route which Mrs. Rusk and I had followed. We did not reach timber-line that night; but we did camp well up the ridge, so that the following forenoon we were able to pitch our tent under the very same clump of little firs where Mrs. Rusk and I had camped nearly two months before.

From this place the mountain looks forbidding enough. The whole eastern side, with the exception of a few sharp rocky outcroppings and some bold lava-cliffs, is covered by a great burden of snow and ice. The glistening white slopes are torn by tremendous crevasse-chasms and piled with enormous séracs. The other part is sufficiently steep to satisfy the desires of the most ardent alpinist. Two peaks can be seen from this camp, the southern one, a pointed pinnacle, being several hundred feet lower that the more dome-like summit-mass. On the east side we do not find the beautiful park-meadows that have been described as existing on Mount Adams, although on other portions of Kulshan parks of rare charm abound. The ridge which we had followed from the Morovits ranch narrows with its upward climb until it finally pinches out between the two glaciers. Its final stretches are free of trees, except a few stunted sub-Alpine groups, and its beauty is enhanced by grassy swards and a profusion of mountain flowers.

Cantwell had a large and a small camera. After we had established our camp, we spent the afternoon in a reconnoissance trip up the side of the mountain. Some remarkable crevasse pictures were secured, and we returned to our tent in the evening to prepare for the great climb on the morrow.

Daylight does not come so very early on the 3d of September, and it was five o'clock when we got away from camp. For a short distance we followed the upper part of the ridge which finally merged into a moraine between Park Creek and Boulder Creek Glaciers. We soon came to the end of this, however, and had to take to the snow. Before long we were among the big crevasses, some of which were of remarkable size and beauty. Owing to the lateness of the season, the snow was very hard and firm. None apparently had fallen in many weeks. Therefore, there was little danger from hidden crevasses.

The most practicable route looked to be along the depression leading up between the two peaks. But Morovits had told us that his party had been turned back by an enormous crevasse, just as they were about to pass into the saddle between the peaks. They had then been forced to pick out a precarious route up on to the south shoulder of the main peak. This had undoubtedly been the only ascent ever made of the east side of the mountain.

Profiting by the experience of the Morovits party, we decided to keep away from the depression and to climb directly up the east side of the main peak, a route never before attempted. To accomplish our purpose we bore toward a low lava ridge or cleaver which sprang from the snow-mass and led well up the mountain-side in the direct line we wished to follow. Before reaching this we passed within sight of a lava spire which rose grotesquely out of the snow. Because of its peculiar shape I called it "The Penguin."

We had a sharp scramble along the cleaver and the rocks were rough and trying to the patience; but the way was free of crevasses and we were relieved of the danger of an involuntary glissade into the depths of a snowy cavern.

The ridge finally ended beneath steep, hard snow-slopes; but directly above was a similar though shorter one, which led still farther in the way we wished to go. We had a bit of ticklish work in getting up the icy incline from the upper end of one cleaver to the lower end of the other; but we succeeded without accident by bringing our hundred-foot rope into play.

The somewhat monotonous climb up the last cleaver brought us well on to the side of the mountain, but into a position that rather appalled us. The ridge ended under a jumbled ice-fall so seamed and broken by hummocks and chasms and knife-like edges that it looked impossible for any human being to creep up its jagged surface. But we must go over it or abandon the climb.

Alexander had for some time been suffering from mountain sickness and he now felt so ill that he decided to remain on the last point of rocks while Cantwell and I went on without him. We were out of water, and Cantwell crept down over the rocks to a place directly beneath an overhanging wall of ice and there filled the canteen.

We looked with misgiving at the ice-fall above. But suddenly we caught inspiration to dare its dangers. Glancing upward, we saw large volumes of smoke rolling from between the two peaks. The knowledge was forced home to us that we stood upon an active volcano, and we felt that we must risk much to look upon the crater from which that black cloud rolled.

It was now eleven o'clock and in distance we had accomplished two thirds of the ascent of the mountain; but our actual difficulties had only begun. We left Alexander to make himself as comfortable as possible until our return. With the hundred-foot rope around my waist I straddled a knife-like ridge of ice and crawled along it until I gained a more solid footing well up on the ice-fall. Cantwell followed. As we stood upon his irregular sky-line, Alexander secured an excellent snap-shot of us with the kodak which had been left with him.

It now became a problem of working back and forth in a maze of ice-crevasses, and of crawling up over hard, slippery protuberances. The rope was here of little benefit, as the crevasses were so close together that it was seldom possible to bring it into play. We had a few narrow escapes from slipping in spite of the extreme care we used. Notwithstanding the difficulty and danger of the work, it was extremely interesting and the zest of mountaineering lured us on to increasing endeavor. A half or three quarters of an hour was sufficient for us to overcome the ice-fall. It merged into a great, crevassed snow-slope which led up to the eastern cliffs directly beneath the summit.

The whole east face of Mount Baker from the snow-line to the top is so seamed and broken by big ice-falls and crevasses that a view of it from an eminence a few miles away gives it the appearance of an immense white ruffled skirt.

Instead of ice we now had snow to contend with. The cracks were not so numerous nor so close together; but they were immeasurably bigger, and we were confronted by the danger of the blind crevasse. Some of the chasms were clear-cut and well-defined; but others were choked at the surface by masses of rotten snow, while some were completely hidden by treacherous white coverings. For hours our course was a zigzag one. Back and forth we went, crossing now a rent on a precarious snow-bridge; working now clear around the end of one; occasionally stepping or jumping a narrow one; but gaining ever slowly in altitude.

The general slope of the mountain was growing exceedingly steep. By the time we had reached the foot of the cliffs, we had to use the utmost care to maintain a footing. We knew that it was only a few hundred feet now to the summit; but we looked at the columnar crags with considerable apprehension. A chimney just above us offered the best prospect of scaling them. To reach this we had to scale a steep, rocky slope slightly coated with ice. It was slippery work and we made judicious use of the rope. When we got to the foot of the chimney, we found our progress blocked by an overhanging bulge of rock about breast-high. Ordinarily this would have been no obstacle, for I could easily have boosted Cantwell up it; but with such footing as could be secured on that treacherous incline such an attempt was not to be thought of. Cantwell found that, by going slightly to the right, he could climb to a position about level with the top of the overhang, and but for the absence of one foothold he could easily swing himself around. I supplied the deficiency. Hugging close to the rock, I turned my right shoulder, Cantwell stepped lightly on it with his left foot, and swung into the chimney. When he had firmly anchored, it was but the work of a few moments for me to ascend with the aid of the rope, and we were ready for the next stage.

It was a short but exhausting climb up the chimney. We had to be careful to avoid slipping and dislodging loose stones. We came out presently on to the southern slope of the summit dome, with but a short climb farther to bring us to the top.

For several hours the smoke from the crater had been hidden from us by the south shoulder of the main peak. But as we emerged from the chimney there burst upon our sight the most thrillingly weird spectacle I had ever seen.

In the bowl-like depression immediately between the two peaks was a great orifice in the snow. It was perhaps fifty feet across, although the western side was partly blocked with snow so that the opening had somewhat the shape of a half-moon. At a distance of possibly two hundred feet a semicircular crevasse swept halfway around it. From the unknown depths of this abyss the black smoke rolled. It drifted away, shifting with the wind, until it was finally dissipated in the rarefied air. The wild, unearthly loneliness of the scene impressed us profoundly, for its counterpart perhaps does not exist on earth.

But it was getting late, and we could not linger long to gaze upon this awe-inspiring place, nor could we take the time for a closer investigation. We turned summitward once more. We skirted the upper fringe of the cliffs, partly upon frozen gravel, partly on crystallized snow, both of which were steep and slippery. We soon topped the highest point of the cliffs. To the west rose the final dome of snow. A sharp climb brought Cantwell, who was in the lead, to a cornice, shoulder-high. Over this he peered.

"What can you see?" I asked.

"Nothing!" answered he.

I came up to him, and gave him a boost. He drew me up with the rope. We were on the level snow-plateau of Kulshan's great summit.

"Four o'clock," said Cantwell, and this remark was plainly heard by Alexander fifteen hundred feet below.

It had taken us eleven tremendous hours from our camp

at timber-line. We well might marvel at the old prospector who could have covered the same distance in ten minutes.

The sun was shining brightly, but it was dropping toward the Pacific at an alarming rate. We turned to the marvelous view which rolled away on every side. Westward and southward the great timbered earth-folds stretched away to the sinuous sheen of Puget Sound, with the serrated Olympics beyond. Eastward the white billows of the rugged Cascades swept to a far horizon, with regal Glacier Peak their dominant feature. Away to the north a silvery thread marked the winding course of Frazer River in British Columbia. Nine miles to the east Shuksan lifted his pointed crown in a brave effort to rival his brother Titan. Far below, Baker Lake, beauteous water gem, shimmered in the evening sunlight. And almost at our feet rolled up the smoke from Kulshan's lingering crater.

Cantwell worked rapidly with his camera. He got some wonderful pictures; but by the time he was through, a half-hour of valuable time had been sacrificed. With a last glance at the marvelous panorama and the smoking chimney of earth's internal fires, we dropped over the cornice and started down. We were soon in the rocky cleft again, descending carefully, for care was an essential now, even more than it had been on the ascent. When we reached the overhang, I slid over the edge, dangling by the rope which Cantwell held firmly from above. I groped with my feet until I at last found a footing. I was then able to ease Cantwell down.

Cantwell now led down the slippery rock-slope while I firmly held the rope. When he had gone thirty or forty feet, he stopped to give me a chance to rearrange my affairs. When I slid down the overhang, the strap to my canteen had caught on a rock and was broken. In trying to fasten this some way so the canteen would not fall, I dropped my alpenstock. It shot down the slope point-first, directly toward Cantwell. I shouted a warning; but he dared not make a quick movement to avoid it. For an instant it looked as though disaster had overtaken us. The sharp steel point struck his foot and penetrated the laces of his boot doing no greater damage than to leave an angry-looking red mark on the flesh. It was a close shave, partly due to accident and partly to carelessness on my part.

Soon after this little incident, which quickened our pulses for a time, we came again to the snow and the dangers of the crevasses. We were able to follow our ascending tracks and this was a great help. We got one good thrill, however. I was in the lead with Cantwell behind on a taut rope. I had passed over a swell out of his sight. I started across a crevasse, the top of which was filled by a mass of snow. This had afforded us a safe passage on the way up; but now the snow gave way beneath me and I sank to my hips. Feeling the sudden jerk on the rope, Cantwell naturally thought that I had fallen into the crevasse. He braced himself to keep me from plunging any farther into the depths. This brought the rope so tight that I was unable to move forward. It was some time before I could make him understand the situation sufficiently to slacken the rope enough to give me a chance to scramble out on to the firmer snow on the lower lip of the crevasse. I did not at all fancy the yawning holes my legs had made clear through the flimsy covering of that dark chasm.

The remaining crevasses were passed without further mishap, and we came again to the ice-fall down which we worked our way cautiously. We found Alexander on the rocks where we had left him, feeling much better. He had had an interesting time during the hours of our absence in watching the various moods of the mountain. A large mass of ice had suddenly given way and had crashed down on the very spot where Cantwell had stood, that forenoon, while filling the canteen.

By the time we reached Alexander, it was growing desperately late. We saw that we should hardly get down before night overtook us. We hurried as much as possible; but we had no more than got off of the lower rock ridge when darkness came. We still had many big crevasses to pass.

A snow-field is deceptive after night. There is no way to tell the steepness of the slope and one is apt to walk over the brink of a frightful declivity under the impression that he is stepping out on to a comparatively level area. We were afraid of losing the way and of bearing too far to the right or the left and eventually finding ourselves in a maze of crevasses from which we could not extricate ourselves. There was danger also of walking into a crevasse without seeing it or of stepping upon a frail snow-bridge without knowing what was beneath. And there was the peril of suddenly coming on to a place that was so steep we could not hold ourselves, and of sliding into we knew not what.

I have long made it a practice when climbing an unfamiliar peak to pick out and mentally note a number of landmarks during the lower part of the ascent, so as to have something to go by in case of being overtaken by night on the descent. I think this practice has once or twice saved my party from unpleasant, if not disastrous, results. Although we were now unable to determine the proper direction by means of the contour of that part of the mountain we were on, we were finally able dimly to distinguish the outline of the ridge on which our camp was situated. Keeping this constantly in view, we bore toward it, continually on the lookout for pitfalls for the unwary. But at the best we could do, we were an hour or more among the big crevasses before we heaved a mighty sigh of relief and stepped upon the upper moraine.

Darkness had no more terrors for us, for we were now in our own front yard, and soon we were gladdened by the sight of the little tent beneath the tiny trees that were scarcely taller than it.

We tumbled into bed too tired and sleepy to prepare a meal.

In the morning we hurried down to the Morovits ranch. The weather had begun to threaten, and we had probably climbed Kulshan on the last day of the season upon which the ascent could have been made.

Our climb of Kulshan seems to have been the seventh recorded ascent. Since then many others have climbed it. Some noted mountaineering clubs have conquered it. For several years it was the object of the annual Mount Baker Marathon, an event wherein hardy climbers competed for a prize in being the first to make the trip from the city of Bellingham to the summit of the mountain and back again. The southern side was eventually found to be by far the easiest route of ascent. It is doubtful if the route used by Cantwell and me has ever been entirely followed by any other climber.

Cantwell's picture of the crater, probably the last ever taken of it in activity, was an excellent one, although, strange to say, the great rolls of black smoke scarcely showed on the prints. A photograph taken by Mr. Lee's party on their previous ascent, already mentioned, shows the crater in practically the same condition in which it was at the time of our visit. Still earlier pictures gave substantially the same results. But a fine photograph taken from the summit in August, 1906, nearly three years after our climb, by F. H. Kiser, the noted photographer of Western scenery, gives no sign either of orifice in the snow or smoke. An apparently firm field of snow covered the great mysterious hole we saw, and the only remaining traces of it were a slight depression in the snow and a remnant of the circular crevasse. The weird crater was seemingly dead.

Among the party on Kiser's memorable ascent was Asahel Curtis, so the personnel included two of the most distinguished mountain photographers in the United States. Cantwell was in their class; but he later took up other lines of work in which he became equally prominent.

At the time of our ascent I was under the impression that Professor George Davidson, the eminent California scientist, was the first man to climb Mount Baker. I sent him a copy of Cantwell's photograph of the crater. In acknowledging its receipt he designated it as unique and expressed much interest in the matter. However, he said he had never climbed Kulshan. He had seen it in very active eruption in the early fifties.

Both this mountain and Mount Saint Helens, in the southern part of the State, enlivened the days of the early pioneers by awe-inspiring displays of volcanic activity; but of late years they have been slumbering—perhaps forever.

One day, twelve years after the ascent of Kulshan, I was on a vessel bound from Port Angeles to Seattle. We landed at a small town to pick up some new passengers. Among them was a little fat man. Seeing me standing on the deck, he walked up to me and asked: "Isn't your name Rusk?"

I couldn't deny the accusation.

"I guess I went up Mount Baker with you, one time," continued he.

"I guess not," I replied, a little resentfully. "The only man I ever went up Mount Baker with was a fellow named Cantwell."

"Well," said the little fat man, "I'm Cantwell."

IX

THE GATHERING OF THE MOUNTAIN CLANS

THE summer of 1905 was marked by a remarkable gathering of mountaineers on the slopes of that wonderful giant which an English explorer named Rainier, which an enterprising Western city maintains should be known as Tacoma, and which the Indians called Ta-ho-ma.

They came as the guests of the Mazamas, that splendid organization of good fellows and good climbers which has done so much to popularize the sport of mountaineering in the United States. From the far Atlantic seaboard came the Appalachians; from California, to the south, home of big trees and granite domes, came the Sierras; from many points throughout the country came members of the American Alpine Club; from far and near they came, lovers of the wild, the enthusiasts of the crags. Two hundred strong they camped upon the ramparts of the mountain. Some among them were famous; others have since acquired fame; while possibly a few have fame still to win.

Such an appeal was not for me to resist. From my home on Lake Chelan I hurried to the scene of this joyous assemblage—a free-lance knowing neither a time of going nor of coming. Thus it happened that the train put me down at Ashford, then the nearest railroad point to the mountain, one hot day in the latter half of July. This was before the time of rapid transit by automobile, and, aside from one's own good legs, horses were the only motive power for getting from Ashford to the end of the wagon-road. Naturally the four-horse stage was crowded that day; but the driver consented to take my bed, for a certain compensation, and

MOUNT RAINIER FROM NEAR TIMBER-LINE ON MOUNT ADAMS

EAST SIDE OF GLACIER PEAK FROM TIMBER-LINE

I set out on foot to walk the fourteen miles to Longmire's Springs.

The afternoon was very warm. I took a good pace upon the highway through the open spaces that were found along the first part of the journey. After I had traveled several miles I suddenly realized that I had been guilty of over-exerting myself and that I was overheated. Having been generously assured many, many times in the past, on the best of authority, that it never got uncomfortably hot in the Puget Sound country and that heat prostrations were there unknown, I had been reckless, and now here I was on the point of heat-prostration myself. Fortunately, I soon came to a mountain stream tumbling down over moss-covered rocks. Sitting down beside it I drank what seemed to me to be gallons of the cool water.

By all the rules, I presume, of both popular tradition and medical science, I should have died on the spot. But, instead, I soon began to revive. In a short time I resumed my journey, more moderately. Presently, I came into the magnificent primeval forest of the Nesqually River. The tramp through this glorious woodland, with its cooling shades and the redolence of the giant evergreens, was a never-ending delight, and I reached Longmire's Springs in the evening, ahead of the stage which had started at about the same time I did.

The Longmire Mineral Springs were at that time the terminus of vehicle travel, and the nine miles from there to Paradise Park had to be made on foot or horseback, over a trail. The hotel at the Springs was constructed of material split from the surrounding forest—a rude but hospitable shelter for those who sought the beauties of the mountain.

I was a late comer. Practically all of the mountain clans were encamped in Paradise Park, well up toward the timber-line. But mystery was a foot. At supper-time I met C. H. Sholes, president of the Mazamas; F. H. Kiser, expert photographer; E. P. Sheldon, enthusiastic botanist; and W. T. Patton, a member of Kiser's photographic staff, who had just come down from camp on a secret mission.

They were looking for a safer route by which to take a large party up the mountain. The way beneath Gibraltar Rock was particularly dangerous because of the falling stones that were apt to drop unceremoniously upon the head of the unwary climber at any time, and this peril, of course, increased in proportion to the size of the party. So the four men had come down to Longmire Springs with the intention of making a hurried trip to the west side of the mountain in search of a practicable way of getting up from that starting-point.

In answer to my somewhat doubtful request to be allowed to go along, Mr. Sholes very readily consented to my joining them. I knew that I should be under more or less of a handicap on this trip, as the other four had already had several days of scrambling at high altitudes, while I was comparatively soft, having done very little hard traveling as yet that season.

Next morning we started. We put in a grueling day crossing glacial torrents and surmounting high ridges. We had a trail; but a mountain trail is a mountain trail, and unless you can go leisurely it involves the acquisition of much fatigue. But in the afternoon we came into that marvelously beautiful parkland known as Indian Henry's Hunting-Ground.

As our little procession was winding its way slowly along the side of a ridge, it came to a sudden and unceremonious halt. Patton was filling the air with cuss-words *de luxe.* A bottle he carried in one of his pockets, dropping out, had fallen squarely upon a hard, heartless rock. The glass was shattered and most of the contents irretrievably lost. I could only surmise what the contents had been; but from color, smell, and other symptoms I concluded that it was a certain well-known antidote for rattlesnake bites, although, of course, rattlesnakes are unknown on Mount Rainier. We all offered poor Patton such consolation as we could give; but unfortunately nothing we had to proffer could take the place of what had been spilled.

Up where the last stunted evergreens maintained their everlasting battle with Arctic conditions we found a great, springy bed of low-lying heather upon which we spread our blankets. On our left a banded glacier plunged downward into a big gorge. Directly in front the mighty mountain rose to its sky-crowned heights with its ice-falls and terrace upon terrace of beetling crags. Behind, the gentle, flower-decked slopes of the parkland fell away to the darker forests below.

We were away at dawn. First along the rocky ridges; then across the snow-covered glacier we went, holding to the rope for fear of hidden crevasses. Then up the great snow-slopes of the central ridge, we picked our way, glad at times to follow in the steps of the wild goat, king of mountaineers. Up and still up we climbed, until at twelve or thirteen thousand feet a giant crag blocked the way.

Kiser, who had been elected leader, after a brief reconnoissance, announced that it was impracticable, if not impossible, to go farther. We were looking for a feasible route for a large, mixed party, and we saw that it was not here. It must be Gibraltar or nothing.

So down we went by the way we had come. The descent did not take us so long as the climb had taken, and we were soon across the glacier and on to dirt-going once more.

I had on a comparatively new pair of shoes. These had heretofore given me no trouble; but when we got back on to the ground again, with the inevitable wetting that pedal extremities always get from prolonged traveling through mountain snows, my feet began to blister. Soon the smoothest going became agony to me. Upon reaching our camp of the night before, we immediately started for Longmire Springs. For a time, in spite of the pain I was suffering, I kept up with the others; but at last I had to tell them to go on without me, and I stopped to treat my feet. When I took off my shoes, I found that both of the feet were literally covered with blisters. A bath in the icy waters of a glacial stream relieved them greatly, and late in the evening I limped up to the hotel at the Springs to find that the other four had already gone on to the camps in Paradise Park.

Remaining at the hotel overnight, the next forenoon I made a leisurely trip up the long trail to Paradise Park, although my feet were still bothering me considerably. Arriving at the Mazama camp, I found all eagerly preparing for the big climb.

The Sierras and the Mazamas had camps near each other. The Appalachians and the members of the American Alpine Club, being represented by smaller numbers, did not have separate camps of their own, but were distributed between the two camps of the other clubs.

In those days there were no hotels in Paradise Park, the tourist trade being largely taken care of at Reese's tent camp. I was then a member of the American Alpine Club, having been honored a few years before by being included as one of the founders of the organization.

As I looked upon the parks of Mount Rainier, with their wonderful sub-Alpine evergreens, their great natural lawns, and their splendid expanses of brilliant flowers, I could not help contrasting the treatment accorded to this darling of the Government with that accorded to my own Mount Adams. On the latter mountain's slopes, for more than a generation, thousands of sheep and other domestic animals had been allowed to ravage the beauty of the parklands; while here not even a single bud might be plucked from the limitless acres of bloom. Mount Rainier had for several years been included in a National Park; but there had not then been expended the vast sums that have since been spent in its protection and development.

The Mazama ascent began on the afternoon of July 25th. We were to go up to Camp Muir, at an elevation of ten thousand feet, spend the night there, and complete the climb the following forenoon. The Sierras had preceded us. They had spent the night before at Camp Muir and were finishing the climb the day we started. To avoid any more packing than necessary, it was arranged for the Sierras to leave their blankets and sleeping-bags at Camp Muir for the use of the Mazamas, while the Mazamas would leave their sleeping-outfits at the main camp for the Sierras when they got back from their arduous trip up the mountain. Horses had been used to pack the beds to Camp Muir.

The Mazamas were divided into four companies of about nine each. Mr. Sholes was leader of the party and captain of Company A. E. H. Loomis, our human toboggan on Mount Adams, was captain of Company B; E. P. Sheldon, of Company C; and C. E. Forsyth, of Company D. Captain Sholes appointed me rear-guard of Company A. Two advanced parties had made the ascent on previous days. In one of these was General Hazzard Stevens, who with P. B. Van Trump had made the first ascent of the mountain thirty-five years before.

In our party were two distinguished members of the American Alpine Club, traveling together. One was Professor Charles E. Fay, of Boston, president of that club and also of the Appalachian Club; the other was John H. Cameron, a banker of Chicago.

The camps in Paradise Park were situated at an elevation of about fifty-five hundred feet. The climb from there to Camp Muir is a long, gradual one; first over grassy, flower-decked slopes, then up rocky ridges and vast snow-fields to the lower end of the great backbone known as Cowlitz Cleaver. Part of the route overlooks Nesqually Glacier, winding its sinuous way in its mighty canyon far below. Ever in front is the tremendous dome of Rainier pushing its crown into the very blue of the heavens, its glistening white ice-falls in marked contrast to the darker aspect of its frowning cliffs.

When we were well up toward Camp Muir we met the returning Sierras on their way back to Paradise Park, after sixty-one of them had made a successful ascent of the mountain. Hearty greetings were shouted back and forth, and each party resumed its journey.

It was quite late, as we intended it should be, when we reached Camp Muir. The place did not appeal to one for a longer stay than necessary. Here one had to make the best of a bad situation by spending the night among angular boulders at the lower end of Cowlitz Cleaver, far above the line of vegetation. There was no shelter, although a stone hut has since been built there by the Government. The principal object in passing the night at this spot was to enable a party to reach Gibraltar in the morning before the sun's warmth had loosened the rocks on the great cliffs; as the danger from falling stones was at the minimum during the night and earlier hours of the day.

We found the sleeping-bags of the Sierras, and each picked his or her means of lessening the discomforts of the night. As soon as it was fairly dark we sought such repose as we might find among the volcanic blocks. I have spent few more miserable nights. It was cold, and my bed was woefully hard and uneven. If you have ever tried sleeping under such conditions you will know that the degree of comfort you attain will depend largely upon your ability to make the sinuosities of your body conform to the convolutions of the rocks.

In such circumstances early rising is easy. It is not then a virtue; it is more nearly like a necessity. We were all astir long before daylight. A cold breakfast was snatched from our pack-sacks. Dawn found us starting the long pull up the cleaver.

The ascent of Cowlitz Cleaver is tedious; but neither difficult nor dangerous. It is a sharp ridge; not broad like the great lava ridge on the lower part of the southern route up Mount Adams. At places along the crest are rather prominent spires. It is sometimes necessary, or at least advisable, to détour on to the snow-slopes on the east side. But at no place will an accident be found due to anything but carelessness. Our party of nearly twoscore, under the skillful leadership of Mr. Sholes, had no difficulty whatever, although a few weeks later one of the regular mountain guides on one of the snow-détours, slipped into a crevasse and broke his leg.

As we were passing along the upper part of the cleaver, we had a stroke of rare good fortune. A magnificent avalanche broke from its moorings on the higher ice-falls of Nesqually Glacier and came thundering down in a splendid white flood. It was almost directly opposite us on the far side of the great depression, and our view of it was unobscured. From terrace to terrace the mighty cataract poured, and we stood entranced until the crystal stream had spent its force and had come to rest on a lessened slope, leaving a pure, white track where it had cut a wide swath in the darker snow.

And finally we came to Gibraltar. The dangers of Gibraltar, aside from the falling stones, have often been greatly exaggerated. But for the one menace, it is not a particularly dangerous place when proper care is used. Of the peril of the dropping rocks too much cannot be said. Sooner or later a terrible tragedy is going to occur at this place.

Gibraltar has been described by a noted geologist as "a black cliff of bedded lava and breccia, a thousand feet in horizontal thickness." It stands upon the face of the mountain at the head of Cowlitz Cleaver, as a great square tower, dividing the upper part of Nesqually Glacier from the upper part of Cowlitz Glacier. The route of ascent passes to the left at the foot of the perpendicular, and often overhanging, face of the cliff. Beneath are tremendously steep talus slopes and solid cliffs leading down to Nesqually Glacier several hundred feet below. A sort of narrow shelf marks the dividing-line between the sheer wall and the slope, and along this the climber makes his way. The footing is comparatively safe; but there is little protection from the falling rocks. When one is beneath an overhanging part of the wall, of course, he is safe; but once upon an exposed portion he is at the mercy of whatever may come from above. Whenever it is cold, as is generally the case during the night, all of the rocks are held in frosty fetters; but whenever it warms up, as it does when the sun's rays strike the face of the precipice, they are released and are apt to come crashing down singly or in companies. Whenever a stone starts, it is very liable to persuade many others to accompany it, so that by the time the line of ascent is reached, there is pretty sure to be a veritable avalanche of volcanic chunks, ready and able to sweep a whole party to oblivion. Of course, the disintegration of Gibraltar is going on year after year, otherwise all of the loose rocks would finally come down and there would be no further danger from them.

Our start had been early, and we reached Gibraltar before the rocks had become very active. We passed safely beneath the greater part of the great cliff and came to the ice-chute which marked the end of our rock-work. The ice-chute lies between the rock and the broken snow-slope that sweeps around the upper end of Gibraltar and on down to Nesqually Glacier. While the chute itself is perhaps several hundred feet long, we had to cross it diagonally, ascending for probably seventy-five feet to the snowslope above. Mr. Sholes asked me to carry a rope up to an anchorage in the snow. The Sierras the day before had cut steps in the ice; but no trace of these remained. The slope was exceedingly steep, but the surface was quite rough, as is often the case with ice that has alternately thawed and frozen.

Taking the rope in my hand, I started across the chute on my hands and knees. When I was about halfway up, a rock the size of a hazelnut came whizzing down from above and struck me on the knee. It stung like a bullet; but did no particular damage. Had it been as large as my head, I should have refrained from writing this story.

I reached the snow which was soft on top and firm beneath. Kicking a solid anchorage with my feet, I sat down in the snow, braced my alpenstock across my knees with the rope wrapped securely around it, and called to Sholes to send them on. Up they came, one at a time, and as they reached me I passed them on to the safety of the snow-slope. It was rather trying on the nerves to watch them come thus; but it was safer so, as there was not so much danger of some one being struck by a rock with only one on the slope at a time. Of course, there was the danger of a rock avalanche catching the rope and sweeping it and everything attached to it to the glacier below. But there is no safe way of passing Gibraltar.

A young woman came up the rope. When her feet were planted safely in the snow, she looked at me in astonishment and exclaimed: "Why, I didn't know *that's* all there was at this end of the rope!"

To this day I have been unable to determine whether or not to regard that as a compliment.

At last all were up. A few minutes more brought the entire party safely to the upper end of Gibraltar, where the snow-cornice connects with the final rocks of the great lava-bastion. Between us and the summit were now only easy snow-slopes.

The southern side of Mount Rainier is the easiest to climb. The same is true of Mount Adams. Although Rainier is two thousand feet higher than Adams, there is really more steep climbing on Adams than on Rainier. There are at least three thousand feet of actually steep climbing on the south side of Adams; while on Mount Rainier, aside from a few steep pitches on the cleaver and the ice-chute at Gibraltar, there is comparatively little. Therefore, for a mountain of its great height, we may classify Rainier as being tolerably easy to climb.

When we reached the top of Gibraltar, Professor Fay decided to go no farther. He was suffering from mountain sickness and an old injury to his knee was giving him trouble. After a light lunch, the rest of us went on for the final two thousand feet. It was simply a long grind up the great snow-slope. The only difficulties we encountered were a few narrow crevasses which were crossed with little trouble. By noon the entire thirty-seven that had started from Gibraltar were at the crater's rim ready to inscribe their names in the record-box. Fifteen of them were women. There were not as many of us as there had been of the Sierras the day before, but, on the other hand, there had not been as many of us who had tried it.

The great extinct crater of Rainier is from a quarter to a half-mile in diameter enclosed by bare cliffs thirty or ,forty feet high. The bottom is filled with snow which makes of the interior a comparatively level field. Around the rim are many small vents in the rock, from which jets of steam issue. In places, and at times, this steam melts the snow, leaving cavern-like fissures between the snow and the wall of the crater.

The record-box is placed on the south rim of the crater. The highest point on the mountain is a dome of snow just west of the crater, the apex being about two hundred and fifty feet higher than the record-box. Most parties making the ascent go no higher than the record-box, and I think it safe to say that a majority of those who climb Rainier never reach the extreme summit.

While the Mazamas were resting around the record-box, I crossed the crater alone. On the farther side I was surprised to find lichens clinging to the bare rock-surface. I found a jet of steam issuing from a small hole in the sloping face of the rock. I stooped to see if I could detect any odor coming from the place and received a little steam-scald for my pains. The rocks were quite warm, and I have no doubt one could place a frying-pan over some of these orifices and there do considerable elementary cooking.

I scrambled out of the crater and a short, easy climb brought me to the highest point on the snowy dome and consequently the actual summit of Rainier. "Columbia's Crest" it is called. Since I was alone at the time, I am convinced that for a few minutes I occupied the highest position of any person in the United States.

Strange to say, I have no vivid remembrance of the view from the top of this great mountain. I have an impression, though, that a smoky haze filled the distance. Needless to remark, however, the view from the summit is a tremendous one, involving, as it does, a large portion of the State of Washington and a part of Oregon. Possibly on an absolutely clear day some of British Columbia would fall within the vision. Nevertheless, the mighty panorama is not so extended as some have imagined it to be. I recently read a book written by an English traveler who visited the Pacific Coast very many years ago. In describing a journey down the Columbia River, he tells how the great form of Rainier was almost constantly in view; and when he had come into the Puget Sound country there was the other side of Rainier dominating the entire region. So he dilates upon the vast expanse of country over which the great mountain is the dominant feature.

Since Mount Adams is the Washington peak most prominently seen from points along the Columbia River, for many score miles east of the Cascades, of course, it was this mountain the Englishman saw and thought to be Rainier. He evidently never knew there was such a peak as Mount Adams.

The Mazamas rested for an hour and a half, and then preparations were made for the descent. According to previous plans, two members of the party, W. T. Patton and R. C. Trengove, of Kiser's photographic staff, remained on top to burn red fire that night. We made a quick trip down to Gibraltar without special incident.

We found Professor Fay there awaiting our return. Our leader was apprehensive of the danger of falling rocks, for it was now one of the most perilous parts of the day. After consultation with some of the other experienced mountaineers, Mr. Sholes asked me to go with him for a reconnoissance. With a long rope we proceeded down to the ice-chute, leaving the rest of the party on top of the rock, out of sight. When we reached the chute, I remained behind with the rope well in hand for an emergency while Mr. Sholes, with the other end, crept cautiously down the steep slope. His feet suddenly went from under him and he shot toward the glacier. Fortunately I was well planted in the snow and saw the accident the instant of its happening.

A quick tightening of the rope was all that was necessary. Mr. Sholes was brought to an abrupt stop, and the glacier was cheated of a victim.

Miss Gertrude Metcalf, historian of the Mazamas, who years afterwards became the wife of Mr. Sholes, at that particular moment was at camp in Paradise Park watching the mountain through field-glasses. She saw Mr. Sholes's sudden glissade, and told others she feared an accident had occurred; but, of course, the distance was so great she could not recognize any of the actors.

Mr. Sholes reached the farther side of the chute at the foot of the rock-wall without further mishap and the call was sent up to the main party to advance. Mr. Forsyth, one of the best mountaineers the West ever saw, came on ahead of the others and took his place on the rope with me. We anchored ourselves very firmly so that we might hold any one in case of a slip.

The party was now started down the chute on the rope, one or two at a time. It was slow business, for each had to proceed with the utmost caution. To Forsyth and me, who had to watch them descend one by one, it was the most trying nerve-work. We were constantly on the alert, scanning the precipice for the first sign of rattling stones that might spell disaster to some member of the slowly moving mountaineers. Our feet buried deep in the snow became numb with the cold, but we dared not move them, for we were the anchors upon which the stability of the rope and the safety of the others depended.

As soon as the first ones had reached the rocks, Mr. Sholes put C. E. Cutter in charge of the lower end of the rope and he himself took charge of the advance along the face of Gibraltar. It required forty-five minutes to get all thirty-six down that treacherous declivity and on to the safer rocks below. Fortunately the giant cliff above refrained from casting stones upon us while we were doing it. Professor Fay, himself a noted mountain-climber, in a subsequent letter to me characterized the descent of the ice-chute, by this three dozen men and women in the face of constant peril from falling stones, as the most dangerous bit of mountaineering he had ever seen.

When they were all across, Forsyth and I tied our end of the rope to a rocky spire, and made a quick trip down the chute. The rope was left for the use of Patton and Trengove in the morning. We found that all except Cutter had preceded us on the way along the face of the cliff. As we afterwards learned, there were one or two narrow escapes from rock-showers that had come down on exposed portions of the precipice.

Cutter, who was an expert photographer and had started up the mountain with a heavy camera, had suffered considerably from mountain sickness during the day. When Forsyth and I reached him we found him feeling very ill. Forsyth hurried on to be of assistance to the others while I remained with Cutter to be of what help I could to him. Owing to his condition we had to travel very slowly, especially in places that were in any way bad. Consequently it was late when we came in sight of Camp Muir. The other members of the party had already gathered up their duffel and had advanced quite a distance down the snow-slopes. I shouted to Sholes, told him of Cutter's illness, and that I would remain with him to help him into camp.

Cutter and I picked up our sleeping-bags at Camp Muir and trailed homeward far behind the others. Presently we met the horses that had been sent up to get the dunnage, and so we were relieved of our burdens. Cutter was unable to go rapidly. Our progress was terribly slow. By the time we were off the snow, darkness was upon us.

And it was a very dark night that set in. We still had

a mile or two to go. There was no trail. I had been over the route but once; and that was the day before on the ascent. Cutter was of the opinion that we should have to stop for the night; but I told him we should make it into camp if he could keep going. I took a general direction toward Mazama headquarters and trusted much to luck.

My chief fear was that we might slide into one of the sharp-cut gullies I had noticed on the way up. Some of the grass-slopes, too, I had seen, were very slippery, for often one finds that nothing is harder to keep footing on that a steep hillside covered with grass. So we were not entirely beyond danger of meeting with an accident, although we were well below what was generally regarded as the danger-line. But Cutter kept resolutely on in spite of his suffering, and, at last, we heard a cheery halloo from the men who had come out from camp to the aid of any stragglers that might need their assistance.

So we were safely home and had had opportunity for much rest and reminiscence by the side of the great camp-fire when a shout called attention to a red flare, seemingly high in the sky, which gave token that Patton and Trengove on the lonely, distant summit had fulfilled their mission.

X

REGAL GLACIER PEAK, ICE-KING OF THE NORTHERN CASCADES

Glacier Peak came to my attention through the descriptions written by Professor Lyman, who had seen it from Cloudy Pass and other points at the rim of the great Railroad Creek amphitheater. He was tremendously impressed by this noble mountain, and he did not hesitate to designate it as a possible rival of Rainier. Measurements placed it fourth among the snow-clads of Washington; but in grandeur it suffers little by comparison with any of them. Although set in the midst of hundreds of snowy mountains, it dominates them all, and I think it may well be called Ice-King of the Northern Cascades. It is only about 10,400 feet high, yet, being well north, it is a snowy dome and it is girdled by beautiful glaciers.

Glacier Peak has been the great unknown among Washington mountains. Set almost on the crest-line of the Cascade Range, it is reached by no road, and there is no populated district from which a near view of it may be had. Many who pride themselves upon a knowledge of Washington's scenic wonders do not even know of its existence.

I first saw this noble peak from the slopes of Mount Baker when Cantwell and I climbed the latter in 1903. There is a strong resemblance between the two mountains, and there is a difference of only a few hundred feet in their height. There is also a strong resemblance between Rainier and Adams; but these two are ponderous and gigantic while Baker and Glacier Peak are more pointed and of far less bulk.

In the summer of 1904 we had a magnificent view of Glacier Peak from Cloudy Pass and vicinity. It was easy to see that the country about its base is extremely rugged; but such surroundings only added to the piquancy of the challenge it flashed to me. A noble peak with noble allies is more desirable of conquest than one which must fight its battles alone. But not until midsummer of 1906 did my opportunity come.

A. L. Cool, of Domke's Lake, invited me to make a trip to the mountain with him. Just below the mouth of Railroad Creek is a dome-shaped mountain rising from the edge of Lake Chelan. It is longer than it is wide and has the appearance of having, some time in the long-past ages, slid down from the main wall of mountains that border the western side of the lake. A valley is thus formed between the smaller and the larger eminences, and in this valley lies Domke's Lake. It is a mile or so in length and about half as wide, and lies several hundred feet above the surface of the larger lake. It is very picturesque, full of fish, and withal an attractive place for the sportsman, or lover of nature. On the shore of Domke's Lake, Cool had a homestead, and there he lived in an environment sufficiently primitive to satisfy any man who had heard the call of the wild.

So one day in late August I landed from one of the lake steamers at the mouth of Railroad Creek, and soon met Cool with his two wise mountain ponies, Benny and Johnny, well loaded with eatables and camp equipment. Everything had been provided, and I had brought only what I was expected to bring, my alpenstock and myself.

We were quickly started and our night camp was made well up the creek in the midst of the ghost-forest. We were traveling by easy stages, and the following day we went only so far as North Star Park and camped just below Cloudy Pass. Here the ponies reveled in an abundance of succulent grass, and we had everything desirable for an ideal camp, not the least of which was a plentitude of marvelous scenery. Just before daylight next morning it suddenly seemed that all the demons of the lower regions had broken loose. A series of diabolical shrieks pierced the air, and the silence was shattered by wild wailings. The commotion arose quite close to us, and continued for several seconds before it resolved itself into the well-known coyote chorus. At times these queer, little animals will break forth in such unearthly noises that even one who is used to their vagaries will be for the moment startled, before realizing what it is that has caused his heart to jump into his throat. Sometimes only two or three are required to do the trick; but you are apt to imagine there are a thousand.

Before packing up, we made a little reconnoissance trip on to the ridge leading south from Cloudy Pass. This gave us a fine view of Glacier Peak, and we had a chance to look down into the stupendous gorge of the Suiattle Fork. We surprised two or three mountain goats and were much interested in the prompt measures they took to escape. They clattered along the ridge until they came to the slope of Chiwawa Mountain, and in less than five minutes they were far up the side of the peak, scaling the precipitous incline without apparent effort.

Returning to camp we soon had Benny and Johnny under our paraphernalia, and were quickly on our way. We crossed Cloudy Pass, taking the left-hand trail. This led us by devious ups and downs eventually on to a mountain-side where a party of hospitable miners were engaged in developing a mine. Dinner was ready and they invited us to their table. The outstanding feature of the meal was a "mulligan" or mixed stew, the principal ingredient being deliciously cooked mutton.

After dinner we descended into and crossed the canyon

formed by the branch of the Suiattle before mentioned. Of course this was several miles from the source, so that the gorge was here neither so deep nor so rugged as it was farther up. A long, steep ascent brought us into a region that was a succession of ridges and canyons leading down to the tremendous canyon of another branch of the Suiattle that sweeps around the eastern base of Glacier Peak. We were in a fine park-country whose beauty had been marred to a slight extent by the presence of bands of domestic sheep.

We had a magnificent view of the mountain, only a few miles away, across the big canyon. A great peak never appears to grander advantage than when seen across an intervening depression. Three glaciers lay on slopes almost directly facing us, and others were apparent in different positions. From this distance Glacier Peak looked almost as difficult of ascent as had Mount Baker from an equal distance.

We camped on the edge of a side-canyon which we must cross before reaching a position from which to begin our final jaunt to the mountain. As night approached, the storm hosts began to marshal around Glacier Peak. Great thunder-caps rolled about the crags, and the vast snow-fields were blotted from view. Soon the reverberations of distant cannonading were borne to our ears. The fleecy billows swept athwart the face of the peak and the elemental conflict was on. The massed clouds gradually spread over the entire sky, and we were treated to that magnificent spectacle—a summer mountain storm.

Presently rain began to fall; but our tent was up and we were snug, while the horses, near by, regaled themselves on abundance of the freshened grass. Considerable rain fell during the night. In the morning it was still showery. The mists were dragging across the lower peaks, torn to rags by the branches of the upstanding trees. There was a damp fragrance in the air, such as may be sensed only after mountain showers.

In the Western ranges there is generally a short period of stormy weather during the last ten days of August. It is usually brief. It may come slightly earlier in the month as I have found to my discomfort; but as a rule it comes within the last ten days. The latter half of July and the first half of August nearly always may be depended upon for ideal weather conditions, although one cannot be absolutely sure that a mountain storm will not strike him suddenly and furiously at any day in the year. September and October are apt to be almost perfect months in the high hills, except that the days are short and the nights often uncomfortably chilly. Then the atmosphere is almost sure to be clear of smoke, and the wonderful hues of the autumn leaves add brilliancy to the other charms of the forest.

As the forenoon continued stormy, we did not move camp. A promise of a clear-up in the afternoon started us on our way again. We crossed one or two of the side-canyons and came to a parky slope just below Buck Creek Pass. Here was a delightful camping-ground. Gradual, grassy slopes led down from the pass for a half or three-quarters of a mile to the brink of the Suiattle Canyon. The thick mat of green grass in the open spaces was varied by noble groves of sub-Alpine evergreens. We were directly opposite Glacier Peak. The glorious mountain loomed magnificently, six or eight miles away, just across the great chasm. The whole slope of the peak rose from the bottom of the canyon, in one tremendous sweep, through forest, glacier, and snowfield, to the topmost crag of the pinnacle, a vertical height of more than seven thousand feet.

We went down the slopes to the lower end of the open country. Here, surrounded by trees, we found a small mud-wallow. Bear tracks were there in amazing numbers. Big tracks, little tracks, medium tracks, made, it would seem, by a whole drove of bears, were there. Not far off, on a dry ridge, decked with beautiful firs, we found our camping-place. It was evident that we could not take the horses any farther, so we pitched our camp with considerable care. The tent was put up and a thick mat of fir boughs was spread on the floor for a bed. Benny and Johnny were hobbled and turned loose to make an easy living on the grass-covered hills.

Between our camp and the pass, a band of sheep was grazing. When we first put up the tent there were no indications that sheep had ever been on the spot; but within half an hour they were bleating all about us. Since most of our outfit would have to be left alone at this place for several days, we were somewhat apprehensive for its safety, fearing some dishonest herder might molest it or allow his sheep to invade our tent.

"Now," said Cool, "you just watch me put the fear of the Lord into that d——d herder!"

It so happened that Cool had been a ranger in the United States Forest Service. He had with him one of the old notebooks that he had used when so employed. Stamped prominently on the cover of this volume were the words: "U.S. Forest Service." Cool placed the book in not too prominent a position, yet where the words could be plainly read by any one standing near our camp-fire. True to our expectations, before the evening was over, after his sheep had been bedded for the night, the herder paid us a visit. Watching him covertly, I could see him occasionally casting furtive glances toward that innocent-looking little book. He asked many questions concerning our identity, destination, and so forth, to all of which we returned courteous though evasive answers. He finally took his departure; but needless to say, during all the time it stayed there alone nothing of ours was molested by man or sheep.

Notwithstanding the recent rain, enough moisture had not been precipitated to check distant forest fires and our views were often obscured by smoke. Cool's photography was very unsatisfactory and he did not succeed in getting a single good picture of Glacier Peak from this magnificent vantage-ground. The day after our arrival we made a reconnoissance trip along the side of the Suiattle Canyon. We soon saw the utter impossibility of taking horses across. The slopes of the gorge were very steep, besides being heavily timbered, covered with brush, and littered by many fallen logs. We quickly realized that we should have to leave the horses and most of our equipment, and with a few days' provisions on our backs, without bedding, strike boldly across the great canyon, trusting to game to replenish our food supply. Cool had his rifle, and, as he was an excellent shot, we had little fear that we should not get something to keep us from starvation.

Accordingly, on the morning of August 25th, we set forth with a few pounds of the utmost necessities on our backs. We dropped down the side of the Suiattle Canyon. This part of the trip was uninteresting. It was brushy and beset with down timber. But at last we reached the bottom. Here we were confronted by a difficulty that seriously threatened the success of the expedition.

We had feared that this branch of the Suiattle would be a hard stream to cross, for we could see that it received the waters from several large glaciers. When we reached it, we saw that our fears were justified. It was a raging, white torrent. Bearing the silt-laden floods of the ice-fields, with a frightfully rapid fall, the boulders continually rolling in its unstable bed, it was too wide to jump, too deep to wade, and too boisterous to swim. No man could stand against such a wild current. There was but one way to cross. That was by means of a log. If we could not find one already down, we should have laboriously to fell a tree with our small axe.

Following up the bank a short distance, we found a barkless log spanning the creek just at the surface of the water. So low did it lie that the resurgent waves swept over it. The wood was as hard as iron, and, from the constant wettings it received, as slippery as ice. It was not an alluring bridge, for if one should once get into that tumbling flood his life would be beaten out in a few seconds.

Cool had sharp nails in his shoes; but I did not. I felt certain they would not hold on such a slick footing. Cool took a few handfuls of sand and threw them along the top of the log. Most of the sand washed off; but some of it remained. He walked quickly across without a slip. While I was sure I could keep my balance, I dared not risk the possibility of one of my feet slipping and throwing me into the water. So I decided to "coon" it. Even this was not safe. Getting down on my hands and knees, I started, having first thrown my alpenstock over. My pack showed a disconcerting tendency to turn me under. The waves dashed over the top of the log, drenching my legs and arms. So slippery was the trunk that I had difficulty in grasping it with my fingers and hands. But I dared not slip, for to slip meant disaster. It was not far; but I had time for nothing else than those few feet of slick timber. With immense relief I found myself reaching for the safety of the farther shore. When I at last stood upon firm ground, we felt that probably the greatest difficulty of the journey had been overcome.

Once across the Suiattle, we headed for the canyon that bore the stream from the glacier that lies on the east face of the mountain. We crossed a heavily timbered bottom where the primeval forest cast deep shadows, and the damp, woodsy smells regaled the nostrils, and soon came to the entering portals of the gorge. Following around the hill-sides we could hear the glacial torrent beneath. Before long we could catch glimpses up the canyon of the crevassed snow-fields and the rugged expanses of ice. In some ways the view was similar to that of Mount Baker from the Morovits ranch, although we saw we should be able to follow up the canyon to the surface of the glacier. The timber became sparser as we advanced, and consequently the view was less obscured. Presently the ice-front of the glacier stood boldly before us, not more than half a mile away.

I remarked to Cool that there was a fine front of ice.

"That's not ice," he said somewhat derisively; "that's rock!"

I told him to wait, and he would see his mistake.

Before long we were abreast of the snout of the glacier, the ice standing boldly up in a point a hundred or more feet in height, steel-blue beneath a slight covering of gravel and dirt that had been washed down by the trickling rivulets. Cool was a much surprised man to see his supposed rock-cliff resolve itself into a precipice of solid ice. A little farther up, by following the depression between the hillside and the ice, we found a place where we could climb up on to the surface of the glacier. Here we stood upon a beautiful banded ice-field, little crevassed and comparatively free of débris, with a magnificent view of the mountain before us.

Cool was slightly in advance, and as he was probably the first white man who ever stood upon its surface, I called this "Cool Glacier."

Exquisitely clear little streams of water were running in their grooves over the ice, and from these we secured drink so cold that it made the teeth ache.

South of the glacier a great rugged double ridge led up

from the Suiattle Canyon, narrowing in the form of a rude triangle until the upper point became a mere moraine between the glacier we were on and another that led toward the southeast. The higher end of this ridge offered the best base from which to attack the mountain. Almost directly south of us, a steep cleft between cliffs promised a means of ascending the ridge. It was but a pleasant walk over the ice to the farther side of the glacier. Then came a sharp rocky climb up the gully. This brought us to the northern leg of the ridge. Between this and the southern leg, a smaller canyon led down to the greater gorge of the Suiattle. The upper end of this smaller canyon formed a considerable amphitheater, which took on a park-like character as the snow-line was approached. We soon saw that the best camping-place would be found on the southern side of the amphitheater or the southern ridge.

Looking across the big basin, we could see many wild goats feeding, like domestic sheep, on the grassy slopes. We were in a wild, primitive region, a veritable paradise to the lover of the unknown. Since crossing the Suiattle we had seen no sign of man having ever preceded us. No scar of axe or blight of fire marked tree or shrub. No old camping-grounds were apparent. During our entire stay on this side of the mountain, we found not a single thing to indicate that a human being had ever been there. We had every reason to believe that we were the first white men, at least, to visit the region.

We proceeded leisurely, in a semicircle, around the upper edge of the amphitheater, entranced by the marvelous scenery and the wildness of the country. Here were no bleating domestic sheep; no odor of the sheep-camp to offend the nostrils. Everything was unspoiled and unsullied. We were the first disturbing human elements to enter this garden of the wild. Nor could we entirely escape a regret that even we had intruded.

When we reached the southern ridge we were virtually at "timber-line," and near the snow. The trees were here of the usual vine-like character found at great elevations, sprawling along the surface of the ground. In a little bowl-shaped hollow, surrounded by these dwarf evergreens and sheltered from the wind, we made our camp. This process consisted in simply throwing off our packs. A brief rest followed.

And now the necessities of the human race entered into our calculations, and sounded a jarring note in the harmony of this perfect place. Wherever man goes he spreads desolation to something, animate or inanimate. We must have food. To furnish it, the life of some creature must be sacrificed—a denizen of this elysium must give up its life that we might eat.

Cool, experienced hunter that he was, said we could get a goat by following down the ridge a short distance. So we started, he ahead with his rifle, I bringing up the rear. The trees got larger as we descended, and soon they assumed the upstanding qualities that trees are supposed to have. Presently blue-grouse began to fly out of the branches, and before long a veritable shower of them was whirring through the air and whizzing off into the canyon on the south. Never, before or since, have I seen such numbers of these birds in one place. But we were after larger game, and did not attempt to molest them.

Finally Cool, with a warning gesture, turned cautiously toward the north side of the ridge. I crept carefully along behind. Suddenly the rifle rang out, shattering for the first time with gunshot crack the silence of the primeval solitude. I sprang to my feet in time to see half a dozen splendid animals dash madly over a small grassy bench and disappear into the depths of the canyon. I thought Cool had missed; but he shouted that he had one of them. Hurrying forward, I saw a young goat in its death struggles about to precipitate itself over the brink of the canyon. Should it once start sliding on the tremendously steep slope, it would probably slip down hundreds of feet and be irretrievably lost to us. We rushed down and succeeded in grabbing its legs just as it was on the point of taking its glissade. We carried it up to the top of the ridge and cut off such parts of the meat as we thought we could use. These we lugged back to camp. A little stream had made a tunnel in a near-by snow-bank, and this formed an excellent refrigerator ready for our use. I regretted the necessity for killing the goat; but the final success of our expedition seemed to depend upon some such measure.

It was nearly night when we returned from our hunting trip. We found much dry dead wood near camp. We built a roaring fire, for we had no bedding. We must depend upon the cheerful blaze to keep us warm while we snatched such fragments of sleep as were possible under the conditions. Then we broiled goat-steaks on sharpened sticks held to the fire. Never in my life have I had a grander feast. Any one of the famous restaurants of the world could command its own price for steaks tasting as those did, if it were possible for it to furnish them. But no high-priced chef ever produced such a delectable repast for the enjoyment of millionaire gourmand. It simply could not be done. I cannot tell how many of those thick, juicy slices I ate; but I do know that I should hardly be believed if I could give the number. I felt that I should be in no condition to climb the mountain next day; but, strange to say, I suffered no ill-effects from my overindulgence.

We alternately roasted and froze by the fire that night. Although it was summer and the weather perfect, we were but a few hundred feet from vast fields of snow and ice and our elevation was that of the snow-line. We turned first one side and then the other to the blaze. It may be said that some parts of our bodies were comfortable at all times, while the other parts were in all the various degrees of discomfort. We had plenty of wood, and frequently one of us arose to replenish the fire. It being late August, daylight did not come so very early. Our preparations were short, nevertheless it was six o'clock when we got started.

August 26th dawned perfectly. But for the smoke from forest fires, climbing conditions would have been ideal. The air was crisp enough to be sufficiently bracing. We followed up the extreme point of the ridge. It finally became a mere narrow ledge between ice-fields, and presently it quit altogether. We now had before us a vast slope of snow-covered ice which forms a common feeding-ground for the Cool Glacier, flowing to the east and the other one flowing to the southeast.

Followed a couple of hours of interesting crevasse work. The surface of the slope was cut by many chasms, although at this place almost free of séracs. We roped together when we first went upon the ice. Of course it was necessary to do quite a bit of scouting to find a way through the maze of cracks. Some places we crossed on snow-bridges; the smaller ones we stepped; others we went around. One large crevasse, in particular, we had to work down into and cut steps up on the farther side, using a little axe which we had brought along. We worked toward a small saddle in the great rocky ridge that leads up the south side of the mountain to the summit dome. A short, stiff pull took us from the ice-field up into this saddle, and we had only a steep climb through soft volcanic scoria between us and the summit. There was nothing to this but tedious toil.

We threw down the rope, and a half-hour or so of scrambling and sinking into the loose substance, tiresome but not dangerous, brought us to the summit cliff. It was only eleven o'clock. We were surprised at the rapidity with which the ascent had been made. We had found Glacier Peak hard enough to reach; but easy to climb when once there.

The old crater of the mountain is directly on the top. It is from a quarter to a half-mile in diameter. The rim has broken down in many places leaving a number of craggy pinnacles sticking up around the circumference. One of these on the southern edge is the highest point on Glacier Peak. The crater is filled by a big snow-field. The rim is pretty well broken down on the east side and the snow feeds over into a great ice-fall which descends the steep side of the mountain and forms the chief branch of Cool Glacier.

On the summit crag we found the wooden frame that had evidently supported a signal pole of the United States Geological Survey. Apparently some member of the party wanted to be sure of having plenty of nails, for we found a double-handful rusting on a rock.

There was no record-box. We had lost all of our pencils and had no means of leaving a legible account of our climb. I have no definite data of earlier ascents. The late Professor Israel C. Russell, the eminent geologist, was one of the first climbers, if not the first. Aside from his ascent and that of those made by the Geological Survey, I know of none preceding ours. The former climbs had evidently been made from the south, and I am certain ours was the first from the east. The Seattle Mountaineers climbed the mountain in 1910, the Mazamas in 1911, and the Mountaineers again in 1921. These climbs, I think, were by practically the same route we used.

The abominable smoke prevented our enjoying the marvelous view we should have had. The great panorama of mountains spreading away on every hand was lost, except within our little circle, in the hazy mystery of the darkened distance.

But our own peak held plenty of interest. Far below we could see the great glaciers radiating from the base of the mountain like monstrous scaly white serpents penetrating well into the depths of the canyons. Just to the south a range of beetling rock-peaks bore away southeasterly, their bases wrapped in glaciers of vast expanse. We spent an enjoyable half-hour looking hither and yon at the countless entrancing views that appeared on every hand. Then we took a quick departure down into the saddle, letting our heels sink well into the yielding pumice-like covering of the slope, and taking great strides as we went. We retrieved our rope, ate a light lunch, and were ready for the ice again.

We descended the crevassed ice-slope by the same route we had come, taking advantage of our morning's tracks, thus avoiding waste of time in looking out a way. It was still early afternoon when we reached camp. It had been the easiest major climb I had ever made. The ascent of Glacier Peak gave me the four highest peaks in the State of Washington—every peak in the State, in fact, that exceeds ten thousand feet in elevation. For several years I claimed the distinction of being the only person who had climbed its four highest mountains, Rainier, Adams, Baker, and Glacier Peak. Several others have since accomplished the same thing.

The balance of the afternoon we spent at leisure. I looked back with satisfaction on the splendid spire we had conquered with comparatively so little effort. Cool took a short trip down the ridge and sat watching the goats, on the opposite side of the amphitheater, through his field-glasses. He saw an old nannie with her kid playing on the hillside a short distance below her. While he was looking, the kid suddenly showed evidence of great alarm and ran up to its mother's side, as if for protection. Presently a large brown bear came clambering up the slope. This was what had scared the little goat. However, the shaggy fellow had important business of his own, entirely unconnected with the mother and her infant, and he ambled away without offering to molest them.

Later in the evening, Cool and I sat quietly on the ridge, below camp, while a great peace seemed to brood over the tremendous scene. While we were there a small band of goats appeared on the opposite side of the canyon headed down the slope in our direction. We remained absolutely still, hoping to see them at close range. Soon they disappeared in the depths of the gorge. In an incredibly short time—only a few minutes, in fact—they reappeared on the slope below us and passed quite near us without suspecting our presence. From where we first saw them to where we saw them last was a stretch of exceedingly rough country that would have required from a quarter to a half-day for an ordinary man to cover; yet these premier mountaineers traversed it with ease in an astonishingly short interval.

We remained at our camp that night. Next morning we set out to do some exploring on the glaciers southeast of the mountain. I was wearing the same shoes I had worn on Rainier the year before. I had supposed that by this time they would have become sufficiently broken to be easy on my feet. But, for some reason, this particular pair were always more or less hurtful so long as I wore them. During this entire trip they gave me much trouble, and on this day, in particular, I suffered agony at every step. My feet were covered with blisters. Traveling became almost intolerable.

Nevertheless, we had a wonderful trip. Reference has already been made to the chain of rock-peaks extending southeasterly from Glacier Peak. The nearest of these was a bold promontory, probably eight thousand feet high, surrounded by two great glaciers, one on either side with a common névé. The glaciers and the névé form a mighty horseshoe; the snouts of the glaciers corresponding to the calks and the névé corresponding to the toe part.

Passing first through a beautiful park-country into the upper canyon, we visited the snout of the northernmost one of the horseshoe glaciers. We found that this remarkable ice-stream ended without a moraine. The ice-sheet seemed to lie lightly on a bed of gravel and small boulders. There was no ploughed-up disturbance of rock and other débris such as we usually find at the ends of glaciers. The ice terminated in a gradually rounding form, gently crevassed longitudinally, giving the snout the resemblance of a huge lion's paw with many toes.

A short distance above the end we went up on to the ice. We found it a beautiful expanse, sloping gradually upward toward its feeding-ground beneath a high ridge which slopes southward from the main mountain. It is almost absoutey free of débris; the ice is firm and little crevassed; and the scenic settings are immense.

The view of Glacier Peak from this glacier is imposing. Impressive ice-falls come tumbling down between great crags, and the massif of the dome towers high above. Beautiful parks extend far up toward the steeper slopes, and box-canyons bear foaming streams downward from the snow-fields. There are grassy stretches, interspersed with groves of sub-Alpine evergreens, reaching to the bases of commanding cliffs. And there are the flower-beds in all their brilliance, many-hued and fragrant, giving a touch of dainty softness to the stern mountain grandeur.

We followed up the glacier a considerable distance and then swung back along the base of the main mountain.

THE LION'S PAW

End of a big glacier, without terminal moraine, southeast slopes of Glacier Peak

ONE OF TWO HIGH MOUNTAIN LAKES NEAR HEAD OF THE ENTIAT

Showing Pass and Glacier over which Horses were brought on the Return from Glacier Peak to Lake Chelan

Everywhere we saw evidences of the goats that had lived here for ages unmolested by the gun of man. At the crossings of the box-canyons the hoofs of countless generations had worn trails in the solid rock.

We passed beneath the jumbled lower end of the glacier which flows down the southeast face of the peak. From this we found issuing streams of chocolate-colored water and I called it the "Chocolate Glacier."

When we had returned to camp we still had a part of the afternoon left, so we decided to start home. We turned our backs upon the splendid mountain and our primitive campground, and headed down into the great canyon of the Suiattle. We had made up our minds to go back by a different route. This would bring us to the Suiattle far above the place where we had crossed it. At first we had easy slopes, with little timber; but presently the hillside became tremendously steep and covered with dense forest growth. In places we had to let ourselves down by the aid of bushes and small trees, exercising great care to keep from slipping. At last, however, we reached the bottom of the canyon, and found the white, glacial flood churning its way over a boulder-bed.

The scene was here wild in the extreme. A dark forest of tall evergreens lined each side of the rocky swath the torrent had cut, making two high green walls, between which the tortuous, rock-paved stream-course wound its way. Immediately to the south, through the branches of the great trees, could be seen the spires and precipices of the range of rock-peaks already mentioned. The river did not occupy the full width of the course, and there were indications that when in full flood it carried a much more tremendous volume of water than at the time of our visit. Many big drifts indicated the awful force with which it sometimes tore trees from their roots and whirled them downward on its crest.

Now, however, there were many gravel or boulder-strewn bars and numerous islands of varying size. Altogether it was a weird and lonely place. One almost instinctively looked for some fearsome creature, either natural or supernatural, to stalk from the depths of the somber forest.

We saw that the southernmost of the horseshoe glaciers ended in an abrupt ice-fall in a side-canyon quite a distance above the floor of the main canyon, and, of course, it contributed its share to the milky torrent. I regretted very much that a lack of time prevented my making a more extended exploration of these remarkable glaciers and the adjacent peaks.

We followed down the stream for a short distance and made our camp on a gravel-bar where convenient drift offered abundant fuel for the night. We snatched such sleep as we could, moving about from place to place, to utilize to the utmost the warmth of the fire which we replenished from time to time.

Morning brought one of the most gorgeous sunrises I ever saw. Masses of cumulus clouds were hanging about the rock-peaks and as the sun rose these were turned to a flaming glory of red and gold. The whole range seemed to be afire. The great crags, aglow with the living radiance, shone through blazing interstices, while the lower levels were still wrapped in the darkness of departing night. It was a marvelous contrast between the shades of the somber forest and the glowing tints of the crag-pierced cloudland.

Preparations for departure did not take much time. We found a place where a great drift lay completely across the wild river, making an effectual bridge for our passage. Then came the long grind up the canyon-side through the interminable forest, with its fallen logs and impeding brush. Only those who have threaded their way out of a mighty Western canyon, where no trail leads on, can appreciate the task it is. The day was drawing to its close when at last we were gladdened by the sight of our tent, set snugly in its grove of firs, untouched by herder or marauding sheep, with inviting bed laid upon springy boughs.

What a glorious sleep we had that night!

Benny and Johnny were found contentedly grazing on a near-by hill and brought into camp, their holiday over and their toils renewed. We were to go home by a different route, a part of which had never been traversed by horses. We first crossed through Buck Creek Pass, then followed down Buck Creek to the Chiwawa River. On the way we had for some time seen ahead of us the remnants of a forest fire that had evidently burned itself out; but had left many lingering patches from which the smoke was still rising in clouds, more or less dense. We saw that our trail passed through the smouldering embers, and we began to fear for the safety of our horses. We came into it on a little side-hill. The trail was here blocked, and it was necessary to make a slight détour down the hill.

The ground was uncomfortably hot. The smoke was strangling and blinding. Cool was ahead, leading Benny. He essayed a dash through the smoke. Everything went well until he reached the bottom of the hill. Then Benny suddenly broke through into a cavity that had been occupied by a partly submerged log. The wood had been largely burned away; but the hole was full of glowing embers. The poor beast struggled frantically. Cool pulled desperately on the halter rope. Finally through the combined efforts of man and agonized beast, Benny succeeded in getting his front feet on to solid ground and was pulled on to a firm footing.

Meanwhile, urging Johnny to his utmost exertion, I made a dash down the hillside. Luckily we missed all pitfalls, and were soon on the trail again beyond the point of danger. An examination of Benny showed that the poor fellow was terribly burned about the hind legs. Our hearts were torn with pity for the faithful animal. We discussed the advisability of shooting him on the spot; but we could not bring ourselves to do it, and, at last, we decided to give him a chance for his life.

We relieved Benny of his pack, giving to Johnny an added burden, and started on. Our progress was now slow and painful, for we could not be unmindful of the suffering of the horse. Cool had in mind a certain camping-place on Phelps Creek which he thought it necessary to make that night in order that we might have time the following day to traverse the section of country that had never known the hoofs of horses. When we reached the branching of the trails, we turned sharply, and took a course almost in the opposite direction to that we had been pursuing. My feet were giving me intense pain, and poor Benny was not the only one of the party that went his way in misery.

Followed a journey of seemingly endless toil and discomfort. The trail was plain and easy to follow; but an intensely dark night set in. Cool was ahead, leading Benny, with Johnny following, while I and my feet brought up the rear. Notwithstanding the agony he must have been suffering, the injured horse, relieved of his burden, seemed able to travel almost as rapidly as ever. The country was new to me, and after it grew dark I could follow the trail only by its *feel*. Cool and the ponies drew ahead. I was left far behind to make my way as best I could. For hours, it seemed, with protesting pedal extremities, I felt my way along that unknown trail, my difficulties intensified by the deep shades of the silent forest. An occasional stub against a protruding rock by no means served to relieve the unpleasantness of the situation.

But if we are only philosophical enough we can always

assuage our difficulties by reflecting that all things must have an end. So, at last, I came upon Cool, in a little glade, throwing off the packs and turning the horses loose to graze.

In the morning I could see that we were in the upper reaches of Phelps Creek Canyon, well beyond the dense timber growth, with green meadows lining the bottom of the valley. At the head of the gorge towered the red and black peaks about the head of Lyman Glacier, with a pass leading through to the snow-fields of the glacier. Two years before, Mrs. Rusk and I had come through this pass on to the upper Phelps Creek slope.

When we arose, Benny was still on his feet, although he must have been suffering greatly. Cool applied such remedies as he had at hand pinning his faith on a well-known "mustang liniment." After breakfast we struck across trailless mountains, our objective being the headwaters of the Entiat River. The crippled horse was apparently no worse off while traveling than when standing still, and he surprised us by the agility with which he negotiated difficult situations. The first stage of our day's journey led up a steep, timbered mountain-side, boggy in places, and generally covered with grass. Finally we came into the higher, rockier region. Wherever we went the going was rough enough. There was no trail, and there could be no doubt that these were the first horses that had come this way. But Benny, little hero that he was, kept on calmly and stoically, steadfastly earning his right to a chance for life.

As evening advanced, we made for a high pass beneath rocky peaks. We came to a great shell-rock slide. There was no way but across it. We spent considerable time in making a trail with our bare hands, lifting the loose slabs and replacing them as best we could. Eventually we had a makeshift trail over which the courageous ponies picked a precarious footing. At last we topped the pass and, looking down the other side, the way we must go, saw a glacier.

The ice filled all of the available space between the peaks. There was no way to get down but over the glacier. To go back the way we had come was out of the question. Fortunately the ice was not badly crevassed and the slope was not excessively steep. Each carefully leading a horse, we took the right-hand side and started cautiously down. The surface of the ice was rather rough and sprinkled with gravel, so the ponies secured footholds without much trouble. It was not a large glacier and the distance down the face of it was perhaps from a quarter to a half-mile. We zigzagged slowly back and forth. The total drop was several hundred feet; but we negotiated it safely, coming finally into a wonderful mountain basin wherein lay two lake gems of rare beauty. These lakes, one lying slightly above the other, were almost entirely above the timber-line, only a few hardy dwarfed trees appearing here and there; while the shores were margined by grassy swards. Each translucent body of water was about half a mile across. This was no summer land. The great elevation, probably exceeding seven thousand feet, gave it an autumn climate throughout the summer months, and winter came on when fall arrived in the lower levels.

We pitched our camp upon the grassy shore of one of the lakes. There was abundance of feed for the tired horses. The gnarled trunks of dead trees furnished fuel for our fire. Altogether it was a delightful camping-spot, yet one for chattering teeth and frosted toes, for the night chill came on apace.

We spread our bed upon a mattress of grass. We did not put up the tent, for the weather was fair and we had plenty of covering. In the morning, however, the lake was margined with ice. So crisp and winter-like was the air that we did not have the courage to crawl out and start a fire. We waited patiently while the sun crawled slowly up over the great earth-folds of the Cascades. The peaks were tinted with a delicate pink glow as the golden sunlight crept nearer and nearer down the glorified crags. At last came radiant warmth, and with it the energy to creep from between the blankets and prepare breakfast.

It was a day of splendid beauty. After the morning meal, we climbed several hundred feet up over green terraces and stood looking across the awe-inspiring spectacle that marks the head of the Entiat River. Immediately beneath lay the jagged ice-falls of Entiat Glacier. The wildly broken masses of snow and ice, at the upper end, clung with precarious tenacity to a thousand-foot precipice-rim that swung around the glacier-head in a perpendicular amphitheater. Directly opposite were the ramparts of the great peaks that look down on Railroad Creek. I know of few scenes of more awful, savage grandeur.

In the afternoon came the resumption of our homeward journey. It was a serious question whether or not we should be able to get poor Benny down into the great canyon of the Entiat. The slope was very steep and long. Heretofore, since the accident, our traveling had been mostly uphill and it is easier for an animal in his condition to go uphill than down. Moreover, he now seemed less able to walk than at any time after being burned. We feared that we should have to leave his body on that rugged canyon-side. But the trial must be made.

We started down immediately after leaving camp. I went ahead leading Johnny; Cool came behind with Benny. Although I did not tell Cool so at the time, I had made up my mind that if it became necessary to shoot the animal I would take the unpleasant duty off of his hands. To a man of even ordinary sensibilities, it is a heart-breaking thing to have to kill a horse; and to the owner of the faithful beast it is almost unbearable. Such a necessity, it would seem to me, would be next to having to kill a human being.

But we did not have to kill Benny. It was a nerve-racking task to get him down, and, at times, it seemed we should have to give it up; but perseverance on the part of man and beast finally won, and after an interminable time we reached the bottom of the canyon and consequent easier going. And before bidding adieu to the brave little horse it may be well to state that he completed the journey in safety, regained his former strength, and lived through many days of future usefulness.

From the Entiat Canyon on to Lake Chelan the trip was still replete with mountain interest. In fact, I have made but few excursions into the wilderness that were so full, from start to finish, as this one. But for my suffering feet and the accident to Benny, it would have been ideal. Even with these unpleasant memories it was one of the outstanding journeys of my life. When we had gone the last remaining miles; past Emerald Park, mountain gem of rarest beauty; by many a rugged feature of the wild, tame only because of what we had already seen; and had come at last, in sight of Cool's snug cabin nestling on the shores of Domke's Lake, I could look back upon it all and say that it had been a thousand times worth while.

XI

CAMP OF THE STARS

THE desire to climb the great eastern face of Mount Adams persisted after an absence of sixteen years from the mountain. Early in September, 1918, with Joe G. Hill and S. E. Sampson, I made a brief visit to this side of the peak and we confirmed my previous observation of the impracticability of Battlement Ridge as a possible route of ascent. I decided to spend ten days on the mountain in the summer of 1919, not with the intention of trying the hazardous climb; but for the purpose of studying conditions and making reconnoissances. I planned to remain a night at a high elevation on one of the big ridges, for I knew that when the feat was finally attempted it would be necessary for the party to stay all night far above sea-level without fire or beds.

I was then living at Yakima, Washington. I intended to make the trip alone; but, the day before I started, J. Howard Green, another resident of that city, upon the suggestion of O. C. Soots, executive secretary of the Yakima Commercial Club, came to me and asked if he might go also. The Commercial Club, under the vigorous and able leadership of Mr. Soots, was pushing the development of the Mount Adams region as a public playground, and I had been asked to furnish such data as I might obtain, from time to time, to aid in the publicity work of the scheme. As part of the programme it was proposed to build a highway through the Yakima Indian reservation, which would cross the Klickitat River east of the mountain, swing around the southeastern base to Glenwood, and there connect with roads leading to White Salmon and connecting with the North Bank Highway and the famous Columbia River Highway. Thus would the distance between Yakima and Portland be greatly shortened and a wonderful scenic area opened to easy public access.

On the afternoon of August 11th, Green and I set out on our adventure with provisions for a ten days' sojourn in the wilds. A Ford was brought into use, and we were taken to the little reservation town of White Swan by L. M. Holt and W. A. Walker of the Indian Reclamation Service. Here we stayed all night. White Swan was intensely interested in the building of the new road, and, when he learned our destination, A. C. Coburn, a prominent citizen of that place, volunteered to get us as far as the Klickitat River. Accordingly, the following forenoon he accompanied us to the river, in a Stephens car driven by the owner, Jim Olney, a young Indian, member of a leading reservation family. At this time a steep grade, which had been built by the Forest Service, led down into the Klickitat Canyon, directly east of Mount Adams. This, however, was many miles above the road leading from Goldendale to Glenwood, which has been frequently mentioned.

At Surveyor's Creek ranger station, which was as far as the automobile went, we met my old friend Ed Snipes, erstwhile forest ranger, together with Mrs. Snipes, both of them old-time Klickitat pioneers. Their son, Harry Snipes, was in charge of the station and his wife and young son were also there.

Green and I now shouldered our packs and set out on the long, hard trip to "snow-line." Two more miles brought us to our night-camp at Soda Ford on the Klickitat, a place visited by my father, mother, and myself in 1888, thirty-one years before.

Next morning we had to wade the Klickitat, cold,deep, and swift, with our heavy burdens. Then came the seemingly interminable pull up the steep timbered mountain-side, along the old zigzag trail which we had followed on that first memorable trip nearly a third of a century before. Night found us on Cunningham Creek, still far from our prospective permanent camp. At three o'clock next day, we passed below the castellated yellow cliffs of Goat Butte and filed into the fresh green meadows of Avalanche Valley, rich with a profusion of fragrant wild flowers.

At the place where we camped, the stream, which rises in a number of springs at the base of the butte, divided on a steep little hillside, one branch flowing in one direction while the other flowed off, nearly at a right angle; the mouths of the two, which ran into a larger creek, were half a mile or so apart. Since the stream-courses frequently change, it is hard to say for how many seasons this interesting curiosity will exist.

The morning of the 15th was ushered in by a splendid sunrise on the mountain. The golden sheen threw the great cliffs into bold relief and they stood out in jagged detail, every one a direct challenge to my eager desire to climb the east side.

Although our camp was at an elavation of about sixty-five hundred feet, I had higher aspirations for this trip, and at ten o'clock we started for a greater level. We followed up the peninsula between Rusk Glacier and the unnamed glacier north of it. Soon we were in a little parkland valley, among the stunted vine-like evergreens, with a marvelous variety of wild flowers, dwarfed in size but perfect in delicate coloring, blooming all around. Every imaginable tint was represented. There were also blue lupine, wild tansy, and other familiar plants. Robins and several other kinds of birds, chipmunks, ants, bees, and other insects gave a touch of life to the scene. A small, succulent bunch-grass grew abundantly. The trees sprawled along the ground, never reaching a height of more than five or six feet, and in places they were matted like a thick green carpet upon the surface. I called this delightful little country the "Vale of Flowers."

We camped by a tiny crystal stream, at the highest grove of vine-trees. Our elevation was about seven thousand feet. Just to our north was the high, sharp, roof-like moraine of the unnamed glacier. The tremendous eastern wall of the mountain was right at hand, and immediately west of us began the serried steps of the great red ridge leading up to the overwhelming yellow precipices.

In the afternoon we went up on to the moraine and looked out on to the unnamed glacier. We had just emerged victoriously from the World War and I decided to name this the "Wilson Glacier," for the World War President. The mighty red ridge sandwiched between it and the Rusk Glacier I thought might appropriately bear the name of "Victory Ridge." Just beyond the southernmost ice-fall of Wilson Glacier rises a high, abrupt precipice and we agreed that it might well be christened "Roosevelt Cliff."

From the top of the moraine we had a fine view of Mount Rainier and Goat Rocks. The weather was magnificently clear; but much smoke from forest fires was beginning to accumulate in the lower countries.

Our camp was a pleasant one, and we managed to snatch a few hours of quiet enjoyment from it, during our busy stay. I was much amused by the antics of a chipmunk that lived near-neighbor to us. He took a great fancy to the outside canvas covering of my sleeping-bag. He evidently imagined that it would make him a snug bed. Often, when it was spread out on the rocks to air, he would take hold of a corner and try to drag it away. He appeared to be much surprised when he found that he could not move it. He would then secure a hold in another place and try to pull it off from another angle; but always with the same

MOUNT ADAMS OVER CIRCLE LAKE, AVALANCHE VALLEY

CAMP OF THE STARS

The author spent the night leaning against the big boulder at the spot where the point of the alpenstock touches the ground. Two-thousand-foot precipice in the background

GREAT PRECIPICE AND HEAD OF RUSK GLACIER, MOUNT ADAMS, FROM CAMP OF THE STARS

Showing dark track of the avalanches down center of the glacier. The Castle on the left. No other camera has ever been taken to this point

result. He finally gave it up as a bad job; but I am sure that for long afterwards he must have dreamed each night of himself and family defying the rigors of winter within the warm folds of that canvas sleeping-bag. One evening while I was standing near camp this same little friend whisked out right in front of me. Seizing a stalk of grass he cut off the head with his sharp teeth, and, running up on to a large rock within six feet of me, sat up on his haunches and proceeded to eat it, meanwhile watching me out of his tiny bright eyes to be sure that I was looking. I never saw a more palpable example of an effort to "show off."

But the main objective of the trip was to spend a night alone at the highest point on Victory Ridge that I could reach. This would give me a good point of observation from which to study the upper part of Rusk Glacier and the Castle, and I could also gain some idea of the effect upon a party that would have to make a night bivouac on the bleak eastern face of the mountain without fire or bed. Therefore, Green and I started at six-forty-five (daylight-saving time) on the morning of the 16th. I carried sufficient food for several meals and a small canteen. We had easy going at first up snowbanks and along old moraines. Between eight and nine o'clock, we passed above the first high point of the ridge, and looked down on Rusk Glacier. I went a short distance out on to the edge of the ice. From here we had a wonderful view of the great ice-fall that marks the middle course of the glacier. We then started up the steep slide slope of the second point of the ridge; but found the traveling very tedious. Finally we bore to the Wilson Glacier side and clambered up the cliffs, getting a magnificent sight of the savage ice-fall of its southern branch. Just opposite us appeared the splendid colored wall of Roosevelt Cliff.

We climbed the cliffs to the top of the second point, and there, at an elevation of over nine thousand feet, found the ridge so narrow and shattered that it would have been dangerous in the extreme to have attempted further progress. Here I decided should be my bivouac; while Green was equally certain he would return to the lower camp. I called this lofty perch "Camp of the Stars."

We had the feelings of discoverers, for, so far as I am aware, no other human beings had ever stood upon the narrow ledge nor looked upon the stupendous scene. On the south the cliffs dropped sheer to Rusk Glacier; on the north the descent was so precipitous to Wilson Glacier that none might find footing upon its crumbling slope. One could cast a stone down to the ice on either hand; but no one could descend and live. Just to the west, the avalanche-hurling crags of the great precipice loomed, their frowning front crowned by a two-hundred-foot wall of snow. From their northern ramparts the ice-falls of Wilson Glacier plunged wildly downward. Forming the southern buttress of the magnificent amphitheater that swings around the head of Rusk Glacier, the Castle towered to a forbidding sky-line. Here in ages past had been, no doubt, the seething cauldron of the great volcano; and still the red and black and yellow walls gave mute reminder of the fires that once had been.

We ate lunch, and shortly before two o'clock Green started back to the lower camp. I watched him disappear behind the abrupt cliffs and waited for him to reappear on the gentler slopes far below.

I was now left alone for my twenty-hour vigil, free to take photographs, gain experiences, and collect impressions from my unique situation. I saw that I must conserve my water supply, for Green and I had already drawn rather copiously from the little canteen and there was no chance to get more until I descended the ridge next day. True, there were hundreds of thousands of tons of cold, pure ice almost within a stone's throw of me; but it might have been a hundred miles away, so far as present access was concerned. It was comfortably warm, for the sun was shining brightly, and I have already spoken of the heat that prevails on these great eastern ridges on a summer day. The heat-waves were pulsating in visible, wavering lines from the rocks. Although it was far above the zone of any vegetation, many flies were buzzing about. I saw several little birds and a chipmunk near by. Presently a small green squirrel-like animal appeared a short distance from me, hurrying down the ridge as though he had urgent business at the lower levels. At first, I was at a loss to know what this was; but I finally decided it was a Douglas squirrel. What he was doing there I cannot imagine, as he could not have come over the mountain, and he was certainly high above any source of food supply. Possibly, like me, he had come up the ridge on an exploring expedition, and, not finding the region to his liking, was losing no time in getting down to more congenial surroundings.

Below, on each side of me, was a great ice-fall. The near-by view was certainly tremendous and inspiring; but the lower country was filled with a miserable pall of smoke. But for that, the eastward panorama would have been marvelous. The great colored cliffs, with their overhanging snow-wall, towered directly above me, right at hand. I estimated that they could not be over a quarter of a mile away in a direct line.

After Green left, I got a good scare. I started out to determine the feasibility of making my way along the ridge at the place where it narrowed down. I worked my way over the treacherous rocks for several yards. Glancing backward, I saw that I was in a precarious position. I could not see how I got there, and I could not see how I was going to get back. It began to look like a choice between Wilson Glacier and Rusk Glacier for me. For a brief time

I lost my nerve. The cold perspiration stood out upon my body and my knees grew weak. Then, collecting my wavering will power, I started carefully back. In a few minutes I was safe once more on the dependable rocks of the broader portion of the ridge, content to forego future exploration in that direction, alone. A party with ropes could pass this dangerous part of the backbone and go on up the ridge for a considerable distance; but it is not a one-man job.

More than an hour had passed since Green left me and I had not seen him on the slopes below. I began to be a little worried, fearing he had met with an accident, for I thought that he should be easily visible once he had passed from behind the cliffs.

About three o'clock wonderful somber shadows began to gather around the great precipice, and the sharp serrated snow- and rock-spires stood out in remarkable relief on the sky-line. The sun was almost directly over the mountain. Its rays fell in queer bars through the interstices of the cliffs. The faint roar of distant streams came droning through the air. A great peace seemed to brood over the big peak, broken occasionally by the far-away crash of an avalanche.

Another half-hour passed, and still no sign of Green. No stir in the camp below. What could be the matter?

The air continued warm and pleasant. I sat in comfort and drank in the glory that lay around me. I studied the Castle and the upper glacier, from this new position and under light-angles I had never seen before. But there was no promise of success in these observations. The Castle looked to be unscalable.

I ate a can of oysters and couple of hardtacks. I drank sparingly of the water. Then at a quarter to five o'clock, a smoke arose from camp and I knew that Green was safe. It was a great relief.

The solitude was intense. The lower country looked

ghostly and unreal through the dense smoky haze, and the pinnacles of Goat Rocks could be but faintly seen. But for the stream-roar it would have been oppressively still. At two minutes after five the sun dropped behind the great snow-wall above me. The dark shadow of Mount Adams had started on its afternoon journey eastward across the country. The cliffs were magnificent in the growing twilight.

Twenty minutes later I observed some remarkable smoke-wreaths coming over the summit of the mountain. They looked like immense blue ribbons about to fall on me. One, for a moment, took the form of a cupid's bow. They twisted and twirled into all kinds of fantastic shapes. I could see the shadows of these wreaths drifting across the Vale of Flowers and Avalanche Valley, casting a peculiar reddish tinge upon the ground.

At five-forty-five a stiff evening breeze began to sweep down from the snow-mass above the cliffs. I saw that I was in for some disagreeable hours if it should continue all night. Bereft of the genial sunlight, the warmth was departing from the rocks.

An hour later a great wall of red and gray smoke rose around the mountain. The upper lines were clear-cut and distinctly separated from the sky; but the highest edges assumed peculiar designs, one appearing, briefly, as a giant Liberty cap. The lower country was almost blotted out. The shadow of the mountain had reached the top of Goat Butte. The chill wind was still blowing from the summit dome. I selected the lee of a huge boulder as my bivouac place.

And then the marvelous night came on.

Profound darkness closed rapidly around the mountain. Soon looking downward was like looking into an inky void. Green's camp-fire shone brightly through the black density like a great lower star, while overhead the natural stars came out in brilliant multitudes, with Polaris in the north and the evening star directly over the mountain dome. Never had I seen those distant suns glitter with deeper intensity against the black curtain of boundless space, and their number was infinite. Constellation upon constellation blazed like diamond setting in the Crown of Night. A myriad master-orbs, each with its mighty retinue of attendant satellites, whirled their ceaseless flight across the dome of Heaven. Cumbering earth-smoke had no place in the firmanent above.

The noises of the mountain were subdued in the solemnity of the fathomless night. The roar of the distant streams came now but faintly, as if to intensify the stillness. Now and then came a sharp crack from a tortured glacier, and occasionally the dull chug of an ice-area settling more firmly in its uneven bed. At times could be heard the clatter of rocks that broke from their fetters and plunged into the depths of yawning crevasses. Erosion was doing its age-long work.

The solitude was oppressive. Above, the great cliffs were wrapped in a dark mystery.

Far to the north a massive shape appeared suddenly suspended in the sky between two layers of smoke. At first I could not make it out; and I could but conjecture upon what this strange thing might be; but finally I sensed that it was the tremendous bulk of Mount Rainier, hanging like a giant bell, its crown and base cut off by the black bands of haze.

Adams itself seemed to be detached from all earthly connection, and to be a separate planet floating alone in the immensity of space. Only two points of light were visible to remind me that I was still a part of the terrestrial sphere. A mile and a half away, down below, Green's fire still flickered brightly, and miles to the northward a glowing spot marked the remnant of a dying forest fire. Except for these, the lower world was but a void. And then Green's tiny light finally faded and died, even as suns fade and die in the galaxies of the universe.

It was a time for solemn thought—a time to impress man with the knowledge of his own littleness. Here was I, alone and helpless, a mere human atom, surrounded by the tremendous forces of nature that had been working ceaselessly for untold ages, grinding out the destiny of the great mountain, preparing the earth to be the abode of mankind. And compared with the life of the mountain my life was but as the snuff of a candle—compared to the bulk of the mountain my frame was but a microscopic molecule. And Adams, mighty peak with its precipices and chasms, its ice-fields and snow-cliffs, was but a grain of sand upon the unthinkably enormous earth.

And what of earth itself? There gleaming in the north was Polaris, casting less light upon us than a firefly's glow, yet a blazing sun so immeasurably far away that it remains a fixed point while the Solar System wings its flight through billions of miles of cold immensity; and presently there would come flaming across my little horizon our own sun, a million times as large as earth. But away off there in the Constellation of Orion gleamed red Betelgeuse, so incalculably big that, if it were a hollow ball, our sun might be placed in its center and earth have room to revolve upon its orbit within the shell and still have millions of miles to spare on either side. Yet Betelgeuse was but a speck impinged against that mighty white bank across the zenith, the Milky Way, appearing, to the naked eye, as a dim cloud which we know to be in reality millions of blazing suns, each perhaps as big as our own sun or Betelgeuse; and beyond that, seen by man's most powerful telescopes, are other stars, so far away that it takes their light more than three quarters of a million years to reach the earth!

And yet what are all of these—earth, sun, Pole star, Betelgeuse, constellations, Milky Way, the awful aggregation of our stellar universe—but a needle-point of light in the black immensity of unending space.

At eleven o'clock came a wonderful change. The half-moon, red as blood, rose, leaden and dead, over the black wall of smoke. It gradually got brighter as it reached the clearer sky above. Landmarks far below began to take on dim shapes. I could see that the canyons and valleys were filled with heavier smoke, the white arms reaching out like great octopus tentacles from the higher points. All through the balance of the night the cliffs and the glaciers glowed with the mellow moonlight, and their savage grandeur seemed softened and subdued.

Frequent blasts of chilling wind swept down the ridge. The rocks were now thoroughly cold, and I shivered behind my boulder. I stuck my feet in my pack-bag to keep them as warm as possible. I was thirsty, but I dared take only a few swallows occasionally from my canteen, for my scanty store of water must be conserved.

Morning was long in coming; but at last a red glow tinged the smoke-wall in the east. Finally the sun appeared, like a glowing red ball rising through it. The weird dark world below began to show through its fetters, the canyons and valleys completely obscured, the higher hills and ridges lying in long lines in darker contrast. It was a strange, unreal world. The multicolored cliffs above caught the glow of the sun and sprang to life; the gold-tipped snow-fields flashed back their morning greetings; a million glittering diamonds sparkled on the awakening ice-points; and my marvelous night was ended.

It had been one of much discomfort, but every minute had been full, and the rewards were worth the cost.

The sun and moon now both hung in the sky between the

crest of the mountain and the eastern pall of smoke; the latter paled under the brilliance of its great neighbor. The rich sunbeams began to play with exquisite effect on the great precipice; the stream-roars took courage, and came with increasing volume; and I wondered if this marvelous symphony of sound, light, and color could be excelled at any other place on earth. This, indeed, was a box seat in the grand opera of the gods.

I had been cheered early in the morning by the sight of Green's smoke at the camp below. Because his light had gleamed for me through the hours of intense darkness, like a star of the lower world, I decided that this must be known as "Camp Lower Star." I wanted to get some pictures of the great precipices under favorable conditions, so I waited until the sun was well up in the sky. It was nearly ten o'clock when I left Camp of the Stars. The going down was easy. I ate breakfast at the first snow I found by the side of Rusk Glacier. A little lower down I met Green who had come up to meet me. We reached Camp Lower Star just two hours from the time I left Camp of the Stars. Green explained that the evening before, after returning from the ridge, he had made a trip to the top of Goat Butte before starting his camp-fire, and this was the reason why I was so long seeing a sign of him.

We enjoyed camp life the balance of that day, but early on the morning of the 18th we started to explore the region about the sources of Wilson and Lyman Glaciers. We followed up the slope for about an hour, crossed the upper end of the moraine and passed on to Wilson Glacier just below the ice-fall of its southern branch. We went immediately to the foot of Roosevelt Cliff, where I reached across the crevasse, touched the rock with my alpenstock, and christened it "Roosevelt."

We passed on to the ice-falls just north of the cliff, which form a glacier-branch that divides; part flowing to the right and forming a stream of Wilson Glacier; that flowing to the north forming part of the Lyman Glacier. Here was a totally unexplored part of the mountain, terribly rugged and characterized by ice-falls of tremendous size.

We started up the séracs north of Roosevelt Cliff, it being my intention to reach the upper end of the cliff, if possible. We found the going very difficult among the hummocks and crevasses. I had to cut many steps in the ice, and I had only a small pocket-axe with which to work. When we were on the second sérac, Green said he would not go any farther, as he feared passing above big crevasses. He said he would either wait for me or go down alone. I proceeded by myself, and, immediately above, encountered a dangerous steep slope up which I had to proceed with great care, cutting steps as I went.

Just above this I found a large crevasse with a knife-like lower edge and a very steep slope below. I proceeded along this edge for a few hundred feet and finally succeeded in getting around the end of the chasm. Forty minutes after leaving Green I reached a broken ice-sérac. More difficulty with crevasses ensued, and I found that I was about level with the top of Roosevelt Cliff, at a probable elevation of ten thousand feet. There was firm ice beyond, but I could not reach this because of some troublesome small crevasses. I saw, by making a long ascent, I could get over to the cliffs. But there were indications that avalanches might, at any time, begin to fall from the great snow-wall above, and, if a large one should start, I should probably be in its track. This, coupled with the fear that Green might start down alone and thus increase the danger for both of us, decided me to return. Calling to Green, I started back, and reached him in twenty minutes. We got down safely on to the main part of the glacier and crossed toward the north so as to get a good view of Lyman Glacier.

The view of Mount Adams from near the divisional moraine of Wilson and Lyman Glaciers is one of the most magnificent to be seen, involving, as it does, the glorious ice-falls and precipices of this slope of the peak. Two branch glaciers unite to form a large glacial body which divides to form the two glaciers, the water-streams from which flow into separate watersheds, one finding its way into the Columbia River in eastern Washington, the other reaching the Columbia River in western Washington. The mouths of the rivers into which they respectively empty are more than a hundred miles apart. It would be possible to divide one of the rivulets flowing on the surface of the main glacial body, so that part of the water would reach the Columbia in eastern Washington while part of it would reach the same stream in western Washington. It is a curious fact that some of the snow falling on the east side of the mountain finds its way, as water, into the Columbia on the western side of the Cascade Mountains in western Washington; although most of the snow falling on that side reaches the great river in eastern Washington. Likewise, the water from most of the snow falling on the western side of the mountain reaches the Columbia in eastern Washington, although some of it gets to the big stream in the western part of the State. These vagaries are because of the peculiar shape and situation of Mount Adams.

At another place on the mountain a glacial body divides, helping to form two glaciers, the Klickitat and the Mazama. The point of separation is marked by a large divisional moraine. The Mazama Glacier again divides; the water from one branch flowing to the Klickitat River; the waters from the other flowing to the White Salmon River.

That night a strong wind blew down from the mountain.

The stars were very brilliant, the Milky Way seeming like a great haze. In the morning the smoke had settled into the valleys and we could see the distant Columbia hills and far into Oregon. The high region between us and the Yakima Valley stood out distinctly, and we could see the hills beyond. This was another camp-day. In the afternoon we noticed a heavy smoke rising from the timbered country north of Red Butte. Going over on to the moraine we saw a tremendous forest fire sweeping through the woods. At times the flames leaped high into the air, and we could see that the unfortunate trees were being stripped by the hundreds. It was a pitiful sight, but one too often seen throughout the West. Since this fire was in a region not frequented by campers, and it was not the open season for hunting, there was little doubt in our minds that it had been deliberately set by some miscreant, possibly with the idea that the devastated area might furnish future range for his stock. Of course, the better class of stockmen earnestly coöperate in the efforts to save our forests, but unfortunately there are some who undoubtedly set fires with the intention of sweeping away the timber, upon the theory that when it is gone grass will take its place.

On the 20th we made a leisurely trip to the divisional moraine between Wilson and Lyman Glaciers, and later went down the slope a short distance through queer lava formations, and called the region the "Devil's Gardens." In looking at the mountain from this part of the country we decided to attempt an ascent by one of the northern ridges.

Accordingly we left camp next morning at four o'clock (daylight-saving time, three by ordinary time), prepared for another day of adventure. The remnant moon had become a nonentity and we started in darkness. We had virtually to feel our way up the big moraine and out on to the boulder-strewn ice of Wilson Glacier. Daylight found us well out

IN A CREVASSE ON WILSON GLACIER, EAST SIDE OF MT. ADAMS

A JULY VIEW OF MOUNT STUART FROM TURNPIKE CREEK PASS

on the surface of the glacier. We crossed the Wilson and the Lyman, and at seven o'clock reached a great lava ridge leading up between Lyman and Lava Glaciers. The big cleaver just west of Lava Glacier had been climbed several times, but the one we were now trying presented an untried route. We knew that by crossing the Lava Glacier to the other ridge, we should have a sure way to the summit; but we preferred to try a new ascent.

We found the way up the ridge very toilsome; but neither dangerous nor impossible. On our left was a terrific ice-fall coming down from the summit cap. On the right was a smooth, tremendously steep ice-slope lying in the upper amphitheater of Lava Glacier immediately above the Bergschrund. This ice-slope also leads down from the summit ice-cap, and covers, perhaps, a full thousand feet of vertical height. We could see that our rocky ridge ended in a point between the ice-fall and the ice-slope. About noon we approached the upper end of our cleaver. For some time, I had been observing the icy decline closely and with some anxiety saw an occasional small rock come whizzing down from some place above.

When our ridge finally pinched out, I saw that any further progress must be made, if at all, up the ice-slope. Upon examination I found this to be overlaid with a covering of snow about an inch thick. Beneath the snow flowed a thin sheet of water upon hard blue ice of unknown depth. A footing was impossible upon such a surface. A slip meant a lightning glissade to the yawning crevasses of Lava Glacier.

We had a hundred-foot rope. Tying this about my waist, I asked Green to plant himself firmly on the rocks and hold me if I slipped. But Green had never used a rope in mountain work, and, like most men who have never had this experience, he was afraid of it.

With my little hand-axe I started in to cut steps. But

the slope was so steep and the handle of the instrument was so short that my hand was soon bruised and bleeding from its contact with the flinty ice. Nevertheless, I worked my way up for quite a distance in the uncertain footing. My feet were soon chilled by the ice-water. Below the prospect of a swift toboggan slide on to the glacier was not alluring. It did not take an expert mathematician to see that the element of danger was rather large. Just then a rock hurtled down the slope with the speed of a rifle-ball, and whizzed just over our heads, between us. We could not see from whence it came, and so could not determine the source of bombardment.

I decided that the risk was too great to justify my further persistence. I was aided to this conclusion by the thought that Green did not realize just wherein our danger lay, and I was reluctant to lead any man into a danger he did not fully understand. The increasing heat of the day would naturally accentuate the falling of the rocks, and our peril would soon be greater than ever.

So I worked back to the point of the ridge. This was a somewhat ticklish job; but I got down without accident.

Earlier in the season when the ice-cap is covered with firm snow, the ascent by this route could be made without especial difficulty. Even at the time of our trial, an experienced party, properly equipped with ropes and facilities for cutting steps, could have made it, especially if the slope had been reached before the sun's heat had started the rocks to rolling.

The return to camp was made without unusual incident.

August 22d, the last day of our stay on the mountain, was marked by an interesting trip to the upper ice-plateau of Klickitat Glacier. From beneath the great sérac a wonderful view was obtained of the Castle, towering four thousand feet above. I was fortunate enough to secure a fairly good snap-shot of a great rock-slide as it thundered for two thousand feet down the cliffs of Battlement Ridge from a point near the junction of the ridge and the Castle. The dust rose in a thick, gray cloud and floated across the crest of the ridge.

On the almost level surface of the glacier I found a curious thing that I had never seen before. I called it a spouting crevasse. From a small stream-channel in the ice the water gushed in intermittent spouts; now surging back almost out of sight, then shooting upward into the air for several inches above the cavity. Evidently the stream was flowing in surges, beneath the ice, and whenever a greater volume forced its way downward the crevasse was not large enough to hold it all and a portion was ejected with a gurgling sound that had attracted my attention from a considerable distance. The possibility of coming unexpectedly upon unusual features, like this, always adds to the interest of glacier travel.

We went in the afternoon to the snout of the glacier and the head of the Big Muddy. There had been a remarkable change since the visit of Professor Reid and myself, in 1901. All of the lower, shallow portion of the ice had disappeared. The Big Muddy emerged, in a mighty flood, from beneath a two hundred foot ice-cliff.

I estimated that the glacier had retreated nearly a quarter of a mile since I had first seen it twenty-nine years before.

XII

THE MOUNTAIN OF THRILLS

THE CASCADIANS, mountaineering club, was organized at Yakima, Washington, in the spring of 1920. A few enthusiasts, feeling the need of such an organization, pushed the work vigorously, with the result that the club was brought into existence with a charter membership of about one hundred. It flourished from the first. Soon ambitious plans were being laid for the conquest of snow-peaks and the exploration of unknown wilds. I had the honor of being the first president.

In the summer of 1894, I had my first sight of Mount Stuart, that great granite rock-peak which is situated almost in the geographical center of the State of Washington. Its jagged outlines appealed to me strongly and henceforth I cherished a fervent desire to stand upon its crest. I should have made the attempt in 1910, had I not undertaken a greater journey to Mount McKinley. Several times subsequently I was on the point of going; but something always intervened.

The organization of the Cascadians brought me in touch with a number of kindred spirits. With Yakima as a base to work from, it was but natural that I soon saw my chance to carry out my long-cherished plan for an assault on Mount Stuart.

A preliminary trip the first of June gave me much needed information concerning routes of approach. The programme as finally outlined involved the taking of a Cascadian record-box to the summit and its deposit in a rock-cairn there. The Fourth of July was considered an appropriate time for such an undertaking.

A big celebration in Yakima kept some from going who were eager to go. There were but two of us when the start was made; the other being Rolfe Whitnall, publicity manager of the Cascadians. The Northern Pacific Railway Company deposited us at the little station of Casway in Kittitas County at five o'clock on the afternoon of July 2d. Here, by previous arrangement, we were met by Jay Contratto, a young farmer, who took us in his Ford truck up the Teanaway River to W. G. Johnson's cabin at the mouth of Beverly Creek. The Teanaway River is one of the most delightful mountain streams I know. Along the lower part a beautiful farming and dairy country is seen; but higher up it runs through a wooded canyon, with level, parky stretches along the banks. A fairly good road leads up for several miles above the mouth of Beverly Creek, so that the journey from the railroad to this point may be made with comparative ease.

From the Johnson cabin the eight- or ten-mile trip to the foot of Mount Stuart must be made on foot or horseback over a mountain trail. Whitnall and I camped on the creek an hour's travel above the mouth. At six o'clock next morning we were away with our packs on our backs. The way up the Beverly Creek gorge is a toilsome one, and we went slowly. As we approached the headwaters of the stream, the rock-peaks of the Wenatchee Range towered far above us. At a quarter-past eleven we topped Turnpike Creek Pass, having risen thirty-five hundred feet in elevation since leaving Johnson's.

Directly before us, not more than four or five miles away, the serrated crags of Mount Stuart stood in menacing ranks, the gullies and depressions seamed with snow, the sharper points black and bare. Stuart is the culminating peak of a rugged range that stands like a great saw with its teeth pointed to the sky.

Drawing water from a rapidly melting snow-bank we cooked and ate our dinner at an altitude of six thousand feet; then hurried down into the valley of Turnpike Creek. The forest that once lined this valley was long ago almost swept away by fire. The trip from the pass down to Ingalls Creek is an easy one, except for fallen logs. The last-named stream sweeps the southern base of Stuart.

Crossing Ingalls Creek on a foot-log, we found a green little park, dotted with immense granite boulders, and pitched our camp at an elevation of forty-five hundred feet. We were right at the foot of Stuart, and there was nothing but mountain between us and the summit.

We had a great part of the afternoon in which to rest up for the next day's climb. But as evening approached, we were assailed by swarms of ravenous mosquitoes. There was no escape from them. They seemed so glad to see us and we appeared to be such tempting viands, that I was led to wonder what they lived on when we were not there. I have been told that it is only the lady mosquito that bites. If this be so, it surely goes a long way toward proving Kipling's contention that the female of the species is more deadly than the male.

The mosquito business was a serious one with us, that night. Never, outside of Alaska, had I seen them such a scourge. And never, even in Alaska, had I been forced to such a contest with them, for, in Alaska, one is generally prepared to combat the pests; but this catastrophe had fallen unexpectedly. Sleep was impossible. In the morning we arose exhausted from the battle with our bloodthirsty enemies. It was doubtful if, in our condition, we could do any extended mountain-climbing.

Nevertheless, at a quarter-past three, we made the start. The mosquitoes went too. They followed us up the long steep slope where the mountain evergreens straggled skyward in the granite soil; they followed us up the crumbling gully to the tremendous boulders heaped high, each upon its under neighbor; they followed us across snow-banks until the timber-line was passed, singing around our heads in hungry hordes; they followed us on and on, traveling easily while we toiled heavily; until far up, at an elevation of more than seven thousand feet, they were forced to give up the chase.

We climbed what may be rightly called the southeast corner of the mountain. We went up the gully that ends almost opposite the mouth of Turnpike Creek. The lower end of this gully is blocked by dense tangles of buckbrush. Higher up it becomes a narrow gorge, broken by occasional waterfalls; but up at the place where the timber almost ends, it broadens into a depression or trough that leads nearly to the first summit. In early summer, as at the time of our visit, this trough, which more technical mountaineers might call a *couloir,* is filled by a broad snow-field that extends well down to the narrower part of the gully.

A high-cliff broken ridge stands to the right of the gully. The timbered portion is rather broad; but the upper part is very narrow and rugged with pinnacles that cannot be climbed over and must be gone around.

We kept to the rocks at the base of the ridge as far as we could; but when we reached the highest point of the ridge, we encountered a very steep snow-slope up which we must go to the sharp crag-line immediately below the first summit. The snow was rather hard and the negotiation of the slope required some care. With the hundred-foot rope about my waist, I slowly kicked steps in the frozen surface and worked my way up, while Whitnall remained anchored to pay out the line. When I had come to the end of the rope, Whitnall would come up to me and anchor, and we would repeat the process.

In this way we reached the lowest rocks, and found above us a climb sufficiently stiff to satisfy the most exacting. This may be described as a great cleaver with crest, in places, almost perpendicular. The surface is of tremendous granite blocks and slabs, between which are chimneys and crevices, some of which are extremely narrow, while others are of greater width. The climber must make his way up these interstices or crawl immediately over the rocks. The trough or couloir, heretofore mentioned, parallels this shattered ridge on the south, but on the north the mountain drops perpendicularly a thousand or two thousand feet to the gashed surface of the glaciers. A glance over the sensational edge is apt to take one's breath, and, as has been said of it, it is no place for nervous people. From a distance this portion of the mountain looks to be absolutely unscalable.

Making free use of the rope, we advanced from block to block. There were frequent occasions when we had to back down and try it again. But the granite here is dependable, the rocks neither roll nor slide, and when a foothold or a handhold is once secured, it can generally be trusted.

A few hundred feet of this work brought us to snow-cornices below the point of the first summit. On the north they broke squarely off on the edge of the great precipice; on the south they fell steeply down to the head of the couloir. It was, therefore, necessary to keep well on their crests, and this we did, taking care that we did not approach too closely the breaking-off place. The last cornice ended beneath an abrupt cliff. Here were several rock-cairns—monuments to past failures. Former parties reaching this point could see no way to surmount the cliff, and, deciding that man could go no farther, piled up stones to mark the highest place attained.

To surmount the cliff, I saw that it was necessary to cross

the steep upper end of the snow-chute to a small chimney. This was a more or less dangerous process, since a slip here was not calculated to produce satisfactory results, and there is always the danger of falling into a cavity when getting from a steep snow-slope on to abrupt rocks. Nevertheless, it was quickly accomplished with the aid of the rope. There were a few loose stones in the chimney; but they were crawled over very tenderly. In a few minutes we stood upon the shattered granite pile that forms the first summit, with the menacing final pinnacle still towering several hundred feet above us, less than a quarter of a mile away.

A narrow backbone, or saddle, leads from the first summit to the foot of the summit dome. The top is of monstrous granite slabs and blocks, which must be climbed over or around for most of the way. On the north it breaks perpendicularly down to the glacier, far beneath, many of the great rock-masses overhanging the edge. On the south it falls, with a perilously steep slope into an immense gully or chasm which rends the southern side of the mountain.

Whitnall, worn out by a night of ceaseless battle with mosquitoes, had been feeling ill for a long time. His condition upon reaching the first summit had become such that he felt incapable of proceeding. I did not insist upon his attempting to go farther.

I left him and faced the problem of climbing the last pinnacle alone. The rope was of no further aid to me, so it remained with Whitnall. With the record-box, on my back, I worked along the sharp ridge, here climbing up the side of a granite block as big as an ordinary house, there working around the face of a great slab, or crawling up a narrow chimney between giant boulders. When near the foot of the pinnacle, I found the top of the backbone surmounted by a narrow snow-cornice which overhung the northern precipice. This must be crossed or the ascent abandoned. Without a rope it was extremely ticklish proposition, since I feared it might give way beneath my weight and precipitate me downward a few hundred fathoms to the uninviting jaws of the glacier. I hesitated a long time; but finally walked gingerly out on to the precarious highway. It held. With a sigh of relief I stepped on to the well-set granite on the farther end, and was ready for the final test.

I swung well to the northern edge of the pinnacle, and this brought me to a position on the verge of the precipice. Availing myself of a few short chimneys in the granite, I worked carefully up and was soon on the summit ridge. A short cautious climb, to the westward, along this brought me to the great, cracked, lichen-covered granite face that culminates in the present actual summit-point of the mountain. At the highest point former climbers had erected a cairn of the granite slabs. After making appropriate notations in the record-book, I placed the box in the cairn to remain as a fitting depository for future historical matter and to take the place of a few tin cans that had formerly performed that function. We had reached the first summit at twelve-fifteen and I got to the top at one-forty-five. The record-box was placed at two o'clock. As I sat basking in the sunshine on the warm rocks, a magnificent golden eagle soared about the cliffs far below me.

The first ascent of Mount Stuart is involved in obscurity, at least so far as I am concerned. Frank Bryant, a well-known wilderness man and miner of Yakima, told me that when he climbed the mountain a number of years ago he found on the summit a stick bearing the name of Angus McPherson and the date 1873. He also saw the same name on a tree near the camping-place on Ingalls Creek. Mr. Johnson, who lived in the cabin at the mouth of Beverly Creek, later told me that Professor I. C. Russell, the eminent geologist and mountaineer, had climbed the peak and had pronounced it the greatest single mass of granite in the United States, if not in the entire world. A small party of Seattle Mountaineers once reached the top; but they found the getting-up sufficiently difficult.

The view from the summit of Mount Stuart is a wonderful one. The near-by features are abundantly thrilling and sensational. From the granite tip the northern face falls sheer, and, looking down, one sees the white floor of the glacier, seemingly miles away. It looks as though a man could in one leap land directly on its surface. The jagged west summit is close at hand; but its crown is considerably lower than the actual top of the mountain. Crags loom upward toward the observer on every hand. At the base are green park lands, dotted with clear lakes; and serrated ridges radiate in all directions. Mountain-waves roll toward the horizon, on every side; some green-crested and with gentle swell; others white-tipped and broken into angry billows. Far to the east stretch the gray farmlands and pastures of eastern Washington and away to the west the green forest-carpet of the western part of the State. The great dominant snow-peaks of the Washington Cascades may all be seen—to the southward, Adams and Saint Helens; to the southwest, Rainier; and northward, Glacier Peak and Baker. Hundreds of sharp peaks in the Monte Cristo and Lake Chelan regions thrust their spires heavenward, and countless glaciers gleam like gems in their rugged settings.

After enjoying the inspiring panorama for some time, I carefully descended the steep granite face and on down the rock-chimneys to the snow-cornice. I followed my tracks in the snow, crossed along the broken top of the ridge, and came to the point where I had left Whitnall three hours before. He was feeling much revived from a nap among the warm rocks. We indulged in a brief period of photography and started down at four-fifteen. When we reached the bottom of the chimney at the foot of the cliff immediately beneath the first summit, we found the snow so much softened by the heat of the afternoon sun that it was safe to travel on, notwithstanding the tremendously steep slope. It was well settled and not in a condition for avalanching. With Whitnall ahead on the rope and myself behind for anchor, we went down rapidly so long as the snow lasted; but when the rocks were reached again we perforce must go more slowly. On the way I suffered an attack of stomach trouble which greatly slackened my pace, and it was eight o'clock when I finally reached camp considerably behind Whitnall. The following day, tired and blistered feet took us over on to the Teanaway from where the kindness of autoists bore us to Ellensburg and the care of the Northern Pacific.

Our account of the wonders of Mount Stuart fired the enthusiasm of other Cascadians, and a second ascent was planned for Labor Day. The entire trip from Yakima to the Johnson cabin was made by automobile. Seven members of the party went on, several days in advance of the balance, and were fortunate enough to find the packer for a sheep-camp at the mouth of Beverly Creek. This man took all of their dunnage on his horses to Ingalls Creek, so that they made the journey over the pass with comparative ease. This advance guard included Mr. and and Mrs. W. E. Richardson, Mr. and Mrs. Rolfe Whitnall, Clarence Truitt, Harold Carey, and Vern Mason. The three lastnamed were enthusiastic young fellows, out for their first real experience in mountaineering. As Clarence will henceforth appear many more times in these tales, he will be passed over for the present. It was not my good fortune to have Harold with me so often, yet I came to know him as a desirable and dependable companion.

Vern Mason was but fifteen years old. His parents, Mr.

CASCADIANS ON FIRST SUMMIT OF MOUNT STUART, LABOR DAY, 1920

JUST ABOVE THE GRANITE CLIFF WHERE VINCENT FELL, MOUNT STUART, LABOR DAY, 1920

Vincent is the center figure

THE TOPMOST PINNACLE OF MOUNT STUART

FIRST SUMMIT OF MOUNT STUART WITH GREAT MAY SNOW CORNICE ON SADDLE

and Mrs. S. H. Mason, had long been very dear friends of mine, and they entrusted him to my care in the hope that I would bring him safely back again, yet, I fear, with many misgivings as to the outcome. Vern was a boy with a standard appetite, and his frequent "When do we eat?" became a by-word with us through numerous days of future mountaineering. It will be noted that a touch of femininity had been added to the complexion of our party, and we were soon to have an exhibition of the remarkable pluck of these two women.

Joseph R. Vincent, Rolland Whitmore, and I, as the last contingent of the little expedition, left Yakima Saturday afternoon, in Vincent's Franklin car. We spent the night at Johnson's cabin on Beverly Creek. Here we met two young men, John S. Brescoe and Albert Mayta, of Cle Elum, Washington, who were returning from a circuit of Mount Stuart. They had had a rough and dangerous trip. Yet, as a sad commentary upon the greater hazards of civilization, it may be told that the day after they reached their home town young Mayta fell beneath the wheels of a train and had both legs severed.

We three, with heavy packs and no accommodating sheepman to help us, had a toilsome journey up Beverly Creek and over the pass. But it was still early in the day when we reached the camp of our friends on Ingalls Creek at the foot of the mountain. It had been our plan to climb up the side of the mountain that afternoon, to the highest point where we could find wood and water. But we found all of the male members of the party, except Richardson, away on a fishing jaunt. They had agreed to return by noon; but the afternoon shadows were growing long when they finally straggled into camp with few fish and tremendous appetites.

Consequently it was five o'clock or later when we got

away. September days are short, and we did not gain more than five hundred feet in elevation on the steep green hillside. We camped in a little pocket among great evergreens, near a spring of ice-cold water that burst from the soddy slope.

There was a sharp tang of autumn frostiness in the air when I crawled from my sleeping-bag at one o'clock in the morning. Soon the light of a cheerful fire gleamed among the big trees and chased the feeble moonbeams into the outer circle of the grove. Most of my companions found it hard to adapt their ideas to such early rising; but I informed them that it is one of the necessities of mountain-climbing. To those of my readers who contemplate taking up mountaineering as a sport or a bad habit, I will say that you must acquire the knack of getting up early in the morning. To accomplish this end I would advise you to purchase either an alarm-clock or a rooster. Personally I recommend the alarm-clock, because you can set an alarm-clock at any hour you wish—but you can't set a rooster.

Breakfast took some time. The start was made at three-thirty. We went up the steep rocky slope by the fitful rays of the waning moon. The white trunks of the dead trees shone ghost-like and weird through the uncertain light. The live evergreens stood dark and somber against the paling glow of departing night. Across the great void the black peaks of the Wenatchee Range loomed mysterious and unreal. We were drifting upward in a phantom world.

Presently a rosy glow began to tinge the east, and the day was slowly ushered in with all the panoply of a mountain dawn.

We kept well up on to the big ridge on the right-hand side of the gully Whitnall and I had followed in our ascent. We found this a considerably easier route. Early in the morning Mrs. Whitnall began to feel very ill; but she refused to give up and courageously kept going. Mrs. Richardson, too, was not feeling well, yet neither of these plucky women ever even suggested the idea of quitting.

The party had been divided into two companies for more convenient handling on the two hundred-foot ropes whenever the use of the life-lines became necessary. In the first company were Mr. and Mrs. Richardson, Whitmore, Mason, and myself; in the second, Mr. and Mrs. Whitnall, Truitt, Carey, and Vincent. We found that conditions were vastly different from what they had been on the Fourth of July. The whole southern side of the mountain was almost entirely bare of snow. The big snow-field in the great couloir had nearly all melted away, leaving in the bottom only a steep, narrow tongue of ice, from fifty to one hundred feet in width, extending from the cliff beneath the first summit to the bottom of the steepest slope which forms the eastern shoulder of the mountain and culminates in the first summit. These conditions made of the ascent a rock climb for the entire distance. That part of the gully lying between the "timber-line" and the lower end of the ice-tongue was completely free of snow. The sides and bottoms were, for a good part of the distance, composed of loose, decomposed granite gravel, exceedingly toilsome to walk in; although, in places, there were fields of great boulders and occasional small cliffs. The climb up this part of the mountain was monotonous enough; but we were soon to have excitement in plenty.

We got on to the broken ridge, or cleaver, leading to the first summit, without once setting foot on snow. Then came an arduous climb up the great rocks and through the narrow chimneys, the ropes being brought into frequent requisition. When we were about halfway up came the adventure of the day.

We had come out on to a great flat-topped shelf of rock

abutting upon the ice-chute. Immediately above the party was a perpendicular wall, eight or ten feet high, which shut off the view upward. It could be seen, however, that we should either have to retrace our steps and find a route to the right or pass around the point of the wall next to the ice-chute. It was a relief to get on to a level surface again, no matter how small, and most of the party paused for a rest. Two or three of us went around the point to reconnoiter. The ice-chute led straight down the bottom of the couloir at a frightfully steep angle, with here and there a jagged point of rocks jutting out into the ice. It was so hard that it would have been folly for any man to hope to get a footing on it without the cutting of deep steps. Above our shelf a very steep incline of rather smooth granite led upward for seventy-five or one hundred feet to a point where there was a promise of secure footing. The slope of this incline was such that it met the surface of the ice-chute at about the same angle it maintained the entire length of its face.

When I came around the point, just out of sight of the party, I saw that Vincent, on his own initiative, had taken the end of a hundred-foot rope in his hand and had started up the incline, climbing with hands and feet. He had reached a point about twenty feet above the ice-chute when he dropped the rope. He grabbed for it and lost his balance. Grasping desperately for handholds, he rolled over and over, down the face of the rock and struck the ice-chute asprawl. His body immediately shot downward on the flinty surface of the ice.

It now seemed that no earthly power could save him from being dashed to death on the jagged rocks below. All of the rest of the party were still around the point out of sight, in blissful unconsciousness of the tragic dénouement. In the swift moment that was given me for decision, I think I did the only thing I could have done under the circumstances. I stepped as far out on the rocks as I could, thrust the point of my alpenstock as firmly as possible into the ice, and yelled to Vincent to catch it as he shot by. Whether or not he heard me and comprehended my meaning, I cannot say. It was never to be known if my action would have helped him any. A near miracle intervened to put an end to the remarkable adventure.

Several days before our visit there had been a considerable fall of fresh snow on the mountain. This had all melted away except in a few nooks well sheltered from the sun. It so happened that a narrow fringe of this snow now filled the crevice between the margin of the ice and the rocky wall. As Vincent shot downward he fought desperately for his life. He attempted to throw himself toward the rocks. He was a large, strong man and he did not intend to give up without a struggle. A mighty thrust with one of his arms brought it down through the soft snow into the crevice. His speed was checked. In the twinkling of an eye he had rolled himself on to the rocks and grasped the friendly projections. A white streak on the surface of the ice, where he had plowed away the dirty covering, was the only reminder of that near-tragedy—mute token of what would have been had that streak continued down the chute.

Vincent was determined not to be balked by that granite incline. I was the only one of the party that had seen the accident. When the others had been told of it, and had felt the resultant thrills run over them, we were ready to proceed. This time Vincent tied the rope around his waist. Selecting a more favorable starting-point, a little farther from the ice-chute, with several of the rest of us grasping the rope, he crept up the slope. He tied the end firmly around a big rock. One by one, the other members of the party went up, hand over hand. From here on to the last cliff beneath the first summit there was little difficulty. There were now no snow-cornices to be passed. We were soon assembled on the first summit prepared for the final climb.

The two women of the party had been improving with the upward advance. The thrills and the enthusiasms of the climb had evidently banished the illness of the morning and by the time the first summit was reached they were as fit as any in the party. A remarkable thing about mountaineering is the wonderful quickness with which one who is apparently "all in" will revive and regain his strength. Many people give up strenuous climbs under the impression that they have come to the limit of endurance; when a few minutes' rest and a little access of fresh courage would put them in fine condition again.

There was no snow on the saddle leading from the first summit to the final pinnacle. There was but a small patch on the south face of the summit dome, where on the Fourth of July there had been a great field clinging to the fearfully steep slope.

The passage of the saddle required considerable care and effort. We had to climb over or around the great blocks and monoliths, with no snow to break the sharp hardness of the rocky projections. To pass some of these granite obstructions, so big that they almost assumed the dignity of cliffs, it was necessary to make use of narrow cracks or crevices which ran diagonally up the faces of the rocks. The ropes here were of much use; for, when the foremost man had securely anchored at a certain point, the other climbers could proceed along the rope with much greater speed and safety. The short chimneys and rock-faces of the summit pinnacles were passed without accident, and, as the top was approached, the party was brought close to the sensational edge overhanging the northern precipice. The final slope of cracked granite was crawled carefully over and the topmost cairn was reached, although the space about it was so limited that only a few could approach at a time. The record-box was found intact. Not an entry had been made in the book since I left it there the Fourth of July.

We had made a hundred per cent climb. We felt that our party was the largest to have reached the summit. Moreover, we were sure that our fifteen-year-old boy, Vern Mason, was the youngest person that had ever made the ascent.

Our toil was rewarded by a marvelous cloud-scene. On three sides a great sea of billowy clouds rolled away to the horizon, its silver-tipped waves receding into the distant haze of September sunlight. The topmost waves were far below us. Looking beneath the lower edge we could see the dark masses of somber mountains in their mantles of silent evergreens. Through great holes in the mist-banks, here and there, the broken earth-folds could be seen. Across the face of the glacier, under our very feet, drifted wisps whose shadows scudded athwart the surface of the ice. Far away, the mighty snow-peaks proudly towered above this shifting ocean, agleam with the sheen of autumn afternoon.

One of the inspiring things to the mountaineer is the frequency with which he may meet with glorious cloud-effects. There is a thrill that comes from a cloud sweeping around the brow of a mountain that cannot be had from any other source. The infinite variety of cloud-form; the constantly changing landscapes of the fleecy world; the gigantic peak-ranges of the upper sky, Pelions piled on Ossas; the unbelievable richness of coloring; the woolly gorges of the cumulus; the mare's-tails of the higher ether; the beauty of the sunrise, the glory of the sunset—all, all go to fill up the climber's life in exquisite measure. Too many men never look up to the clouds at all. Unless they encounter a fog—and then to grumble—they know nothing of the mists. We often speak indiscriminately of cloud and fog, making no distinction between them, and, in truth, the only difference is one of altitude. A fog is a cloud with low aspirations.

Photography prevailed, for a time, that afternoon on the summit of Mount Stuart. But we knew we must not linger too long. So presently down we went, creeping carefully over the upper granite face. The highest reaches of the mountain had no adventures for us that afternoon. Lower down we were to have our fill.

When we reached the upper end of the ice-chute in the couloir, I decided to take a chance on the prospect of saving an hour's time. On the way up I had been carefully observing the opposite side of the chute from the one we were ascending. It was the first time I had seen the rocks along its borders, as they had been deeply covered with snow on the Fourth of July. Now, however, they looked to be considerably easier to traverse than the ones we were on, barring a possibility of their being loose. If they were of sufficient firmness, we should be able to make the descent by that route much more rapidly than over the one we had come up. I stated the situation to the other members of the party and they were all willing to take the chance.

We safely passed the upper part of the chute, going between the cliff and the edge of the ice. The rocks were a little inclined to settle beneath our feet; but we made good time. We came out on to a sort of shelf, with the perpendicular southern face of the couloir on our right, and a steep granite incline dropping toward the chute. Finding it necessary to descend at almost a right angle, we did it by means of a crack in the rock, about six inches wide, which furnished holds for fingers and toes. We now stood eight or ten feet from the surface of the ice, with a perpendicular drop to it.

Below, the rocks adjacent to the chute stood in a broad shelf which should have been easy to travel over. But when

Vincent and I went ahead to reconnoiter, we found them shattered and loose and extremely treacherous. It would seem that a great mass had slid down from the cliffs of the ridge and was now resting on an unstable foundation, either of shifting boulders and gravel or possibly old ice and snow. At one place I was slightly in advance of Vincent. He stepped out on to a point of great boulders, some of them as large as a house. Suddenly, without warning, the whole mass settled beneath him with a dull, grinding noise. The whole subsidence probably was but a few inches; but it was enough to suggest unpleasant possibilities, such, for instance, as a leg ground between unyielding stone jaws, or a body held beneath a cruel weight of slag while frantic companions strove vainly at rescue. Conditions did not improve with our advance. When I reached the place where the shelf pinched out between the lower end of the ice-chute and the great ridge above, the mass was so loose that there seemed danger of starting a rock avalanche at any moment. Here it was not so very far down to the ice, and it looked feasible, once down, foı a party to pass around the lower end of the chute; but there was that treacherous drop of loose scoria to be dealt with. One man alone might have made a dash for it, braving the danger of falling stones and taking a chance of riding an avalanche he might start; but, with a party of ten, including two women, such an attempt would have been madness. To scale the cliffs on the right was impossible. We were trapped. We had deliberately descended into a savage *cul de sac,* from which the only escape now seemed to be to climb back the way we had come. And I felt that I was to blame for the mess, for I had been the one to suggest that we take the chance.

I returned to the place where the balance of the party was waiting. Vincent had already preceded me. The situation had become serious. The sun had dropped behind the big ridge to our right, and the evening chill was in the air. A cold wind was sweeping the mountain-side. Night was rapidly approaching. There were many chattering teeth. We were nearly nine thousand feet above the sea, facing long hours of frigid darkness, with absolutely no shelter, in our summer clothes. Quick action of some sort was imperative. To remain there overnight was out of the question.

When I reached the party, Vincent was working his way down a narrow ledge to the surface of the ice, with the intention of seeing if it were possible to creep along the edge of the chute at the intersection of the rocks and the ice. He held the end of the rope in his hand. I told him he must tie this around his waist, which he did. When he got on to the ice he began a cautious descent along the margin, supporting himself partly with his hands upon the rocky wall and held by the rope from above. A large boulder lay with its lower side embedded in the surface of the ice; but it was impossible to tell how firmly it might be held, and we were afraid it might give way when any one attempted to pass it. But it did not move, and, immediately below it, Vincent passed around a jutting point, out of sight of those who were holding the rope. It was now impossible for us to follow his movements, and all we could do was to keep the rope well in hand so as to stop him if he slipped. Whitnall crept out on to the point of rocks to try to keep track of Vincent's progress.

Suddenly there was a violent jerk on the rope as it snapped taut under the impact of Vincent's one hundred and ninety pounds of flying weight. He had slipped, and for the second time that day had started down that frightful slope. I was almost yanked from my feet. I yelled to the boys above to hold hard, and they threw themselves backward upon the vibrating line. But the impulse of gravity, even aided by the slick treachery of that awful chute, could not prevail against the strength of that bevy of determined young fellows, and Vincent was again persuaded to forego his penchant for the lower regions of the mountain. When he had recovered his breath and his equilibrium, to some extent, he made himself heard sufficiently to make it plain to us above that it was impossible for the party to get down that way, and still maintain its entity as a company of worth-while human beings.

I did some quick thinking. Something had to be done forthwith to get the party across to the more dependable rocks on the opposite side of the chute. We had nothing with which to cut steps in the hard ice. For climbing we had alpenstocks with sharp steel points; but these were almost worthless when it came to gouging out footholds in such an adamantine surface as that chute presented. Later the Cascadians acquired several regular Swiss ice-axes; but up to that time we had been unable to obtain any of these desirable adjuncts of successful mountaineering.

My decision was quickly made. I called to Vincent to try to make his way across the ice to the opposite rocks. The chute here was only fifty or sixty feet wide. We were well above him, yet the only support we could give him on the rope was an oblique support. Nevertheless, it was of some help, and we could keep him from sliding far in case of a slip. He crept slowly in the direction of the coveted rocks, kicking his hob-nails as firmly into the ice as possible and jabbing the point of his alpenstock hard down. He won, inch by inch and foot by foot, until, at last, we saw him reach out and grasp the rocks. To anchor the rope was but the work of a few moments. We now had a slender connection with the world of safety once more.

Mrs. Richardson was now tied to the end of the other rope and let down the cliff on to the ice. Clinging to the one that was stretched across the chasm and supported by the one about her waist, the courageous little woman worked her way down the ice, past the big boulder which interfered considerably with effective use of the ropes, and out on to the forbidding surface of the chute. Hand over hand she went over, her feet touching but lightly on the treacherous ice-face. She often afterwards described it as the greatest thrill of her life as she hung there in uncertainty, supported by two thin lines of hemp, the great, precipitous mountain frowning above and nothing but death yawning below. Slip she did, and frequently, but nothing could break her grip upon that life-line, and eventually she won to the security of the rocks.

We drew back one of the ropes, and Mrs. Whitnall went next. Her going was as the going of Mrs. Richardson, and she, too, was at last upon the rocks.

Three of our party were now safely across the chute, well below the most dangerous part of the rocks. But the transit had taken much valuable time, and seven of us were still within the trap. The lengthening shadows warned me that long before the others could get across night would be upon us. Our company would then be divided in darkness, and those who remained would face a situation serious in the extreme. The last to cross would have to go with practically no support from the ropes, for we were above the others, and the support of ropes, of course, must come from above.

There was but one thing to do, and we did it forthwith.

Shouting to Vincent to get the women down the rocks as quickly as possible, we cast the end of the rope far out on to the ice, and he drew it to him. Then we turned to the task of climbing back to the head of the ice-chute, just beneath the first summit, and a dash down the opposite granite cliffs, in a race against darkness.

The other six were all far younger than I, and I felt

that where I could go they could surely follow. Telling them to come on, every man for himself, I turned and started up the narrow crack in the face of the granite.

I climbed as I have never climbed before or since.

Followed an hour of perhaps the quickest rock-work ever seen in Western America. We forgot that we were nearly nine thousand feet above the sea and that our breath was supposed to come in short gasps upon the slightest extra exertion. We remembered only that we were on one of the most savage mountains in the United States; that an Arctic night was swooping down upon us; and that we must pass around that serpent tongue of ice and down, down, down to help rescue two women from their perilous position.

Twilight had come when we reached the top of the chute. A cornice of white snow leaning against the cliff offered a safe crossing. Along it I went, with Vern Mason close behind. Some of the party were afraid of the snow and hugged into the rocks. One, at least, must have been careless, for a shower of loose stones went bounding down over the ice. Looking to watch them go, we were horrified to see that Vincent and the women, for some reason, had not moved from where we had left them. Their heads were still sticking above the rocky point, and the stones were whizzing straight for them. We shouted wild warnings. The heads ducked, but not enough. A big fragment shot within a few inches of Mrs. Whitnall's face. We went weak in the knees. But it was over almost before we realized that it was happening and we were on our way again. Another tragedy had been averted—there were no precious moments of daylight to be wasted in regaining our equilibrium. We were on the right side of the ice at last; but the cliffs were still below us. Down them we must go. That morning I had slipped my electric flashlight into my pocket, knowing the possibility of being overtaken by darkness. I now brought it forth to light the way. The battery had gone dead. The delicate instrument had been unable to stand the buffeting on the rocks that strenuous day.

We might have been thought reckless as we plunged down the rocks in the gathering gloom. But the occasion demanded risk. Soon it grew so dark that I could not see those in the rear. I knew they were coming only by the sound of the different voices. There was no possibility of following our morning route; for on rocks one makes no tracks, and we could not see far enough to recognize points made familiar in the full light of day. Nevertheless, we frequently passed over places that we had climbed over on the way up. The ridge was but narrow, at best, and we could not stay on it and diverge more than a few feet, one way or another, from our upward line of scramble.

We came to a fifteen-foot chimney. One wall was smooth; the other offered slight irregularities for footholds and handholds. We did not hesitate. Calling warnings, each to the one behind, down we went, bracing bodies against the smooth wall, feeling for holds in the irregular one. It was risky business; but there was no other way. If we had had abundant daylight we could have used the rope, working slowly and surely; but we now had minutes where we should have had hours. There was no time to tie knots and pay out a life-line. Every man must be sufficient unto himself.

All got down the chimney without accident. A few seconds later I came suddenly on to an enormous granite slab, six or eight feet in width, lying at a steep inclination. The outer edge overhung the northern precipice and there was a straight drop of a thousand feet or so which the darkness did not make any more cheerful. We could have here gone to the foot of the mountain in one quick jump, and our troubles would have been over; but we should have been on the wrong side of the mountain when we lit, so by a common, silent impulse we decided to stick to the slower and more toilsome route, if possible. Spread out like a bat, I slid down the incline with feet directed toward a solid anchorage below; but some of the boys preferred to come down with their right legs dangling in a great crack between the inner edge of the slab and an overhanging wall of rock.

Shortly afterward we came to a narrow chimney which I recognized as one we had come up in the forenoon. It was hardly wide enough for the passage of a man's body, and when I was about two thirds of the way down one of my heels jammed into the crevice, and I could not pull it out. I called to Vern, who was just behind, to restrain his precipitancy, so that there would not be an undue congestion of humanity within that limited space. For a time, it looked as though I was there for an indefinite stay, and as the others could not pass me they would have to stay too.

Finally I succeeded in wrenching my heel free. It was now thoroughly dark, and we were perhaps traveling as much by instinct as by anything else. Presently we came to another obstacle we had climbed going up. This was an almost straight granite face with a sharp upper edge. By letting ourselves down to the end of our arms we could just place our feet firmly on a four-inch ledge, below which we could secure a footing on the sloping rocks.

We were now past the more precipitous part of the cleaver; but there still remained a jumble of granite blocks and boulders lying at a precariously steep angle. Calls sent forth into the darkness revealed the fact that Vincent and the woman were a short distance to our right. They seemed to have made very slow progress. The two parties converged toward each other and finally came together at the foot of the steep slope. Below lay the long, broad, middle stretches of the great gully that has been previously described. In places the bottom and sides were covered with boulders of considerable size; but for most of the distance the surface was a loose gravelly deposit, into which the feet sank to the ankles at each step—a toilsome ascent, but an easy route for getting down when daylight lit the way.

Obviously our proper route was down the gully, provided always that we could keep from straying on to unknown and more dangerous parts of the mountain. We were heart-breakingly far above timber-line, and long hours must still elapse before we could hope for the comfort of a fire. We must spend the night on the mountain, that was certain. The best we could plan for was enough wood to assuage the freezing blasts from the upper heights. We were without water and there was but one place to get it. Among the big boulders at the lower end of the ice-chute a stream gurgled far down in the rocks. The boys had filled the canteens there in the forenoon by reaching into the crevices. Now when we came opposite this place I sent Whitmore, Carey, and Mason there again. They had literally to feel their way in the darkness, and it was no easy task to find the hidden water, guided only by the sound of its gurgling.

Meanwhile I was leading the balance of the party down the mountain-side. It was so intensely dark that, although we walked close together, single-file, it was hardly possible for one to see the person next behind him. One of the ropes was cut in two and each piece tied to one of the women with a man holding the other end, so that there was no danger of losing them in the darkness.

That morning while we were coming up I had followed my habit of observing landmarks for use in case of being caught by night. Now I was able dimly to make out a great black rock-dome that marks the upper end of the long rock ridge and the division between our gully and a precipitous canyon to the left. To have gone into the latter would have meant disaster, for it is broken by cliffs and precipices which cannot be passed even by daylight. We passed safely to the right and kept the proper direction.

Since Whitnall had been with me on the Fourth of July climb, I thought he should be more nearly familiar with the route than any of the others of the party. As he alone, or with one companion, could travel more rapidly than the entire company, I now asked him to push on ahead and build a big fire in the first available timber. Truitt volunteered to accompany him. They were quickly swallowed in the darkness.

The boys who had gone for water rejoined us, with full canteens, and we continued our seemingly endless journey down that rugged, pathless desolation. We were now beset by one of the greatest perils of the day. So steep was the slope and so dark was the night that those in the rear were in constant danger of starting loose rocks to bound down on to those in front. One considerable fragment came hurtling toward the foremost members of the party. Vern Mason, warned by the shouts of those above, with quick presence of mind, threw himself flat upon the ground; but luckily the rock missed us by a few feet and crashed on into the lower darkness. To lessen the danger as much as possible, I kept the party angling across the slope, whenever practicable; but, of course, there were times when this could not be done, and the foremost ones had to take their chances.

I could dimly observe the peaks of the Wenatchee Range, beyond Ingalls Creek Canyon against a misty sky-line, and, as I had marked certain ones to be my guides, I managed to keep the direction fairly well. In the morning I had noted a clump of dwarfed evergreens on the gray side of the granite ridge to our right. This was to mark the point at which we must turn toward the timbered ridge on our left. I knew that we must keep to the depression until this landmark appeared. There was no use, no matter how long the way might seem, to seek wood or shelter until it appeared.

It was virtually a matter of feeling our way. As I have said before, there were several jump-offs or low cliffs across the gully. While none of these was very high, any of them was high enough to cause serious injury to any one falling over. Farther down, we knew, the gully broke off into a narrow gorge containing what were considerable waterfalls at times when the melting snows were precipitating their floods down the mountain-side. But I knew that before we came to this dangerous part of the gully I must see the dark patch of evergreens upon the gray slope of the ridge.

Our anxiety for Whitnall and Truitt increased. No cheering gleam pierced the night. We began to fear they had met with accident. There were so many things that could have happened.

After we had been going, it seemed for hours, we suddenly heard Whitnall's voice below us. We answered, and he called back that they were waiting for us. Finally we came to them sitting in the shelter of some rocks. They had been working back and forth across the face of the mountain unable to find either themselves or wood for a fire. Although it seemed that we must have come several times the distance we should have come, I could see that we were still a long way from the point I was aiming for. Some of the party now began to argue that we had lost the way; but I was firm in the belief that I was following the right course.

With a reunited party we went on again, down, down, down, ever down, into the jaws of the night. We came out on to one of the small cliffs. A little added care was necessary in getting down. Then we were on our way again.

And then, at last, a dark patch appeared on the gray of the granite ridge. It was my landmark clump of tiny trees. The slope had become perceptibly less.

I turned to the left at almost a right angle to our former course. One member of the party protested that we were too low down. The way now lay across a broad field of immense gray granite boulders. These I knew from former acquaintance. As I led the way over the broken rocks my eyesight played peculiar tricks. The granite masses appeared to be nearer than they were. Often I would put out my hand for support upon a boulder and find it a foot or two forther away than it had looked to be. Thus I narrowly escaped some bad falls. At first I thought it was a trick peculiar to my own eyes; but other members of the party told me they had experienced the same thing.

It was not far across the boulder-field, although the going was rough. I came out of the rocks into the sparse trees on the narrow ridge, where the dead snags gleamed with potential warmth and cheer, not fifty feet from the point I had aimed for.

It was eleven o'clock. We had been in almost constant action for nineteen and a half hours.

Vincent, expert fire-builder, was close behind me. Before the last of the party had straggled into our forced encampment, he had a tremendous blaze going. There was plenty of dry wood, and soon the entire granite ridge south of us was lit with a glow that brought the rocks and trees into bold relief. The gleam chased the night-shadows far into the depths of the great canyon immediately on our north. Our light must have shown for many miles over crag and forest, and, no doubt, many a denizen of the wild looked in fear and wonder at the strange glow so far up on the side of the rugged peak. In fact, we had some apprehension that our conflagration might spread to the living trees near by and make of us a band of outlaws instead of a bunch of innocent, though belated, mountaineers.

Yet there was little comfort for us the balance of the

night. An icy gale swept across the ridge. There was no escape from it. While we roasted on one side, we froze on the other. We had only the remnants of the day's food supply, and the water the boys had brought in the canteens. We snatched fitful naps between the times we had to turn alternate sides to the fire. Daylight had scarcely manifested itself when we threw dirt upon the fire and hurried down the ridge to our hillside camp. A half-hour more brought us to the main camp on Ingalls Creek. We rested and slept most of the day and brought it to a close with a wonderful "mulligan" concocted from ingredients including every edible thing in camp.

Next day our sheepman took all of our stuff on his horses across the pass to Johnson's cabin. Left free to pursue our way untrammeled, we made a wonderful fourteen-mile hike up Ingalls Creek and across the upper trail to the Teanaway. We thus had a marvelous view of the entire southern rock-face of Mount Stuart and a trip through a splendid mountain park where great fields of glaciated rock show that an immense glacier once swept down the gorge of Ingalls Creek.

In the spring of 1921, a few of the Cascadians began to form more ambitious plans in connection with Mount Stuart. Many people held firmly to the belief that this mountain could be climbed only late in the season after the summer suns had melted the snow from its forbidding crags. Some claimed that the ascent could not be made at all when its great dome was sheeted with snow and ice in the spring or early summer. Our Fourth-of-July climb had been looked upon as unprecedentedly early—it was even doubted by a few.

Now a few of us decided to make the ascent on the 29th of May—the day before Decoration Day. Six of us set forth in the afternoon of the 27th—W. E. Richardson, Clarence Truitt, Rolfe Whitnall, Max Hiscock, fifteen-year-old Jimmie Frisque, and myself. As we passed through Ellensburg on a Northern Pacific train, Whitnall saw a reporter and told him where we were going. The same evening the paper announced an interview with a United States Forest Service man in which that individual expressed the opinion that there was so much snow on Mount Stuart that it would probably be impossible for any one to climb it that year at all.

Recent floods on the Teanaway had incapacitated bridges, created détours, and made portions of the road impassable, so that our going from Casway was uncertain and devious. About dark the taxi we had chartered from Cle Elum, brought to a stop by a fallen tree, put us down several miles from the Johnson cabin to make our way as best we could to that haven for the night.

So we enjoyed a two hours' tramp in the darkness with our packs on our backs. It was half-past ten when we reached Johnson's cabin. Nobody was at home, and we bunked on the porch.

Beverly Creek, like all mountain streams, is alluring at all times of the year. In its six- or eight-mile course, it tumbles down over a myriad moss-covered rocks, some four thousand feet, with many pools and shallows and white-foamed cascades, fringed with deep-hued evergreens, the home of speckled, red-lined trout.

And it was still early spring on the middle reaches of Beverly Creek. Farther up it was winter. After we passed the boisterous tributary, Bean Creek, we began to encounter snowbanks. The streams were full from the melting snows, and we feared that a few warm days might make them uncrossable. The peaks of the Wenatchee Range were still heavily laden with their winter mantle, and we could see many sun-carved cornices lying on the sky-lines far above us. As we approached the headwaters of the creek, the snow-banks became more frequent, finally merging into a continuous field, deep and firm, broken only by the tree-trunks and an occasional projecting boulder. The creek was lost beneath this white covering; completely arched over by solid masses of snow; and only an occasional gurgling far down in the frozen depths reminded us that it was still in existence.

The snow was hard and we walked upon its surface as upon a marble boulevard. In the high mountain passes in early summer some interesting things may be seen. The winter snow falls deep—sometimes twenty or thirty feet. The young evergreens are bent over, pressed downward and completely covered by the great weight, and there they sleep for months to await the coming of warmth and sunshine again. When the snow begins its melting in late spring and early summer, it gradually settles lower and lower; the green branch-tips appear, one by one; then the bow of the slender bending trunks may be seen above the snow; and finally comes a time when each little tree has strength to break its fetters and snap suddenly into upright position with the resiliency of a steel spring. It is not always safe to pass near one of these trees when it is ready for its "snap-up," as a whip-like blow from it as it leaps into place might seriously injure or even kill a man.

It was half an hour past noon when we stood in Turnpike Creek Pass and saw before us the great bulk of Mount Stuart sheethed in snow from foot to crown, except where the crags were so steep that no snow could cling. Cold and repellent it looked—surely no man could scale that white-robed giant. Our trip must have been in vain.

We dropped quickly down into the broad valley of Turnpike Creek. The upper crust of snow was now sufficiently soft to give us firm footing on the steep hillside. We ate our lunch on a gravel bar beside the little stream which alternately flowed through long snow-tunnels and open spaces, where it caught the glint of the sunlight.

An hour or so later we crossed Ingalls Creek and climbed to the place where we had made our Labor Day camp. Here a spring avalanche had plowed down through the trees, leaving a swath of broken trunks and windrows of mud in its wake. We dug in the hillside a shelf for our beds and built a big fire below. We spent the night in rather cold comfort, and were early away on the ascent. During the early morning the snow in the timber was quite hard and we had to use some caution. Now, however, we had a couple of Swiss ice-axes and the cutting of steps was not so great a problem as it had formerly been.

Near the point where we had spent the night on our descent the previous September, Whitnall, who was feeling ill, abandoned the ascent. We found before us almost an entirely snow-climb, as different from that of the preceding autumn as two climbs could well be. Where we had spent long hours in darkness working down the gully over gravel and loose rocks, we now climbed steadily on firm snow from twenty to fifty feet in depth. By the time we reached the foot of the great rock cleaver where the ice-chute had given us so many adventures, the day had developed into the hottest one I have ever seen on a mountain. The sun beat down upon the snow with blistering intensity. We had recourse to the usual devices for preventing sunburn. We wore colored glasses, and we smeared our faces with grease-paint, yet we subsequently suffered from puffed-up countenances and peeled noses.

But the heat made the success of our expedition possible. The snow was softened so that we could easily make steps in it with our feet. So long and so steep were the slopes that we could never have climbed them without cutting steps had the snow been hard, and we should not have had time, in one day, to cut enough steps to take us to the top. A cool day would have made the ascent impossible.

To give the reader an idea of the steepness of Mount Stuart I will say that from the foot of the mountain on Ingalls Creek to the first summit, along the route of ascent, approximately forty-five hundred feet in elevation, the slope averages more than forty-five degrees. On the shoulder just below the first summit in several places it runs from eighty to ninety degrees. And it must be remembered that this is the only route so far discovered by which the rugged peak may be climbed.

As we went up, it was so steep that we often supported ourselves by placing our hands on the snow on the upper side, without stooping, as we zigzagged back and forth. We did very little rock-work below the first summit.

We found the saddle between the first summit and the foot of the final pinnacle topped by an immense snow-cornice, which at some points extended out over the edge of the northern precipice as much as twenty feet. It was necessary for us to travel along the top of this cornice, occasionally dropping down on the south side to climb around a jutting point of rocks. We had been roped together since leaving the timber; Truitt coming just behind me, Jimmie Frisque next, then Hiscock, with Richardson in the rear.

We were passing along the crest of the cornice, taking care not to get too near the northern edge. Suddenly there was a sharp crack in the distance, as a mass of snow broke loose and hurtled down the cliffs.

"There she goes!" yelled Clarence, and he promptly jumped down the south side, followed closely by Jimmie. The rest of us were taken by surprise; but we held our places and we soon had the boys back in line where they belonged. Clarence thought the cornice had given way beneath us, and he made his leap, resolved to save the party while the saving was good. He had showed himself a young man of quick decision, and had really done the right thing, if the right thing had been at all necessary; but we had been in no danger, as the avalanche started several hundred yards from us.

The little incident gave us a lot of amusement, and none enjoyed the joke more than Truitt.

As we approached the summit, instead of walking gingerly over a steep face of cracked granite, we had to negotiate carefully a thin covering of snow, the stability of which gave us none too much confidence. We kept the rope taut to be ready for accident in case any member of the party should slip. The record-box was buried beneath two or three feet of ice and snow and had to be dug out with one of the ice-axes. The records had survived the long winter in good shape and were perfectly dry. No names had been added since our Labor Day visit.

The descent was merely a matter of following our tracks back, using, of course, such caution as was necessary to prevent accident.

The going from Ingalls Creek to the mouth of Beverly Creek was a great deal like the coming from the mouth of Beverly Creek to Ingalls Creek had been.

Five days after our ascent, in the opening days of June, Mount Stuart was again climbed by two young men who wrote that they saw our tracks in many places. Thus was doubly exploded the idea that the mountain could not be climbed in the early part of the season.

Still more ambitiously the Cascadians assaulted Mount Stuart on the 29th of the following May. On that day the mountain was successfully climbed by a party consisting of Mr. and Mrs. W. E. Richardson, Miss Carrie Grosenbaugh, Miss Bessie Simmons, Miss Pearl Snyder, Rolfe Whitnall, J. H. Renfro, Clarence Starcher, Sam Kelsey, Clarence Truitt, Arthur Renspie, J. Mason Streeter, and myself. Included in the party, but not climbing the mountain, were Mrs. Rolfe Whitnall, who had made the ascent before and did not care to go up again; Mrs. J. H. Renfro, who found that she had not done sufficient training for such strenuous work; and Roy Neilan, who was ill.

The climb was similar to our May ascent of the year before, except for the greater number participating, although there were thrills enough to satisfy everybody.

Whitnall, president of the Cascadians, scattered flowers from the summit in memory of mountaineers who had died in the World War or had lost their lives in mountain adventure. The magnificent and unusual settings made of it an impressive ceremony.

XIII

CONQUEST OF THE GREAT EAST SIDE

THE CASCADIANS were going to Mount Adams. They were going to visit the scenes, or a part of the scenes, that my mother, sister, and I had visited thirty-one years before; they were eager to see the glaciers, the crags and the waterfalls I had so often told them of. It was a far cry from 1890 to 1921; but the wonders were there unchanged, and now a bunch of outdoor enthusiasts were planning to revel in the glories I had seen before several of them were born. The club's 1921 summer outing was to be devoted to the eastern face of the mountain.

And I had ulterior motives in the plans of the Cascadians. From among the vigorous men who would be sure to go on that trip I knew that I could recruit a suitable party to aid me in a final assault upon the Great East Side. The time had come when I must accept the challenge of the mighty precipice. The doubts of twenty years must now be set at rest.

And so we were assembled, twenty strong, on the morning of August 7, 1921, in front of the Masonic Temple in Yakima, ready for the start. From Portland had come Edgar E. Coursen, seasoned veteran of many strenuous climbs; Mr. and Mrs. Maurice H. Barnes, his son-in-law and daughter; and Miss Mary Gene Smith; the last three young in years, but old at the mountain game. Yakima furnished as its contingent: Mr. and Mrs. W. E. Richardson, Mr. and Mrs. J. R. Vincent, Mrs. J. V. Ellis, Mrs. Rolfe Whitnall, Miss Carrie Grosenbaugh, Clarence Truitt, Clarence Starcher, Rolland Whitmore, Robert E. Williams,

J. Mason Streeter, and myself. From Warden in the eastern Washington wheat-belt came two teachers, the Misses Helen Whitnall and Gladys McDowell, and from her home on the Columbia River came fourteen-year-old Eudora Mitchell. In that company were novices and experienced mountaineers; but all had the enthusiasm that is necessary to make mountaineers.

Vincent had his own car and provided transportation for six. The rest of the party was carried in two seven-passenger cars, furnished by a local automobile company. We were away promptly at eight o'clock for the long dusty ride across the Yakima Indian Reservation to the little town of White Swan. From there on, there was less dust and the roads were more picturesque, for, after ascending the rocky, Toppenish Creek hill, we came to the park-like timber-lands. We aimed to take lunch at noon at the Signal Peak Ranger Station; but one of the machines had trouble and it was considerably past that hour when we sat down to the appetizing meal prepared by Mrs. Morse and her mother, Mrs. Hause. After lunch the beautiful twelve miles to the Klickitat River were soon run off, and we thought little of the steep, narrow grade which led us down into Surveyor Creek Canyon.

Soda Ford on the Klickitat was then the terminus of automobile transportation. Here we were committed to the care of a pack-train owned by Asa H. Morse, a young White Swan farmer. For the next two weeks our transient culinary department was to be under the control of Morse and his charming wife, who, the women of our party declared, when her hair was done in a certain way, looked like the picture of a Gibson girl. Mrs. Hale was head cook, and, for fear the reader may be anxious to know how we fared, it may be well to say, without giving further suspense, that never was a camping party more thoroughly and delightfully fed. Our meals were all that could be desired, both as to quality and quantity, and, notwithstanding that all of the provisions were transported, first by wagon for fifty miles and the balance of the way on horses, they were furnished to us about one third of the price of meals at some of the much-advertised mountain resorts where the transportation problem is comparatively simple.

Chief engineer of the cayuse department—otherwise known as the pack-train—was Pete, expert horseman and teamster. A few years before, Pete, while in the Government service, had discovered a forest fire on the reservation. He undertook the rather large task of putting it out unaided. He was rewarded for his temerity by a crack on the head from a falling limb. He dropped unconscious and the advancing fire would have consumed him but for the timely arrival of our old friend, Ed Snipes, who, with great difficulty, dragged him to safety and took a leading part in getting him out of the wilderness to medical attention. Since then there had often been times that Pete's physical faculties refused for a brief period to function; and when such a spell came on he had to suspend operations and await the return of his efficiency. Notwithstanding, he was an invaluable aid to Morse in the conduct of the pack-train.

Pete had brought our dunnage to the Klickitat with his four-horse team, and we were ready for the joys of camp life. After breakfast in the morning there was considerable excitement when the party was ferried across the swift channel of the Klickitat on the pack-horses. Some of the young women—and some of the young men, too, for that matter—were more than a little nervous over this method of getting to the opposite side of the stream; but the transit was made without accident, amid considerable hilarity on the part of the seasoned mountain travelers. I little thought that in less than a year I should cross the river at this place on a substantial bridge which had been constructed as a part of the great Mount Adams Highway, an important link in the shortening of the auto route from Yakima to Portland.

When we had been put safely across the river, the pack-train returned to camp to pick up our outfit, while we took the long steep trail up to Mount Adams Lake, which required a climb of two thousand feet. It was well along in the afternoon when we reached this beautiful little sheet of water. Shortly afterward the pack-train arrived in charge of Morse and Pete, accompanied by Mrs. Morse, Mrs. Hale, her daughter Gladys, and her son Milt Hale who was the ranger in charge of the Surveyor Creek Ranger Station.

The balance of the afternoon was pleasantly spent by the various members of the party, some of whom enjoyed a swim in the lake. Mount Adams Lake, having neither inlet nor outlet in the summer—it probably occupies an extinct crater—becomes quite warm and agreeable for swimming. It has an unknown depth and is about half a mile in diameter. The great mountain from which it takes its name is reflected clearly in its waters; and altogether it is a most picturesque spot in a land of picturesqueness.

The troubles that camping parties have with the pack-horses are proverbial, and we were no exception to the rule. On the morning of the 9th our outfit was thrown into a state between hilarity and apprehension by the sight of a recalcitrant cayuse dashing madly through camp with Pete clinging for dear life to its tail. Pete dared not let go, and it looked as though he could not hold on much longer. It seemed to be one of those problems that has no solution. But Morse, expert ropeman, solved the difficulty by bringing his lasso into play and neatly throwing a noose over the head of the fleeing bronco. The action was quick and de-

MOUNT ADAMS FROM MOUNT ADAMS LAKE

CASCADIAN PARTY ON EDGE OF THE GREAT SNOW WALL, LEAVING BIVOUAC FOR THE SUMMIT, FIRST EAST-SIDE ASCENT OF MOUNT ADAMS

Upper portion of the Castle seen at the right

THE CASCADIAN PARTY THAT MADE THE FIRST ASCENT OF THE EAST SIDE OF MOUNT ADAMS, AUGUST 13–14, 1921

Left to right: Richardson, Starcher, Truitt, Williams, Whitmore, Coursen, Rusk

cisive and it summarily relieved a tense situation.

The walk from Mount Adams Lake to Avalanche Valley is rather tedious. It was mid-afternoon when the last of us—having remained at the morning camp to help get the pack-train in motion—filed into the valley. The horses had outtraveled us, and we found camp pitched on the natural lawns where the stream divided—the spot where Green and I had camped for a night two years before. I was the only one of the party that had ever been in this delightful spot before, and they were all entranced by the grandeur and the beauty of the place.

For the next eleven days this was to be our home. The cooks made preparations to prepare and serve the meals with the greatest convenience possible, and the members of the party selected their sleeping-quarters in the near-by groves. A large tent was set up for the women, and another was erected as a place of general assembly and refuge in case of storm. The married couples had small tents of their own; while the unattached men slept in the open beneath the stars. The horses were turned loose to graze on the short nutritious bunch-grass that covered the foothills between camp and the main mountain. Our appetites developed as mountain appetites usually develop, and the cry of "Come and get it!" was always a welcome one. Nevertheless, so well were we provided for that there was always plenty and to spare.

"This is the life!" Truitt would inform us on frequent occasions, and we would generally concur. If the tramp had been a hard one and the party had stopped for a rest, it would be aroused to renewed activity by his cheery:

"Is everybody happy? Is anybody mad? All right, let's go!"

The forenoon of the day following our arrival at permanent camp was spent in a trip to the top of Goat Butte from which commanding position the party was inspired by the marvelous view of the mountain. A cairn had been erected on the summit of the butte, and in a tin can, on various scraps of paper, were inscribed the names of former visitors. Unfortunately, we were compelled to destroy some of these records because some senseless vandal had written thereon unprintable things. We returned to camp by way of the remarkable yellow castellated cliffs on the south slope of the butte. I was struck by the great amount of disintegration that had here taken place since my visit with Professor Reid twenty years before. We had then walked easily along the top of the cliffs; but now the crest was broken down in many places, forming great spires with sharp clefts between.

In the afternoon we crossed the stream from Rusk Glacier by means of a great snow-bank that completely overlay the upper part of the turbulent flood, and made a journey to the lower end of Klickitat Glacier and the source of the Big Muddy. Conditions here were practically the same as Green and I had found them two years before, except that the stream was more divided and not so nearly confined in one channel where it came from the ice.

A couple of hundred yards below our permanent camp a small colony of whistling marmots had its home in a jumble of immense boulders that had slid down from the butte above. The members of the party derived much entertainment from watching these interesting animals. One or two old patriarchs became so tame that they could be viewed at close range, and Mr. Williams secured some excellent photographs of them. Here the ubiquitous fool with a gun came into evidence. One morning while strolling a short distance below camp I heard a shot. Upon investigation I found a sheepman and his wife who were riding horseback to their camp north of the mountain. They were accompanied by a friend and his wife, guests out for a camping trip in the wilds. The friend had a big revolver strapped to his hip, and, seeing one of our benevolent old marmots gazing from a rock confidently in their direction, had blazed away at the unoffending animal. His intentions were murderous; but his aim was poor, and the mormot, with outraged faith in mankind, ducked into his hole. When I appeared on the scene the man had dismounted and was scrambling over the rocks to ascertain the result of his marksmanship. I made a few pointed remarks concerning the folly and the uselessness of slaying unoffending animals; but such admonitions generally fall on unresponsive ears when addressed to the fool with a gun.

On the 11th, practically the whole party put in the day on a visit to the Wilson and the Lyman Glaciers. To our keen disappointment, we found that there was an unusual amount of snow on the mountain; more, in fact, than I had seen in any previous year except in 1901. Much of the beauty of the ice-formations was, therefore, lost to us. Of the curiously interesting ice-wells, none was in evidence.

As we crossed the upper part of Wilson Glacier near the foot of Roosevelt Cliff, we saw two great snowballs that had rolled down the steep slope and had lodged on a flat place. The under part of one of these, which stood about as high as an ordinary man's shoulders, had melted away, leaving it standing on two legs or columns, with a hole between. Coursen lay down on the snow and stuck his head through the hole and one of the party took his picture. Then Miss Eudora was lifted to the top of the mass to have her picture taken. When she was lifted down, it was seen that the big snowball swayed slightly. A light push with the hand toppled it over. Cold shudders went through the whole party as we realized what might have happened had those frail snow-legs given way and let hundreds of pounds of congealed weight crunch down on Coursen's head!

The 12th had been scheduled as the day on which to begin our attempt to climb the Great East Side. As upon all occasions when I visited this part of the mountain, I had been closely studying the Castle and the other stupendous cliffs. More strongly than ever before, doubts now assailed me. The Castle looked to be impregnable. Not only did I have little hope of success; but the presentiment of accident was strong upon me. I think I should have been glad if something had occurred to make the attempt impossible.

After we returned to camp on the afternoon of the 11th, threatening clouds began to fly around the summit. It seemed certain that a storm was impending. And for the adventure we were about to undertake good weather was imperative. We should have to spend a night at some place on that forbidding face. Retreat in the teeth of a storm would be impossible. So the start on the following morning was abandoned, to await the pleasure of meteorological conditions. I began to feel that the attempt would never be made.

But the weather settled on the 12th. The sun set in a perfect sky, and all indications pointed to a considerable period of unbroken calm. It was now or never. We decided that dawn should see us far on our way.

Our party had been forming for several days. As finally arranged, it consisted of Mr. Coursen, Mr. Richardson, Mr. Truitt, Mr. Starcher, Mr. Whitmore, Mr. Williams, and myself as leader. Some of these had had little or no experience as climbers; but they were all strong, reliable men and I had no doubt that they would give a good account of themselves. For various reasons the other men of the main party could not or did not want to go. We were to go as light as possible; taking only enough provisions for two days; no beds or sleeping-bags; a couple of cameras; as little clothing as possible; a few extra necessities; and our climbing equipment. It was to be a rough trip, and we neither could take nor expect luxuries. In fact we anticipated a shortage of ordinary comforts.

We went to bed on the night of the 12th with the knowledge that we were to try a thing that had long been regarded as impossible. Professor Lyman, who has been frequently mentioned in these tales as one of the earliest and most painstaking of the Mount Adams enthusiasts, was one of those who had regarded the east side as unscalable. John H. Williams, in his interesting book, "Guardians of the Columbia," had said: "Mount Adams is ascended without difficulty by either its north or south slope. On the east and west faces, the cliffs and ice-cascades appall even the expert alpinist. As yet, so far as I can learn, no ascents have been made over these slopes."

Morse's lusty shout aroused us at two o'clock in the morning. We crawled from our beds and gathered, shivering, around the fire. We snatched a hasty breakfast from the fare he had provided. We blinked up at the frosty stars that gave us their promise of a perfect day. Three of the women were also up. They were Mrs. Richardson, Miss Grosenbaugh, and Miss Smith. They planned to climb Goat Butte, see the sunrise, and watch our progress up the mountain.

At three-thirty we were away. The women also started at about the same time. It was still extremely dark. We stumbled up the grassy ridges toward the snow-fields, with such uncertain aid as a small electric flashlight could give us. Daylight found us just below the snow-fields on the north side of Rusk Glacier. We struck the glacier at the lower end of Victory Ridge.

Before taking to the ice we stopped for a few minutes to prepare for the final test. I took occasion to impress upon the party the uncertainty and danger of the undertaking, and suggested that this was the last chance any one would have to turn back, as it would be next to impossible for a man to return alone after we were well launched upon the real climb.

But there were no quitters in that party. I was never with a better bunch of men. From the start to the finish every one uncomplainingly stood up to the work, and not a one once faltered in the most trying situations.

Briefly outlined, our plan of ascent was to go straight up the center of Rusk Glacier to the great Bergschrund at the foot of the Castle; work from the end of the Bergschrund up the cliffs on to Battlement Ridge near where it joins the Castle; climb right over the Castle to the terribly crevassed snow-field below the summit dome; then up this snow-field, through the maze of canyon-like snow-gorges to the top. Described in a few words, it is true, yet this route meant incalculable toil and danger, involving every class of climbing known to mountaineers—glacier-work, rock-work, and snow-work, each of which presented some of the most difficult features in its line.

About the center of Rusk Glacier is a rock island or cliff. It is on the dividing-line between the white or southern portion of the glacier and the dark northern part which forms the track of the avalanches. The southern half of the glacier is protected from the great snow-slides by the dominating bulk of the Castle, and here the snow lies white and unsullied by the débris hurled from the crags. Over the lower end of the island-cliff a considerable ice-fall tumbles, and the glacier here is greatly crevassed and broken.

Before taking to the glacier we roped together on one of our hundred-foot ropes. We climbed in the following order: Myself as leader, Coursen, Whitmore, Williams, Truitt, Starcher, and Richardson. Richardson and I had

Swiss ice-axes; the others had steel-pointed alpenstocks, each from six to seven feet in length. Our heavy-soled shoes were thickly hobnailed, and we also had a number of long calks in heels and soles.

After taking to the ice our route for a time was over a comparatively smooth surface, toward the island. Soon the slope became steeper and we swung to the right, passed close to the ice-fall, and bore slightly to the left of the island. There was some danger from rocks falling down the precipitous ice-slope; but it was still early in the morning and they had not yet started to fall rapidly.

We made unexpectedly quick progress up the face of the glacier. We kept quite close to the island until we were past it. The snow was hard and little of the ice surface was here exposed. Frequently it was necessary to cut steps, and the rope was kept well in hand to preclude the possibility of a slip. The snow was greatly "cupped"; that is, there were many cup-like depressions in it caused by uneven alternate melting and freezing. This condition was a considerable aid to us in climbing, as a "cup" would give the head man on the rope a chance to anchor and assist those following in getting up a steep pull. There was not the danger of taking an involuntary slide on a rough surface of this kind that there would have been on a smooth steep surface of snow.

Owing to the fact that there was an unusual amount of snow on the mountain in the summer of 1921, the upper part of the glacier was almost completely covered, and in only a few places did the bare ice appear. The Rusk Glacier is very steep and badly crevassed, and we had to exercise considerable caution to avoid hidden traps. Our course was mostly a zigzag one. Numerous détours were made to get around the ends of open crevasses. We kept completely on the white surface, that part protected from avalanches by the Castle; but on our right, not so very far away, we could see the dark, dirty ice that marked the track of a thousand terrific slides.

When we were pretty well up, we began to use our trench mirrors to flash signals back to camp. We were not long in receiving answers, and during the entire day whenever we were in a position visible to our friends below, and the sun was shining, this exchange of greetings was kept up. Meantime, the women on top of Goat Butte had been watching us for hours. The excitement there, as well as at camp, was keen, and it increased, of course, the higher we got, in proportion to our prospects for success.

As we advanced, the great precipice and the Castle loomed menacingly above us. To the left, Battlement Ridge, with its serrated crest, frowned grimly. Its wall rose perpendicularly from the glacier and masses of snow leaned against the cliffs. The uneven snow-slope above us was thickly studded with rocks that had fallen from the Castle. At the foot of this mighty bastion the great Bergschrund yawned, a tremendous gash across the face of the glacier. We looked apprehensively at the Castle, for we did not know at what moment it might begin bombarding us with rocks. This was a danger that no skill could avoid, a peril that must be met by the mountaineer if he would accomplish things worth while in moutaineering. Yet I calculated that the percentage of risk was little, if any, greater than that taken by any man in crossing a busy street in this time of reckless automobiles.

Shortly before reaching the Castle we passed the end of a very large crevasse. It was but an infant compared with some we were to see the following day. From there we angled to the left, up the steep slope of the pock-marked snow, to the lower lip of the great Bergschrund. The upper side of the Bergschrund was an overhanging snow-wall

BERGSCHRUND AT FOOT OF CASTLE, RUSK GLACIER, MOUNT ADAMS

Showing Great Precipice and Overlying Snow Wall

THE CASTLE, MOUNT ADAMS, WITH RUSK GLACIER IN FOREGROUND

Telephoto from Avalanche Valley

EAST SIDE OF MOUNT ADAMS BY MOONLIGHT FROM AVALANCHE VALLEY

The Castle is the highest pinnacle of rock in upper center. The tents of the Cascadians show in foreground. Note path of star that set over right end of the mountain during the two hours of exposure of the negative.

in places forty feet high. This formed the lower edge of a broad cornice that clung to the almost perpendicular lower walls of the Castle. The Castle itself towered fifteen hundred feet directly above us with its constant menace of unstable rocks.

We had reached a probable elevation of ten thousand feet, and it was not later than ten o'clock in the forenoon.

We proceeded to the left along the lower lip of the Bergschrund. It was exceedingly jumbled, and we went with extreme caution, not unmindful of the great snow-wall hanging directly over us. Our problem was now to get from the end of the Bergschrund on to the cliffs of Battlement Ridge. Where the Bergschrund touched the rocky wall of the ridge, the snow was broken and shattered into big blocks, with soft patches of rotten snow between. The rock-face rose abruptly, in places perpendicularly, for fully fifty feet before giving way to a more negotiable slope. Large sheets of ice, standing edgewise, clung precariously to the sheer rocks. Our only way of advance was to cut steps along the upper edge of the ice, and to trust to its being strong enough to hold our weight.

The situation now demanded the utmost caution. Except where the ice was attached to the rock, there was a considerable space between it and the cliff. The thought that it might give way or that one of the party might fall in between was not reassuring. Foot by foot, with my Swiss ice-axe, I hewed steps along the sharp top of the brittle ice, he fragments rattling down into the frozen caverns with an minous sound. The others coming behind, with extreme are, kept the rope taut to guard against accident as much as possible. We were not sure how much cohesion, or affinity, or whatever one has a mind to call it, existed between the ice and the rock, and we did not know at what moment the whole frail slab-like white sheet might give way and crash downward bearing with it every member of the party that happened to be standing on it at the moment of disaster. Luckily, however—I say luckily advisedly, for it was as much a matter of luck as anything else—nothing of the kind happened. Soon the foremost men were firmly anchored on the cliff waiting for the others to get off of the dangerous armor of ice as quickly as they could.

We were now ready to essay the first of a series of steps in the ridge above the ice. These steps were formed by perpendicular places in the cliff, each ten or a dozen feet in height and topped by a sort of bench covered with loose stones. Some of the steps had to be surmounted by climbing straight up over a point of rock; but others could be climbed by means of short chimneys.

Telling Coursen to see that I had plenty of rope, as I had to go in a hurry when I started, I made a dash up the first point of rock. I gained some slight advantage from my momentum, and my rapid climbing lessened the danger of the handholds and footholds giving way beneath my weight. I was thus able to get far enough up to grasp the upper projections and draw myself to the top, where I clung, for a time, panting for breath. When the first man has surmounted a bad place, it is comparatively easy for the others to come up on a rope, and it was not long until this difficulty was behind us.

The intermediate steps were passed without great difficulty; but when the last one was reached, a narrow chimney was seen leading up. As there appeared to be considerable danger from loose stones, I cautioned those below to stand well to one side, sheltered as much as possible by projecting points of the cliff. As I climbed up through the chimney, I had to pass directly over the boulder which had lodged in the cleft. When I was fairly on top of it, the rock suddenly gave way. I braced myself desperately, from wall to wall, across the chasm. The rock went out from under me. Fortunately, it did not catch the rope, and, as the rest of the party was sheltered to one side behind the bluff, it crashed harmlessly on to the ice below.

The surmounting of the last chimney brought us on to the steep, rock-covered north slope of Battlement Ridge, and we could now see our way clear to the Castle. Looking backward and downward, we could see a great part of our recent route up the glacier, our line of march being marked in many places by our tracks in the hard surface of the snow.

We unroped. Here each man could do better unhampered by the restraint of the life-line. There was little chance of slipping, the chief danger now being in the starting of a rock-slide. Clambering diagonally up the steep boulder-strewn slope, we soon reached the crest of the ridge at the point of its junction with the Castle. We were hundreds of feet above the Bergschrund.

Here a marvelous view, never before seen by human eyes, burst upon us. Peering over the escarpment of jagged cliffs, we looked down two thousand feet on to the gashed surface of Klickitat Glacier. The tremendous séracs lay like white marble ruins of some ancient city shattered by an earthquake. Directly opposite, not more than half a mile away, towered the three thousand-foot precipice that looms so terrifically above the great glacier. A thousand-foot waterfall was creeping down a gorge in the red cliff, another thousand feet of its course hidden beneath a big snow-field that clung tenaciously to the uncertain crags. Were this fall exposed entirely to the view, it would probably show from two to three thousand feet of height—possibly higher than Yosemite—one of the highest in the world. It—as well as one north of the Castle—can be seen only from the Castle, the ridge, or the upper glacier; so these two wonders will always remain hidden from all except those who wish to brave the dangers of a hazardous climb.

The very top of the ridge was so loose and narrow that we did not feel justified in setting foot upon it, but contented ourselves by standing beneath the crest and using the upper few feet as a breastwork, over which we gazed at the awe-inspiring spectacle beyond.

Turning, we had a magnificent sweep of the glacier we had just left; the great dark track of the avalanches blackening its northern part, with the pure white snow of the protected portion nearer at hand.

Thus far had we come; but the end was not yet. The terrific ramparts of the Castle still loomed for more than a thousand feet above us; and beyond lay the awful snow-field of the upper dome. The difficulty of getting up on to the ridge would probably vary, at different times, according to the amount of snow and ice encountered. It might be less difficult than we found it; it might be more difficult; or it might be impossible.

A steeper continuation of Battlement Ridge now led from our position well up toward the more precipitous crags of the higher part of the Castle. The whole formation, both above and below us, showed the results of a one-time tremendous heat. The history of the old volcano is here writ in graphic characters for him who has the skill to read.

Now came a tedious climb up the lower part of the Castle. The rock-surface was, for the most part, a rough conglomerate formation. At times we could walk upright; but frequently we found it prudent to use hands as well as feet. As we went we continued to flash signals back to our friends in camp. We could make out the tents, far, far away, and it seemed a fearfully long time since we had left them.

The first stage of the Castle ascent would have been rather monotonous—as well as toilsome and somewhat dangerous—if it had not been for the marvelous scenery that was constantly unfolding on every hand. We attempted to pass to the south of the main turrets of the Castle; but soon found the crags hanging perpendicularly over the great ice-fall of Klickitat Glacier. This condition forced us to traverse to the northern slope. Crossing a sharp saddle, between a minor spire and the higher cliffs above, we reached a narrow snow-chute leading down between the ridge we had been following and a less pronounced one just to the north. At the upper end, this chute was attached to a considerable snow-field clinging to the eastern face of the Castle. Directly beneath the snow-field a five-hundred-foot, perpendicular cliff led around to the northern side of the Castle. Between the brink of this cliff and the sheer upper columns of the Castle is a very steep rock-slope, partly occupied by the above-mentioned snow-field at the time of our visit.

Putting on the rope, we cautiously crossed the slippery snow-chute to the upper point of the farther ridge. From here we angled up the main snow-field to some minor cliffs just beneath the main ramparts of the upper Castle. Then came a ticklish, step-cutting process up the steepening snow-field past a jutting point of rock. When directly at the foot of a great black column, we again swung to the south in another effort to pass the southern face of the Castle. We went immediately beneath a rock-face that towered straight above us for hundreds of feet. Reaching another saddle in our southern sky-line, one glance was enough. From there the side of the mighty dome broke down even more precipitously than before. We must gain the crest of the Castle either on the east or on the north side.

We retraced our steps to the snow-field. Here an effort was made to ascend a broad chimney or gully, partially snow-choked, down which a considerable stream came plunging from a hidden snow-bank above. This was impracticable. By cutting steps in the snow, I advanced twenty feet or so, with the stream tunnel directly beneath me; but when the snow ended, the water falling over an almost perpendicular section of the chimney cut off further progress.

I climbed down and we started a traverse to the north. On leaving the snow- and ice-field it was difficult to find footing on the steep rock-face. I slipped and had to jump for a rocky projection; the shortness of the rope almost prevented my reaching it, and I narrowly escaped a bad fall. Richardson, being last man on the rope, had to cut steps before he could get across from the ice to the rocks.

Carefully picking our way along the side of the cliffs, we crossed the face of the Castle, almost on a level, to about the northeast corner. Here we paused on a sort of ridge or shelf projecting from the side of the massif. A large part of the northern wall of the Castle could here be seen. We could look in against the great chute down which the avalanches seemed to have a regular route. Precipitous enough it was, and we soon saw that further progress upon the northern face was impossible. Beneath, the cliffs fell away perpendicularly, and in some places overhangingly, for hundreds of feet to the glacier. We looked directly against the sulphur-colored precipice, overtopped by its two-hundred-foot wall of snow. The scene here was scarcely less awe-inspiring than the one from the southern side of the Castle had been.

Above, the black and yellow conglomerate columns rose for three hundred feet more of vertical height. Between these columns great broad chimneys led to the very crest of the Castle. If we could successfully negotiate one of them, the battle would be won.

It was now two o'clock in the afternoon, and the others of the party felt the need of lunch. I wanted nothing to eat. As it often does on a hard trip, my appetite had failed me. I have never suffered from mountain sickness; but my stomach generally goes bad for a day or so when I start out on a particularly strenuous journey, although altitude seems to have no effect on it one way or another. Having once become adjusted to changed conditions, my digestive forces resume their normal operations and my appetite again assumes stability and is ample for all requirements.

But on this day, while the others ate, I sized up the situation. For the only time during the climb, I felt doubtful of the outcome. The prospect above did not look inviting. Gloomy forebodings assailed me.

There was little time for misgivings. The lunch was soon eaten and we were ready to go. Immediately above, a broad double chimney—so broad, in fact, that it might be called a gorge—led upward. In places the way was almost perpendicular. We approached it by means of a sharp rocky ridge, up which we clambered on hands and knees. It was now a question of using the hands as well as the feet.

Leaving the ridge, I swung toward the opposite side of the chimney for the purpose of determining which was the more feasible branch, the right or the left. Coursen, who was second on the rope, after a look at the situation, said he liked best the appearance of the route along the left-hand wall of the chimney and wished to climb that way. Accordingly, I threw off the rope, and the rest of the party proceeded up the left wall. Consequently, during the first half of the climb, I was not roped to the others.

As we entered the chimney, probably few of us let our minds linger on the obvious fact that a slip here would result in a rough tumble of a hundred feet or so and then a thousand-foot plunge to the glacier. It was no time to speculate on the consequence of a fall. The all-important thing was not to fall.

We were now climbing over a yellow, conglomerate, cement-like formation—breccia, I think the geologists call it. Here and there, in this natural cement, small black rocks were embedded. They often made excellent hand-holds and footholds; but great care was necessary to be sure of their solidity.

A small stream was falling down the right branch of the chimney. After convincing myself that the left branch was the more feasible route, I traversed to the left and re-joined my companions when about half of the ascent had been accomplished. Shortly after this, we were startled by the crash of two avalanches, in quick succession, as they rushed down the track beneath us. They were hidden by the overhanging crags, and we were safe from their rush; but they gave us one of the thrills of the climb.

We climbed carefully and surely. Williams received a nasty knock on one of his hands from a small stone that hurtled down from above. As we approached the top, the chimney again divided. We discussed the best route to take. On the right, at the top, was a slightly overhanging projection, which looked possible, but not desirable. On the left, the way led sharply up to the top where a large chunk of the conglomerate had broken from one of the walls, blocking the extreme upper end of the chimney, but leaving beneath an aperture large enough for a man to crawl through. Thither we went. As I crawled through the hole, I saw that I was on the shattered edge of the plateau and that a short scramble over broken fragments would bring us to the very crest of the Castle.

Encouraged by my shout of victory, the rest of the party scrambled quickly up, although we did not for an instant relax our vigilance on the rope. When all were through the hole, it required but a few minutes to clamber over the loose fragments, and we were walking across the flat top of the Castle. My twenty-year goal was won.

We had been on the way twelve hours from camp.

But before I had time for anything else, I must know the answer to an all-important question. The top of the Castle is flat surface, an acre or so in extent, covered with a compact volcanic scoria. A number of times in the past I had looked down upon it from the summit of the mountain. It had always appeared to me that one could easily walk from the Castle's crest to the great snow-field behind it, which would be necessary for a party to do, in making the east-side ascent, in order to reach the summit. Yet there was a strong possibility that there was a sheer drop-off on the west side of the Castle that would prevent a climber's reaching the snow-field at all. If such were the case our defeat was certain. Therefore, the first thing I did when we came out on to the plateau was to walk straight across to the west side to settle the question.

Sure enough, there was a drop-off of perhaps seventy-five feet. At first glance it looked as though we were stumped. Coursen was with me, and we began a careful examination of the wall to determine the possibility of getting down. It was not perpendicular, although very nearly so, and we soon were able to pick out what was doubtless a practicable route to the bottom. At the foot was a small area of sloping rock partly covered with broken detritus. Here the tremendous snow- and ice-fall, tumbling down the terrific slope below the summit, divided. The southern portion dropped off, to our left, into the awful ice-cascade of Klickitat Glacier. The northern part pressed on, to our right, to the verge of the great precipice and lay there, the two-hundred-foot snow-wall so often heretofore mentioned. At the point of division, where the Castle and the snow-mass met, a little moraine jutted gently out in defiance of the crushing weight that bore down on either side. To the south of it the snow ground down to Klickitat Glacier; to the north it avalanched to the Rusk.

No words can describe the confusion of that snow-mass beneath the summit dome. In mighty séracs it lay, wild beyond the power of human conception; pile upon pile; ice-pinnacle, tower and minaret; block tumbled on to block; marble domes impinged against crystal walls; frozen gorges gashing fields of dazzling white; scintillating icicles flashing diamonds back to the afternoon sun—all blending into one lawless whole of majesty and might.

After satisfying ourselves that we could get down, Coursen and I returned to the other members of the party. The men with the cameras were soon busy. We decided to build a rock monument and place in it a record of our achievement to this point. We had completed all of our glacier-work and most of the rock-work; but the snow-work was still before us, and the outcome was by no means certain. We went to each edge of the Castle and looked into the awful depths below us. We realized our great height by looking down. We were approximately eleven thousand, five hundred feet above the sea—an elevation greater than the summit of any other peak in Washington or Oregon, except Rainier. The top of the Castle did not look to be so very far away when looking up to it from camp at the foot of Goat Butte; but that camp seemed infinitely far away to us now.

We carried rocks and built our "stoneman" on the eastern edge of the plateau at a point from which our camp could be seen. We wrote a record of what we had done so far, put it in a small tin box, and placed it in the cairn. Up to this time we had been too busy seriously to note the storm-clouds that had been gathering around the mountain. But before the monument was fully completed, it began to

pitable crags. Within a hundred yards of the spot where we must drag out the hours of darkness, the snow-wall clung to the verge of the giant cliffs. Now and again tons of the congealed mass broke loose and thundered down the awful declivity with a crash and a roar that made the blood run cold. Avalanche followed avalanche throughout the night. Possibly the wind helped to free the slumbering demons. Startling though each manifestation of this terrible power might be, the effect was awe-inspiring to the watchers of our little band, and such a night could not grow dull.

The others ate of our cold store of provisions. Still I could not eat. Once Coursen handed me a cracker and I tried to eat it; but my stomach instantly rejected the proffered morsel. So they had the advantage of adding fuel to their waning fires; while I must draw upon the energy stored from previous meals in camp.

We put on all our extra clothing. We had three light, hooded parkas made of balloon silk, and these were quite a help to those who wore them to keep out the wind. Richardson and Truitt each had a carbide lamp, which was of considerable use after darkness set in. My electric flashlight, like the one on Mount Stuart, had been unable to withstand the rough usage and the battery had gone dead.

When it was fairly dark we huddled together in our rocky nest beneath the overhanging cliff, and tried to sleep. But the attempt was attended with little success. We might have slept in spite of the hardness of the rocks—and even the crash of the avalanches might not have kept us awake had it not been for the cold. But if any of us slept, it was only in fitful dozes of a few minutes at a time. We lay and shivered as long as we could stand it; then we rose, by ones or twos or threes, and worked our way down to the little moraine and walked along it, back and forth—

always back and forth—with the wind and the snow smiting us mightily from the north. Then, when circulation was partially restored and we were on the point of exhaustion, we would creep back again to the nest behind the improvised stone wall and try once more to sleep—only to rise again in a short time and repeat the walking process.

We all walked but Whitmore. He shivered it out. Possibly his shivering was violent enough to pass for exercise and keep his blood from congealing. It is often a help to fold one's arms tightly when very cold, and maybe the contortions of Whitmore's muscles served the same purpose for him that our walking did for the rest of us. At any rate, he kept his place with his back against the cliff. Whitmore was a remarkably sturdy young fellow, full of mountain enthusiasm. I had noticed him on our other trips. Generally when the balance of the party sat down to rest he remained standing or walked about in search of something interesting. It seemed that his restless energy would not allow him to remain quiet, even for a few minutes. But, this night, he was the one who wooed quietude. Whether or not he slept any more than the others, I cannot say.

The night was laggard. When some one thought it was midnight and asked the time, it was only ten o'clock. When it should have been one o'clock, it was only eleven; and when we were ready to greet the sun as it burst across the horizon, it was but midnight. For several hours there was moonlight, yet I cannot now recall what hours they were. The moonbeams had sufficient strength to force their way through the interstices of the scudding clouds, and to flood the great snow-cap with a weird, uncertain light, through which the dark shadows rushed like portents of impending doom.

But we were cheerful through it all. We laughed and

joked; although it need not be supposed that we were not duly impressed with the immensity of our surroundings. Truitt frequently admonished us that "This is the life!" I do not believe there was one of us who did not feel that he was fortunate to be there, and probably not a man but would have resented the insinuation that he would be glad to change his situation to one in his warm sleeping-bag at camp so far below. Such levity as we expressed was for the purpose of making each other forget, as far as possible, the discomforts we were going through.

Toward morning some of the party deserted the nest and sought shelter from the wind in a crevice on the lee side of the low rocky ridge; but their new quarters were rather cramped and very little warmer than the old place.

And, as the night advanced and the storm did not increase in severity, we had every reason to feel that we should win. The driving snow continued unabated until nearly morning. When, at last, day broke in all the glory of a mountain dawn, we saw that the clouds were breaking away. There was promise of fair weather.

The sun rose clear; but we could not start at once. We must wait until its warmth should soften the surface of the snow sufficiently to enable us to hold our footing. The storm had plastered the northern side of the rocks with a thin coating of snow and the old snow surface had a new covering of several inches; but apparently the fall had not been heavy enough to interfere with our climbing.

Our repeated marchings up and down the little moraine had flattened the top of it until it looked like a graveled highway, and there were several yards of it over which a Ford could have been driven with ease. At different times, ever since our arrival, we had noticed a strong smell of sulphur. This part of the great precipice undoubtedly formed the rim of one of the principal craters of the mountain, and the Castle is probably a subsidiary cone built up after the main crater had broken down.

The others made out a cold breakfast; but food for me was not yet. By seven o'clock we decided that conditions were such that we could start.

Directly above us the great snow-mass was piled up in a tremendous ridge-like formation, of unknown depth, the top of which was broken into séracs of inconceivable roughness. The awful pressure that produced this confusion of snow and ice came through countless tons of snow bearing down from the summit. The summit itself we could see, not so far away; but on its edge lay the overhanging cornice where I had stood so often in the past to look down upon the unattainable crest of the Castle. To climb straight up that snow-precipice was impossible. We knew that we must bear to the north of the summit dome and reach the top from that direction.

We roped together in the same order we had kept the day before, and bade our cheerless camp good-bye. The test of the last stage of the climb was now at hand. It was my plan to pass to the left of the great séracs—the Klickitat Glacier side—although Coursen was of the opinion that the right side would be the better route. It was all a gamble, at any rate, for no man could tell what was above.

The snow was still rather hard beneath the thin, newly fallen layer, and the slope broke pretty sharply toward the ice-fall of Klickitat Glacier. More or less caution was required; but we worked carefully and were soon well up on the bulge of the snowy ridge. Between the big blocks and in the crevices was much rotten snow, treacherous, unreliable stuff, fit only to cover man-traps and to invite disaster. Blind crevasses abounded on every hand, and those that were visible were of enormous proportions. There was a blending of ice and snow, and it was frequently impossible to tell where one ended and the other began. The walls of the great crevasses were marked by successive layers, each showing a winter's fall of snow.

In the enormous concavity between the summit and the verge of the great precipice, the snow-mass lies in incredible depths—five hundred, possibly a thousand feet of congealed substance—accumulated through a period of time, no doubt, that antedates human history.

Over this vast accumulation we now had to make our way. We came to the upper end of the séracs and found the snow and ice piled into such prodigious blocks and towers—such an aggregation of fantastic shapes—that we could proceed no farther. On the left an awful snow-gorge cut across the face of the mountain and forbade hope of progress in that direction. Deep ice-valleys floored with rotten snow, hummocks, walls, and ridges, barred a crossing to our right. We must return to our starting-point and try the northern route.

At nine o'clock we were back within a hundred yards of our night's bivouac. The morning's work must be done over again—possibly with no better result.

I had been leading for fourteen hours. I now requested the party to reverse our order of march, thus putting Richardson in the lead. Richardson had begun his mountain-climbing experiences with the Cascadians the year before; but, in the brief time between, he had developed into a real mountaineer. He was one of the coolest, most level-headed and dependable fellows I had ever been with, and his assistance on this ascent was one of the main factors that made success possible.

We now bore to the north of the séracs and passed tolerably close to the snow-wall on the brink of the precipice. To do this we had to work between some big crevasses. The sun was still shining; but angry-looking clouds were again beginning to swirl about the upper part of the mountain. As we slowly worked along the last sunlit stretch, Mrs. Whitnall suddenly created a wave of excitement in the camp below by announcing that she saw us. The others incredulously scoffed the idea, until they were able to confirm it with their own eyes. They had not seen us since the day before, just previous to the storm, and the distant sight of us was a great relief. But they could not follow our movements for long, because we soon passed into a dense cloud and were blotted out in a haze of mystery.

Followed a struggle with adverse conditions, different from any we had already gone through on the ascent. The clouds closed round us so thickly that we could scarcely see farther than the length of the rope. Those ahead looked like phantom men as they crept up the slope in the dimness of the mists. We had before us the tremendous task of finding our way up through the maze of giant crevasses with neither sun nor landmark for a guide. As long as we could keep going up, we knew we were going toward the summit. But we could not always keep going up. A great gorge in the snow would suddenly loom through the uncertain light. Then a way to pass it must be found. Some of these gorges were choked with snow, on which we crossed —gingerly, be it said, for we had no desire to spend the balance of our lives in the depths of an icy cavern. To get by others, we had to make long détours, walking carefully along the lower lips and casting apprehensive glances now and then into the frozen chasms.

The first ones were not so bad; but as we approached the northern shoulder of the mountain the crevasses were of enormous size. No words can describe the impressive grandeur of these wonderful snow-canyons as they loomed through the clouds. Bigger ones I have never seen, and I believe they approach the limit in size for snow-crevasses.

We often read of bottomless cracks in the snow or ice, or ones that are thousands of feet deep. Such descriptions are rank exaggerations. Competent authorities have placed two hundred feet as about the greatest depth attained by crevasses. Some of those we saw that day were undoubtedly nearly or quite that deep, and into their capacious maws, it seemed, a city block could have been cast.

There was no way of judging direction except by the general slope of the mountain. Our aim was upward, ever upward. The clouds still held us in their grasp. We had no means of knowing what we had attained or what we still had to attain. There was a strong chance that we might still come face to face with an obstacle that would defeat all of our plans.

At last we came to a mighty crevasse stretching away into the clouds in either direction. On the left where it cut through a great ridge of snow an awful gap appeared against the grayness of the clouds. We saw that we must pass its northern end, if pass we could at all. We started along the lower lip, a steep slope on our lower side, a vertical drop of two hundred feet above. The space we had to walk on was not wide. We kept the rope tightly drawn; but even so we were none too safe. The chasm was sixty feet or more in width and trending toward the northern break-off of the mountain. Should it cut through the snow-wall on the brink of the precipice or into one of the ice-falls on the northeast corner of the peak, we should be completely balked. With intense anxiety we crept along that icy ledge, peering into the cloud-bank ahead, eager to learn our fate. Retreat seemed almost impossible—to try to get back the way we had come an unthinkable thing. All now depended on the ending of that great crevasse.

Finally we saw it. The end was bridged by a thick layer of snow beneath which the crevasse retreated into darkness.

It was only a question of getting far enough beyond the open vent to be sure of secure snow for the crossing. It was a steep pull up over the icy declivity; but we were so glad to have passed the chasm that we did not mind it. Soon the surface rounded to what I took to be the snow-plateau of the northern shoulder of the mountain. There were no longer any crevasses, and presently we were traveling almost on the level. But as there was now no slope to indicate the direction, and the clouds were as thick as ever, we could not be sure of our bearings. Richardson took out his pocket compass and we set a southerly course by that.

Yet we went through that swirl of mist for a long time without seeming to get anywhere. We began to doubt our position. Nevertheless, I was certain we could not be far wrong. However, Mount Adams is a tremendous mountain and the opportunities to get lost on it, especially in the clouds, are limitless.

And then suddenly the clouds lifted for an instant. To our right a great rock-pyramid loomed. It was the north summit of Mount Adams. We were headed exactly in the right direction.

Gradually the clouds broke away. Before us towered the summit dome, with its negotiable, snow-covered north slope presented for our convenience. It was "now all over but the shouting," and a wearisome climb of a few hundred feet. The snow was soft and rotten. We sank almost to our knees at every step. This was the most tiresome part of the whole ascent with no excitement to relieve the monotony.

When we were almost up we heard the sound of pounding. I thought I knew the cause. In a few minutes more we were floundering triumphantly through the miserably soft snow of the actual summit plateau, and soon we hailed the three men of the United States Forest Service working upon the frame of the lookout station.

These men, Ranger James H. Huffman, Joe Guler, and Arthur Jones, were expecting to finish their work before bad weather forced them to retreat down the mountain, thus completing the Government's four years' task of establishing on this lofty perch a station from which fires could be spotted throughout hundreds of square miles of forest lands below. Their tents were pitched on the first summit eight hundred feet lower down. From here a telephone wire had been stretched on the rocks to the foot of the mountain and in this way communication had been established with the outside world.

Before leaving Yakima I had made arrangements with O. C. Soots, secretary of the Yakima Commerical Club, and W. H. White, connected with the publicity department of the same club, to make an attempt to reach them over this same line and thus give the news of our success to the public. The Forest Service men told me that I should not be able to get any one over this wire later than noon on Sunday. As it had been eleven-thirty when we reached the summit, I now asked the other members of the party to go by the record-boxes and register our names, while I hurried down to the telephone.

I found the tents near the spot where my father and I had been forced back by the great storm in 1891—thirty years before. Entering one of the tents, which were weighted down by big rocks, I soon found the telephone instrument and sent my ring down the mountain-side. Quickly a voice answered, from some place far away on the borders of civilization. I put in my call for the Commercial Club rooms in Yakima. Presently came the answer that neither Soots nor White could be located. We had expected to complete our climb on Saturday—this was Sunday. Consequently, our distant friends would have thought we had failed and had given up hopes of hearing from us. I then tried to relay a message through to them for future delivery; but I could not make the man on the other end of the line understand. I soon realized that static electricity was interfering to such an extent that further intelligible communication would be impossible. By this time the other members of the party had arrived and we prepared to descend.

Our plan of descent was to go from the first summit south a short distance along the usual route and then to swing to the left, descend over the common névé of Klickitat and Mazama Glaciers, cross Klickitat Glacier, and détour around the lower end of Battlement Ridge to camp.

We left the first summit and went rapidly down the steep slope, relieved to find snow with no crevasses in it. After we had swung some distance toward the southeast corner of the mountain, we saw a party on the ascent coming up the lava "stairway" of boulders, from the south. Several of our party, including Coursen, cut across to have a talk with them. Coursen found among them some old friends. He told them we had just climbed the east side.

"But," remonstrated one of the other party, "can that be done?"

"No," was Coursen's laconic reply, "it cannot be done—*but we have just done it.*"

We found our route rougher and steeper than the usual south-side route. When we reached the upper névé of the glaciers we encountered some good-sized crevasses, but ordinary crevasses had no terrors for us now and we passed them with little thought. The morning clouds had long since dispersed and we descended into a sunlit region. As we went down the great swelling snow-slope on to Klickitat Glacier, we heard a distant halloo and soon we saw the glint of the sun on mirrors. Some of our party had made a journey from camp to the lower part of Battlement Ridge. We hurried across the glacier and down the long north moraine; then swung around the point of the ridge. Yet it was six o'clock when we finally trooped into camp and received the enthusiastic welcome of our friends.

It had been thirty-nine hours since I had eaten food!

Ours had not been entirely an accomplishment of young men. Four of the party were young; one was past sixty; another was over fifty; while I was rapidly approaching the half-century mark.

It was rather early when we sought our beds in the evergreen groves. We were soon asleep, making up for our long hours of strenuous wakefulness. Some time in the night I awoke. A gale was tearing through the tops of the stunted trees. Snug in the folds of the blankets, I lay long in my sleeping-bag and listened to the roar of the wind in the branches. A sense of deep satisfaction crept over me. I had reason to rejoice.

Our work was done and we were safe in camp. The Great East Side was conquered and the storm was on the mountain.

XIV

THE ETHEREAL MOUNTAIN

If Earth ever approaches Heaven, in its physical aspects, it must do so through the medium of a great mountain. The glory of the ice-crowned heights alone can lift us to an understanding of the sublime beauty of celestial majesty. The purity and aloofness of the lofty peak; its shining radiance; the golden glow of its sun-tipped dome; the glittering armor of its glacier-girt sides; the sparkle of its jeweled snow-fields; the serene dominion of castellated crags; the auric soul-touch of the resplendent mount; all raise the beholder from the level of the dust and place him athrob with the Infinite.

To one standing upon the shore of that lordly western river, the Columbia, and looking up the Hood River Valley, far beyond the stretch of happy homelands and across the peaceful folds of evergreen hills, there comes a vision of sublime purity, beauty, and grandeur, in perfect blending, a glory seemingly apart from earth, distant and yet near, celestial majesty supreme, white, calm, and lone, evanescent yet substantial gift of God to man—the Ethereal Mountain.

When I first saw it from that point of vantage I could scarcely bring myself to think of it as a thing of this world, so far above and so remote from all human toil and trouble did it seem; the serenity of ages upon its noble brow, untroubled by the passions and the strife of mankind, unchangeable guardian of its city of devoted worshipers, emblem of constancy and strength, yet fair as a maiden on her wedding morn, beautiful though grand, untroubled by the flight of time, a glorified pinnacle of light, it pierced the azure of the sky.

Although Mount Hood had come down to me through the long vista of years, from early childhood, together with that other sublime mountain, Adams, and was linked with it in memory's golden chain, strange to say, the opportunity to visit Oregon's premier peak was never presented to me until after I had said my last farewell to the more northerly giant. So it was not until an early August morning in the summer of 1922 that I, at last, turned my impatient feet toward its glittering spire to add it to my list of ice-kings. Whereas less than twoscore had gone up Adams before me, thousands had gone up Hood. A third of a century, lacking less than three months, had elapsed between my first ascent of one and my first ascent of the other. Yet my enthusiasm had not waned, and "eager-hearted as a boy"—as eager-hearted as the boy that had faced the sunrise on the Washington peak that memorable morning so long ago—I set my face to the Ethereal Mountain.

After breakfast in the beautiful little city of Hood River, I took the "gas car" on the railroad that runs up the valley and in due time arrived at Parkdale, the head of rail "navigation."

Man has few dwelling-places upon this earth more lovely than the Hood River Valley. It stretches along its glacial river, for twenty miles or so, a land of orchards, homes, and prosperity. It has not fully emerged from the dominion of primeval forest, but what remains of unspoiled nature only adds charm to its other attractions. Pretty villages nestle between groves of evergreen; productive fields spread their rich soil to the warming kiss of the sun; and the big red apples blush to the touch of the western winds.

Over all gleams the soul of the heavenly mountain.

Always the mountain. At the head of the valley it looms, in calm or in storm, dominant in quiet majesty, regal guardian of intruding mortals. Even when embattling cloud-hosts wrap about its form and hide its splendid outlines in vaporous mystery, the dwellers below feel its overpowering presence. For the Presence and the Soul are ever there.

But on the day of my journey up the valley, I could see little of it. The fleeting summer clouds drew their veils across its face, and permitted but a glimpse, now and then, of sparkling ice or frowning crag. The day was warm; but there was distant coolness in the intermittent flashes of the snow-fields.

From Parkdale there was no public conveyance to the mountain. I started on foot, my pack upon my back. But good fortune was in store for me. Through the kindness of fellow travelers, who had better means of transportation than my own, I arrived safely at Cloud Cap Inn before it was fairly dark.

Mrs. Schwartz, the charming hostess at the inn, had few guests at this time. So I had no trouble in securing a room for the night. After dinner, the few tourists present gathered around the big stone fireplace in the living-room and discussed mountains and mountain craft. Mr. Moody, the guide, had made the ascent that day with a party of two, a man and a woman. He told me that the north-side route was in about the worst condition he had ever seen. There was less snow than usual above Cooper Spur, and what there was was very hard and icy. There were also a number of troublesome crevasses, which added to the danger. Although there had been a considerable fall of fresh snow recently, this had about all melted away, leaving the old snow exposed and about as soft as so much granite. As this slope of the mountain is tremendously steep, the difficulties of the ascent, at once, became apparent to me. Since I intended to climb alone, I saw that I was in for an interesting time of it.

I borrowed Mr. Moody's alarm-clock and went to bed, intending to get away at four o'clock in the morning, before any one else at the inn was astir. But either the alarm did not go off, or I did not hear it. I was startled to see a little wisp of dawn creeping in through my window, and I knew that I had stayed in bed too long. I dressed quickly and stole out of the house; but it was already half-past four, and morning was feeling its gray way through the forest. With some dismay I saw that the sky was filled with clouds. I could not see the mountain.

There was a hint of dampness in the atmosphere. There was a grateful freshness in the smell of the evergreens. First came a walk along easy trails on forested hillsides. The parklands were reaching upward toward the eternal snows. Presently I came out of the timber to the crossing of a water-torn gully where the floods from melting snows had hurled the boulders about in confusion. Beyond this lay Cooper Spur, the great moraine-like ridge that pushes its nose far up between Eliot and Newton Clark Glaciers and aids so materially in the ascent of the north-side route.

At the place where I came on to the Spur, there are many picturesque groves of the stunted sub-Alpine evergreens, standing little higher than a man's head. It was now entirely daylight, and the weather prospect was not enticing. Broken clouds were drifting in all directions, and in many places the sky was heavily overcast. I did not believe a heavy storm was impending, yet the chances were that the sun would not come out sufficiently bright to soften the snow for safe climbing. I was inclined to the opinion that it would be the part of wisdom to camp in this altogether picturesque spot and wait for a better day. I decided to cook my breakfast, and to determine my future course on a full stomach.

There was plenty of dry wood and I soon had something to eat. Probably an hour was consumed in this operation. I decided to go on as far as possible, and to turn back if it became necessary. A sharp pull brought me well up on to the Spur. The trail was here well marked, for many feet had been there before mine. The clouds did not show any disposition to disperse as I went along the rapidly narrowing ridge. However, it did not look as though there would be either rain or snow—not even severe wind, for that matter; but it was surely destined to be a cool day.

From the sharp roof-like top of the Spur, now scarcely more than wide enough for the well-beaten trail, I could look down upon the crevassed and broken surfaces of Eliot and Newton Clark Glaciers. Little wisps of cloud came drifting up from the latter ice-field, floated over the crest, just in front of my face, in leisurely fashion, and drifted across the Eliot Glacier as though they were looking for some entertaining way in which to spend the day.

Looking backward I could not see the inn. There were clouds between me and it. The terrifically precipitous tower of the mountain seemed almost to lean over me, so near at hand it was. Surely, no man could hope, alone, to climb that frightful snow-slope and the cliffs beyond! From summit ridge to amphitheater of Eliot Glacier it looked to be an almost perpendicular drop. Scarcely less forbidding were the snow-fields and crags by which I must ascend.

By the time I got to the upper point of Cooper Spur, I saw that the sky was underlaid by a thick stratum of high clouds which had a look of permanency not auspicious for softening snow. As a matter of fact I did not wear my colored glasses at all during the day, nor did I use any preparation on my face, yet I suffered neither from snow-blindness nor sunburn.

Upon stepping from the last rocks on to the snow-field I immediately saw the ice-like character of the snow. Yet the first part was not steep. The crest of the swell between the side-slope to Eliot Glacier and the side-slope to Newton

Clark Glacier followed a concave line, gradually steepening as it approached the cliffs.

The tracks made by Mr. Moody and his party the previous day were still visible, and these I followed. The snow was rough, as old snow generally is in the summertime on a mountain-side, lying in humps and ridges and hollows. This roughness makes the climbing easier and safer on a steep slope and one can go up places that would be utterly impossible were the snow both hard and smooth. The lower clouds were now broken and more or less scattered, but the high layer—far above the summit—still held its place in the sky.

Presently the slope grew uncomfortably steep. Yet the old tracks which had been made in soft snow, furnished excellent steps in many places; but soon came a time when I must use my hands as well as my feet. As the angle of ascent became more acute, I was reminded of the story of the mule which I had heard at the inn the evening before. This animal, together with a horse, had been led far up the slope earlier in the season, when the snow was in better condition, during the preparations for the American Legion climb. At a particularly ticklish place the poor brute's halter broke; it slipped, lost its footing, and slid down the terrific slope. Gaining awful speed as it went, the body of the hapless creature swerved toward Eliot Glacier, plunged over the precipice, struck the ice-fields below, jumped one or more crevasses, and finally disappeared in a frozen chasm. Mercifully, of course, the mule was dead, long before it reached the end of its frightful slide.

The crevasses Mr. Moody had told me of cut straight across the face of the mountain, and I had to work around them on the left. The largest, he had referred to as the "big crevasse." It was not extremely large. I had seen many that were infinitely bigger; but it was not nearly so safely and pleasantly situated as had been a number of the giants, for I had to negotiate the very steepest part of the snow-slope immediately above it. If I should take a slide, it might catch me, and again it might not; but it would probably make little difference in my future status whether it caught me or let me go on to the depths of the glacier.

About the time I got beyond the end of the big crevasse, I began to notice a danger that I had never heard or read of in any account of ascents made on the north side of Mount Hood. The day was not warm enough to produce any perceptible softening in the snow, yet it was apparently warm enough to loosen a number of small rocks on the frozen cliffs above. These began to come hurtling down quite frequently in close proximity to my line of march. Fortunately there were no collisions, much to my relief, and probably to the chagrin of the rocks.

Such steep climbing produced results in the way of attaining altitude. It was not a great distance from the big crevasse to the first of the cliff-ridges leading to the summit. It was a decided relief to set foot on rocks again and to look back at the near-ice-precipice I had just come up and to wonder how I had done it. If it had given me a creepy feeling to look up the forbidding incline it surely gave me several creepy feelings to look down it.

But now for the top! Enough of retrospect. Sufficient unto the ascent is the evil thereof—let the descent take care of itself.

I soon found the end of one of the long ropes that are stretched each season from the summit to the lower end of the cliffs to aid climbers in getting up the rocks. At this particular time a rope would have been of far more benefit on the snow-slope I had just come up than on the crags; but, I understand, earlier in the season, just below the top there is a snow-cornice that would be extremely dangerous without some such safeguard. I could have done very well without the rope; but it was a great help and an aid to rapid progress, and I was not too proud to use it. In fact I found several ropes, which evidently had been stretched at different times. The rock-climbing on this part of the mountain reminded me considerably of some of that on Mount Stuart, except that here the formation is volcanic and not nearly so firm and dependable as the granite of the Washington peak. In places there were little patches of ice between the rocks, and these required some care. Occasionally both footholds and handholds had to be used in getting up especially abrupt points; but, on the whole, it was very interesting, and not too dangerous, climbing. From the standpoint of safety it was altogether preferable to the precarious snow-slope below.

I had no watch with me, and, consequently, no way of knowing the time. Under such conditions it always seems later than it really is. By the time I was well up along the rocks I thought it was considerably past noon, and there was no means of telling how far it still was to the summit. The climb up the snow-slope had appeared interminably long.

But suddenly I heard a hail from above. Looking up I saw a man standing on a square tower of rock slightly to my right.

"How far am I from the top?" I called.

"Only about three hundred feet," was the answer.

"What time is it?" was my next question.

"Eleven o'clock."

"I'll be up by noon!" cried I.

"Yes, you'll be up in half an hour," he replied.

I was up in twenty minutes!

The climbing of Hood is surprisingly short, after such monsters as Adams, Rainier, and Shasta. But there is never a dull moment from start to finish, and, on the north side, at least, not an instant when it is advisable for the climber to relax his vigilance.

I was now on the summit—a long, narrow, irregular, gravel-covered backbone, breaking off terribly steep on the south, but frightfully steep on the north. Looking to the west, I saw, at a short distance, the United States Forest Service's fire lookout station, a replica of the one on Mount Adams, lofty watchtower of Uncle Sam's wooded domains, 11,225 feet above the sea. Making my way thither, I found there five other human beings. Two were Eastern tourists—one a scientist who writes F.R.G.S. after his name, the other, his companion, a boy of thirteen years who had already made twelve major ascents in the Canadian Rockies that season. They were in charge of Clem E. Blakney, the southside guide. Mrs. Blakney, who makes many climbs with her husband, was also a member of the little party. The other man present was a summer denizen of this lofty abode. He was Charles A. Phelps, the lookout.

There is always a cordiality in the greetings of mountaineers who meet at great heights. I was soon engaged in pleasant conversation with my new friends. Mr. and Mrs. Blakney were soon to start on a hike to Mount Adams in an effort to win the Mazama's badge bestowed only upon those who have made the ascent of all three of the "Guardians of the Columbia," Hood, Adams, and Saint Helens.

Shortly after my arrival, the south-side party started on its return down the mountain. I accompanied the four climbers westward along the summit ridge, and watched them start their descent of the steep snow-slope, sliding rapidly down along the great rope that was anchored securely to the rocks and stretched as far as I could see toward the lower levels. Far below, near Crater Rock, big jets of steam were rising into the air and drifting upward to mingle with the fleecy clouds that were idling across the face of the peak.

I now had a chance to form an impression of the terrifying grandeur of the north side of Mount Hood. Breaking squarely off, the slope drops in one almost perpendicular sweep to the floor of Eliot Glacier, thousands of feet below. Fascinating as is this awful precipice, one can scarcely look over it for the first time without the hair rising on his head and the cold shivers running over his body. Strong men have gone into hysterics at the sight, it is said, and I doubt if one lives who could gaze at it unmoved. One step from the firm surface of the top would hurl a person down this desperate incline, unable to stop until he had plunged, a shapeless mass, into the maw of the glacier. Although so terrible and forbidding when close at hand, this imposing spectacle when seen from the Hood River Valley, or other distant points, blends into the symmetrical beauty and æsthetic charm of the Ethereal Mountain.

As I looked down this tremendous declivity I recalled to mind the man in Hood River who, the morning before, told me he had slid down the same slope on skis, after having practically carried a woman of national reputation to the summit of the peak. I decided to place this man in the same category with the old-timer who had seen Lake Chelan when it was only a hole in the ground and the old prospector who could have gone from the timber-line to the top of Mount Baker in ten minutes on his snowshoes.

The inspiring distant view from the summit was cut off by clouds. Through interstices in the vapory masses I caught detached glimpses of shadowed earth-stretches, dark, mysterious, and unrecognizable, fragments only of the tremendous empire that lay within the sweep of the mountain's vision.

About the peak itself, a master cloud-drama was in progress. There was an alternate massing and dispersal of the fleecy hosts; first a collecting and then a scattering as though the weather was undecided whether to clear or to produce a storm. The mist-sea was limitless, and its billows rolled away to infinite cloud-horizons. There was a heaving and a swelling motion, far and near, as the unstable ocean rose and fell with the vagaries of a changing atmosphere.

There had been a violent storm but a few days before and traces of it still remained. On the side of the lookout house were some of the white, armadillo ice-scales that we had seen on the frame of the Mount Adams lookout station after the big storm the previous year. But now the crest of the summit ridge was completely bare of snow, although there was plenty of the cold white substance on the slopes near by.

Mr. Phelps and I were now left alone on top of the lofty peak. He invited me to have dinner with him, and, as my appetite had remained stable on this trip, I gladly accepted his hospitality. I ate of the well-prepared meal with relish, and, considering the difficulty of transporting provisions to this high home—everything had to be carried up on some one's back—I was surprised at the variety and excellence of the fare. Some of the delicacies prepared by Mrs. Phelps for the use of her absent husband during his lonely vigil, were especially gratifying to one with mountain hunger. He told me he had more than enough food on hand to last him the balance of the season.

As we ate, Mr. Phelps told me of his life while watching for far away fires from his eyrie above the clouds. He detailed, in interesting way, some of his experiences in the great storms that occasionally swept the mountain. His was a lonely life, but full of adventure and seldom dull. He said that he had seen me through his telescope when I first stepped upon the snow at the end of Cooper Spur that morning, so he had known that a solitary traveler was on his way toward the top. I was the second man that had come up the north side alone that summer. Seldom have I enjoyed a visit more than I did this one with him. All too soon did an hour slip away and the time come when I must think of getting down.

The little lookout station was snug and homelike. It did not look to me to be a bad place to live, for one who could endure the loneliness. In fact Mr. Phelps had many visitors, for Mount Hood is probably the most frequently climbed *snowpeak* in the United States. Nevertheless, I could not help remarking upon the possibility of a tragedy. Although the small building was lashed down with great, steel cables securely fastened to the rocks, it seemed to me that if a gale should catch it from a certain angle it might be torn from its moorings. One could do much speculating upon what might happen to a house suddenly hurled out into space over the brink of that terrible precipice.

At ten minutes past one, I decided it was time to trust my fate once more to the treachery of the northern slope. The clouds still clung around the mountain and there was no hope that the snow had softened. I thought seriously of the wisdom of going down the south side; but I had left most of my personal effects at Hood River, and I could not afford the delay incident to a separation from them.

Mr. Phelps regarded the situation fully as gravely as I did. He said that he would watch for me to emerge upon the more gradual snow-slopes above Cooper Spur, as the most critical part of the descent would be hidden from him by the very abruptness of the mountain that made it difficult for me. If I did not appear upon the lower snow within a reasonable time, he would telephone down to the south base of the peak, from where the message would speed on to Portland, then up the Columbia River, then up the

Hood River Valley and the long wooded foothills to its final destination at Cloud Cap Inn almost within shouting distance of its starting-point. Whereupon a rescue party could be organized at the inn to go out and find what little might be left of me.

And if this rather undesirable contingency should occur, there would be presented the somewhat incongruous spectacle of the faithful lookout's flashing a message in almost a complete rough circle, over a hundred and fifty miles or so of forest, valley, hill, and river, to some people only three or four miles away to inform them of the fact that a man had slid off of a mountain almost into their back yard.

I had been on the summit an hour and forty minutes—one of the most pleasant and interesting periods I had ever spent on a peak—when at last I waved good-bye to Mr. Phelps and dropped over the edge. I was going to trust my fortunes again to the north-side route.

It is usual to refer to it as the north-side route, although this is really a misnomer. The line of ascent from Cooper Spur up the bulge between Eliot and Newton Clark Glaciers is more nearly on the east side of the mountain. Since the approach to the peak for this ascent is generally made from the north, I presume it thus came to be designated as the north-side route. On most of our great Western snow-peaks the south slopes are the most gradual and easy to climb. This condition, no doubt, is owing to the fact that the sun exerts most influence on the southern exposures and erosion works there more effectively. The eastern faces are usually terribly precipitous.

I dropped rapidly down along the ropes. The rocks gave me little trouble. Although I was sure no one was below me I took care not to start any loose stones. I paused now and then to study the picturesque volcanic cliffs north of my route and to note the stern menace of the terrible slope.

Far below the Eliot Glacier spread like a great white map, its corrugated surface gleaming brightly in the half-light until lost in its distant terminal moraines in the edge of the primal forest. From my craggy height the floor of the vast ice-field looked to be almost level, although I knew it to have a steep slope toward the foothills. Feathery clouds were hanging low above the frozen cataract.

Cloud Cap Inn was hidden by the mists.

All too soon I came to the end of the longest rope. I now realized to the full the seriousness of my situation.

There had been but little softening of the snow during the day. What was worse, it was now beginning to harden again. A chilly little breeze was blowing, and, so close that I could almost touch it, a cloud was drifting across the face of the mountain.

Getting the best grip possible upon my nerves, I left the last protecting point of rock, and stepped out on to the icy snow. It seemed hardly possible for a man to work his way unaided down that frightful steep. I had but one ally to help me in my battle with the cruel slope. This was my Swiss ice-axe. After doing valiant service on Adams, Stuart, and Shasta, it had been presented to me by the Cascadians, with inscription engraved on a silver plate, in token of my having been first president of the club. To-day it was to prove its life-saving value.

Although I moved so slowly—for I had to test each foothold ere I trusted my weight to it, and had frequently to reach down and cut steps below me—I was soon a long way from the rocks and upward retreat was cut off by the ice-snow above. I had carefully analyzed my chances in case of accident. The big crevasse was directly below me, yet I did not reckon it as a serious factor. In the event of an unchecked slide I should probably shoot across it as though it were not there. If such a thing should happen, the contour of the mountain would undoubtedly urge me toward Eliot Glacier and I should be hurled over its bordering precipice on to the jagged ice-field, like the poor mule of which I had been told. I realized that if I once lost my footing, I must stop myself within a short distance, for a man sliding over that rough, hard snow, with speed accelerating at every yard, would soon be unconscious or so nearly so as to be absolutely helpless, and gravity would then work its will with him unhindered, bearing him down, down, down, a broken and senseless mass, to the depths of the unfeeling glacier. I must use several ounces of prevention, for there would be no pound of cure.

True, I knew, hundreds, in the past, had glissaded hilariously down this slope, in happy security; but that was when the snow was soft and safe and friendly. On this day it was hard, and as cruel as hell itself, and no man could make that slide and live to tell the tale. Only those who have seen a great snow-slope in good and in bad conditions can know the terrible difference.

As has already been said, there had been a fresh fall of snow on the mountain a short time before. This had nearly all melted away from the slope. However, patches of it still lay in crusty, white sheets, an inch or two thick, in the depressions of the dark, hard, older snow. I found that by stepping on to this new snow I could get a better footing, as my hobnailed shoes sank easily through the thin crust which had enough resistance to retard considerably any tendency to slip. I began to seek out these white patches, working from one to another over the ridges of icy snow. I had almost come to believe that my troubles were over, when, without warning, a sheet on which I was standing started to slide with me. I jabbed the point of my ice-axe down hard into the old snow beneath and succeeded in getting a firm enough hold to keep from going too. I now saw that the new snow was unreliable; I must continue to trust myself to the old—that, at least, would not slide.

So I kept away from the white patches whenever possible; but they continued occasionally to start, sometimes at the touch of my axe, sometimes for no apparent cause. They went slithering down the mountain with an ominous grating sound not at all pacifying to the nerves. My progress was terribly slow. I began to fear I should never get down —or should get down all too quickly. And yet when I ventured to look backwards the rocks I had left seemed a long way above me.

And then it happened.

In spite of all my precautions, my feet suddenly shot from under me. I started on a lightning-like descent toward the lower regions of the mountain, gaining speed as I went, my body bumping over the icy protuberances of the snow. The supreme moment of my mountaineering career was at hand.

But my mind was working clearly and rapidly. I was under no illusions as to what I was up against. I instantly realized that something must be done immediately.

And nobody was there to do it but myself!

I had started on my back, thus presenting my broadest possible sliding surface to the pitiless snow and preventing effective use of my arms. Fortunately, I still retained my hold upon my ice-axe. I turned quickly upon my left side. Grasping the handle of the axe near the middle, with both hands, I brought the point hard down into the snow. My momentum tore the steel tip from its shallow hold, and I shot on unchecked.

It was now or never. I knew that my life hung by seconds. Another minute would be too late. Every foot of flight was adding to my speed. Mustering my last available ounce of strength, I deliberately poised the axe and again thrust the point straight down into the snow. With a thrill I felt the steel penetrate, strain, and hold. With a desperate grasp upon the slender pole, I shot on downward the length of my arms, and lay sprawling, while my feet sought vainly for a niche upon the mountain-side. Fearing the axe might still give way, I kicked with my heels until I was sure I had worked them into the icy surface enough that I might venture to rise. I cautiously and slowly worked my way up on to my feet and stood leaning on the ice-axe, gasping for breath.

It was minutes before my strength came back to me. Looking down the mountain-side, I was surprised to see, far below, my heavy cap, on edge like a hoop, rolling with terrific speed, bounding from point to point of the uneven snow, flying like a thing of life to escape the dangers of that awful slope. For five hundred feet or so it went, with undiminished rapidity, toward Newton Clark Glacier, and then it apparently stopped in one of the depressions in the snow, for I could see it no more. I marked with my eye the place where I thought it would be, in the hope that I might find it when I got that far down.

Then I had leisure to look back to see how far I had come. My track was white and visible, for I had scraped off the dirty surface of the snow. I had slid about fifty feet.

My involuntary descent had undoubtedly taken me over the very worst stretch of the slope; but there was danger enough ahead. I could be no more careful than I had been, and Cooper Spur was still a long way off. But there were no more accidents for me that day. I got safely by the end of the big crevasse. From there on it was not so bad, although still bad enough.

By the time I had come opposite the place where I thought my cap should be, the slope, although still a steep slope,

MOUNT HOOD, ELIOT GLACIER, AND CLOUD CAP INN
FROM THE NORTHEAST

MOUNT HOOD FROM COE GLACIER

MOUNT SHASTA IN HIS SUMMER ROBES AS SEEN THROUGH SMOKY ATMOSPHERE

had diminished so much that it was no longer dangerous. I made a straight traverse in the hope of finding my lost headgear. I could see an object I took to be the missing article, but when I came near to it, it proved to be only a brown rock partly embedded in the snow. I searched for quite a while with no result, and finally turned reluctantly away.

I gave up the cap with deep regret, for I had worn it on many a mountain day. On the far-flung snow-deserts of McKinley; on the ice-swept crags of Adams; on the granite buttresses of Stuart; and on the lava wastes of Shasta I had worn it; and now it was to have its final resting place upon the névé of one of the glaciers of the Ethereal Mountain, a stray relic of the heights like the hat that had been flung into space by that memorable gale thirty-one years before.

Thereafter I made more rapid progress down the slope. I had forgotten everything but my own perplexities and the dawning assurance that I was going to come safely out of it, after all, when I heard a faint halloo dropping from the sky. Then I knew that Phelps had seen me and knew that I was safe. Perhaps he little dreamed how nearly he had come to seeing only a black speck flying downward over the snow with meteor speed toward the mule-filled crevasse on Eliot Glacier.

It was with infinite relief that I finally stepped upon the friendly, dependable rocks of Cooper Spur. The descent from the summit to this point had taken me longer than the ascent. But from here to Cloud Cap Inn was only a pleasant ramble. It was six o'clock when I reached the picturesque log tavern to find them somewhat worried about me. The mountain had been hidden by clouds the entire day and they realized the conditions that were prevailing upon its slopes.

All of Mrs. Schwartz's guests had departed and I was the only non-resident of the inn to sit down to dinner that evening. I went to bed in the same room I had occupied the night before, planning to start at daylight to make the trip afoot down through the forests in order to catch the afternoon train at Parkdale.

When I arose the sweet aroma of dew-kissed woods was in the air. Not a cloud was in the sky. The mountain stood out clear and cold in the glorious freshness of the morning. Gradually its crown turned to gold under the magic alchemy of the dawn. Emblem of purity, big with the supreme dignity of the ages, above all littleness of earth as God is above the littleness of man, this regal pile rose high to the dome of fading stars. Heavenly guardian of the Columbia and its busy shores, it loomed to greet its fellow Titans.

Let the reader take a map of Oregon and Washington and draw a line from the crest of Hood to the crest of Rainier; then draw another line from the crown of Adams to the crown of Saint Helens. The result will be a great cross with a splendid mountain-gem at either tip. On this perfect morning each of these wondrous peaks gleamed white in the growing day. I thrilled to the inspiration of their glory, and knew that there had been granted to me the joy of great heights in fullest measure.

As I turned for a farewell glance at the Ethereal Mountain, there was an unexpressed prayer in my heart that in some way its lovers might save its soul-charm from the fate of poor, old commercialized Rainier; that its heavenly majesty might never be coined into dollars and cents; and that it might be handed down as a blessed heritage, to future generations, in its primal purity.

XV

UNDER THE SHASTAN MOON

I FIRST saw Shasta under the crescent moon. Misty and mysterious it shone through the soft mellow light, just before dawn; as my train wound through the foothills at its base.

After the traveler, going south, has passed the green folds of the Siskiyous, he comes into a broad prairie-valley of fertile farmlands, dotted here and there with little buttes like gray bubbles on a glacial pool. This open country, which comes as a surprise after so much woodland, evidently is the disintegration of a great lava-flow from the old volcano. At the head of this broad gray expanse, looming above high swells of timbered ridges, gleams Shasta, the majestic, mightiest of California snow-clads.

Its glory has been the theme of writers whose names are writ large in the classic literature of the world. And now, I, humble but persistent mountaineer, was going to see this noble peak, made rich in historical interest by the explorations of John Muir, Clarence King, Joaquin Miller, and others who now dwell among the immortals.

But I had not seen it up the long daylight vista, as the train wound through the open valley, growing ever bigger and grander as we approached. It came to me suddenly out of the silver night, with the crescent moon hanging above its glorious crown.

In the cool dawn I left the train at Sisson. Here I must wait for many hours until an afternoon train from the south brought my old Cascadian friends, Mr. and Mrs. W. E. Richardson, Clarence Truitt, and Rolfe Whitnall. They had been to San Francisco to attend the great Masonic convention that had been held by the Golden Gate in June of 1922. From the little town, Shasta looms mightily, its broad summit overtopping the hamlet by nearly eleven thousand feet. Yet, at first, one does not get a true impression of its bigness, and it is apt to prove disappointing. But it grows, hour by hour, as the observer comes to comprehend in detail the immensity of each feature, and, if he should live long enough and intimately enough in its environs, he might eventually grow to an appreciation of its sublime dignity.

Shasta is not so snowy as the big peaks of northern Oregon and Washington, although it bears several considerable glaciers and has great areas covered by perpetual snow. Reference has heretofore been made to the snow-line in southern California and Colorado as compared with that in our more northerly latitudes. But there appears to be no such thing as an actual "snow-line" in southern California and Colorado; such snow as is found on the peaks there lying only in large patches or small detached fields. A definite snow-line in these regions would fall quite a bit higher than the summits of the highest pinnacles. Shasta, however, comes nearer the northern mountains in this respect, and I believe we may consistently speak of its "snow-line" as being between eight and nine thousand feet.

Looking toward the mountain from Sisson one sees a long green slope, bare of trees, leading up toward the rougher parts of the mountain. From a great area here, as upon other parts of the foothills, the timber has all been logged off. From a distance these slopes look to be covered with green grass; but a closer inspection shows the growth to be dense chaparral of scrub-oak, manzanita, mountain balm, buck-brush, and so forth, making a thicket that is almost impenetrable.

From Sisson to the summit of Shasta it is eleven and a

quarter miles. To Horse Camp, at an elevation of eight thousand feet, from which point the ascent is generally made, it is eight miles. Sisson lies at an altitude of 3550 feet, while the highest point on Shasta is given at from 14,162 feet to 14,380 feet. This rise of nearly eleven thousand feet in eleven miles, of which the last six thousand is very abrupt, presents one of the most imposing mountain faces in the world.

There is a road, through the brush thickets, extending from Sisson about three miles toward the mountain. Its surface is the natural gravel, as Nature made it, and the grade is quite stiff. From the end of this road the United States Forest Service has constructed an excellent trail to Horse Camp; leading first up a broad canyon, then up great ridges, covered with primeval evergreen forest, to timber-line. From the town the great, valley-like depression in the side of the mountain, leading from far below tree-line up to Thumb Rock, can be plainly seen. This mighty hollow, filled in past ages, no doubt, by a tremendous glacier, is usually followed by those making the ascent from the Sisson side.

I put in a rather monotonous day waiting for the afternoon train to bring my friends from the south. Several of the local residents to whom I told our plan to climb the mountain said it was an unheard-of thing to attempt the ascent so early in the season. A number of special trains sped through, bearing loads of gayly decked Masons, before I saw alight the four I was interested in. We immediately prepared for a four-dollar advance toward snow-line by means of a hired automobile. As we were gathering our effects to load into the machine, we were comforted by hearing an occasional side remark, passed in low-toned voice, between solicitous residents of the town, which sounded suspiciously like: "Bunch of d——d fools!"

It was well past four o'clock when, after much boiling and sputtering over the steep climb, the automobile set us down at the end of the road, and we had the remnant of the day in which to make the remaining five miles to Horse Camp. We had neither beds nor sleeping-bags, for we were going light, carrying only the food necessary for a two days' stay.

The afternoon was warm and there was little shade in the canyon where the logs had been cut off years before. When we began to climb the ridge it was cooler but steeper. We came into big timber where the woodland fragrance was a delight to the nostrils. There were sign-boards every mile; but they seemed to be three miles apart. There was no water by the wayside, for the wooded slopes of Shasta, on this side, at least, are in summer as dry as a powder house. The supply in our canteens was exhausted long before there was a prospect of finding more. We had much elevation to make, and it began to look as though night would catch us far beow Horse Camp. And there would be no moon until nearly dawn. So we hurried as best we could; but the altitude began to manifest itself in our shortening breath. At last occasional snow-banks began to appear in the deep shadows of the great trees. This was encouraging, for we knew we were getting up in the world when we came to snow in California in the latter half of June.

Hillslope after hillslope was left behind. Finally in the deepening twilight we came out on to an open hillside up which the trail went at an easy grade. Presently this led us on to a plateau, with the great solemn Shasta firs standing about in all the dignity of forest nobility. We crunched through shallow snow and came to a big log beneath a giant tree.

It was dark. While the others gathered dead wood to start a fire, I went farther to reconnoiter. In about a hundred yards I came to a white board nailed high upon a tree-trunk. Dimly I made out its message to the weary traveler. "Horse Camp," it said, and I knew that we could here pass the night with clear conscience.

We were completely surrounded by snow. Some of this we melted. We cooked our supper by the light of our vigorous fire. Then we put on all our extra clothing, assumed graceful recumbency by the side of our blazing log, and fondly expected to sleep. But sleep does not come readily to one, without blankets, surrounded by snow, at an elevation of eight thousand feet. Perhaps we slept oftener than we should have done in comfortable beds; but not so continuously. Once Mrs. Richardson's balloon-silk parka caught fire from too close an association with glowing embers, and excitement was dominant for a few moments until the blaze was extinguished and a competent alpinette saved for future snowy conquests.

It was not hard to get up at one o'clock that morning. The frosty air lent zest to our activity, and we were ready to start at half-past two. The crescent moon came timidly up over one of the great lava ridges of the mountain. We got away in the weird, uncertain light, and, with past experience as our only guide, followed a route with which we were unfamiliar.

The cold dawn found us traversing snow-covered moraines; the full light of early morning upon steepening slopes; and the strong tide of mature forenoon ready for the long hard pull to Thumb Rock.

As we went up the great depression, I was surprised to see that here the climber was not always safe from bounding stones, for I had never heard that rolling rocks were a Shastan menace; but even as I had found this danger unexpectedly on Hood, I now saw that it was, at times, present on the California peak. As a matter of fact, I have climbed upon but two mountain routes—that upon the south side of Adams and ours on Glacier Peak—where this peril was not apparent.

As the great depression bends upward to its ending at Thumb Rock the slopes become terribly steep. A heart-shaped island of volcanic gravel and boulders divides the snow-field below the great rock, and this I shall henceforth refer to as the "Heart." One can climb the Heart; but its surface is so soft and yielding that it is too toilsome and fatiguing for practicable work. Most climbers follow the branch of the snow-field lying on the right side of the Heart, although some prefer to swing on to the great lava ridge. The immense ridges on each side of the depression are broken by many sharp spires and are covered with rough boulders that make the ascent along either very difficult.

From Thumb Rock a double line of low red cliffs leads directly across the face of the mountain. On the left of these cliffs a snow-slope leads up to the summit plateau; but it is too steep to be available for climbing purposes. Consequently all who make the ascent by the ordinary route must pass the red barrier. It is the one real difficulty in the Shasta climb.

On the 17th of June the snow was in very good condition, although it was so hard on some of the steeper pitches that we found it advisable to take to the rocks. We found the final pull to Thumb Rock unexpectedly long and tedious and it sapped our strength woefully. When I finally reached the red cliffs, I had little trouble in getting up the lower row; but the upper row was different. Between the two lines is a narrow, sloping shelf. The rocky surface of this was partly covered with snow; but in places water was running over it, and occasional patches of ice had formed. Both lines of cliffs are rapidly disintegrating. The second line is somewhat higher than the first; both are cut by short gullies or chimneys.

The gullies in the upper cliffs were partly filled with snow; but in each one there was left a rim of almost sheer unstable rock which would have been dangerous to attempt without a rope. Had these depressions been filled to the top with good snow, it would have been comparatively easy to go up, even though it might have been necessary to cut a few steps.

Turning to the right, I followed the shelf to the end of the barrier. Here I found the ends of the red cliffs—as well as Thumb Rock—overhanging the great cirque of McCloud Glacier. The vast, bowl-like amphitheater was filled with a big field of snow which extended up to and leaned against the points of the barrier-cliffs. Although the snow reached, in a sort of cornice, clear to the top of the barrier, I knew there was sure to be a wide chasm beneath, between the rock and the snow; and, since the rock was overhanging, the cavity was certain to be broader and far more treacherous than would have been the case had the snow met a perpendicular or slightly sloping face of rock.

Carefully testing the snow with my ice-axe, and cutting steps as I went, I was soon on top of the sloping barrier-plateau, calling to those below the route to follow. When all were up, it was time to think of lunch. This we ate in discomfort, with a raw wind sweeping us from the west. Leaving part of our things, we started on for the summit.

Shasta is an enormous mountain. The culminating region is a tremendous ridge, from which radiate several other ridges scarcely inferior in size. After we had topped the barrier, we had comparatively good traveling, mostly along ridgy slopes, with occasionally a steeper pull; now in rather soft snow, now on gravel stretches. Far to the south we could see Mount Lassen; but Lassen was on its good behavior and had evidently suspended, for the time being, its bad habit of smoking. I have always thought that this mountain, after passing a sedate and blameless existence for generations, finally became jealous of the adulation bestowed upon its great neighbor, Shasta, and decided to do something desperately sensational to attract attention to itself. It succeeded, even to the extent of having itself included in a National Park, while its greater rival languishes without the favor of Federal appropriations. Perhaps, in ages past, it was Shasta that taught Lassen to smoke and to indulge in wild revelries; but, now, Shasta, grown old and with fiery ardor cooled, must watch in sullen silence while its gay young pupil invokes the gossip of the world with startling pranks.

Finally we reached a point of rocks, and, looking a quarter of a mile or so, across a level field of snow, saw, with consternation, a rugged, upstanding line of cliffs—the culminating pinnacle of Shasta.

The thing that gave us most concern was the fact that these crags were sheeted with ice and we had no rope. We knew that under favorable conditions they were easily scaled—but no one had tried it so early in the season before; consequently we were the first to know the difficulty that was apt to confront the climber here in June.

We hurried across the field of frozen snow, and, as we went, the wind, which had attained the velocity of a near-gale, smote us mightily, chilling our ardor and making us long for lowland comforts. When we got to the foot of the cliffs we saw a danger we had failed to anticipate.

The wind was striking the face of the rocks with great force. The ice clung in thick sheets to the upper part of the pinnacle. Every few seconds a big white slab would be torn loose, to hurtle through the air and fall with a crash on the snow-covered boulders below. It took but a glance

GREAT RIDGE LEADING TOWARD THE SUMMIT OF SHASTA, FROM THE TOP OF THE RED BARRIER

Névé of McCloud Glacier at right

A LONE ALPINETTE NEAR THE SUMMIT OF SHASTA

The ice-sheeted pinnacle to the left is the extreme summit

to show that a person approaching too closely was in constant peril of being struck by one of these cleavers—and to be struck by one meant loss of further interest in the things of this world.

So the last hundred feet of Shasta was not for us that day. Up to this point the early season had presented no unusual difficulties, and but for the icy menace of the upper crags we should have succeeded. But the wise mountaineer knows when to turn back. I made reconnoissance along the talus slope at the base of the cliffs and saw that the ice-sheet apparently extended clear around.

Therefore, not wishing to justify the opinion that had been expressed about us at Sisson, and as it was already three o'clock, we went back the way we had come.

When we got below the red barrier, we took the opposite side of the Heart from the one we had gone up. The snow was soft and smooth. We slid, slid, slid; and so came down rapidly and effectively, albeit somewhat wetly.

I had made sixty-two-sixty-thirds of the ascent of Mount Shasta; but that last one hundred feet would not down. It haunted me and called me back to complete what I had left unfinished. So as the summer of 1923 approached, I knew that it could not pass without my making another attempt.

But in the mean time I had acquired a handicap. It was brought home to me forcibly in the following way: In the spring I unexpectedly met C. E. Forsyth—who had once held the rope with me on Mount Rainier—whom I had not seen for years. Now, Forsyth, having remained *in status quo* so far as avoirdupois was concerned, had the same difficulty—and for the same reason—in recognizing me that I had found in recognizing Cantwell when we met on the boat twelve years subsequent to our ascent of Mount Baker. After Forsyth had penetrated my disguise, he reminded me of the days when I was young and slim—the days of Adams, of Baker, of Rainier—days that were gone forever. My meeting with him was a great surprise to me for several reasons. One of these was the fact, now learned for the first time, that we were both residents of the same county; another was that I had heard years before that he was dead. After talking with him for a while I decided that the report of his death—like that of Mark Twain's death—was greatly exaggerated.

But, fat or lean, I was going back to Mount Shasta. The only difference would be that I should climb alone and so take plenty of time. And I planned to make a large part of the ascent by moonlight.

Thus it came about that on the night of July 27th a Southern Pacific train bore me through the Siskiyous in a flood of silver moonbeams, with long vistas, half seen through mellow light, fading away into mysterious distances.

Sisson was still asleep when I alighted on the depot platform in the early morning. I did not disturb it.

It was four-thirty when I stole quietly out of the slumbering town, seen only by an early-rising resident who was putting his cow out to grass. I was glad of the cool hours in which to traverse the long stretch of dry road through the chaparral, where the old forest had been stripped away, leaving but a few small pines, firs, and cedars of all that once lordly company. The moon was still in the sky; but presently it set directly over Eddy Mountain on the western side of the valley, while the great shadow of Shasta crept across the intervening lowlands. I was well up into the broad canyon when I ate my breakfast at seven o'clock, and the first rays of the sun struck me at about the same time.

Ever mindful of my handicap I took it slowly, for I had my sleeping-bag, as well as several days' provisions and my cooking-kit upon my back. The day grew warm and I was grateful for the deep shade cast by the great trees after I had climbed the switch-back trail from the bare canyon on to the airier ridges. I rested frequently, for I had the entire day to do it in, and there was not the necessity for haste that we had found the previous year when we had only a piece of an afternoon in which to do this same work.

While resting at an elevation of about six thousand feet, I heard the whirr of an aeroplane. I soon located the machine, high in the air, traveling south. It passed directly between me and the mountain with the glint of the sun upon its shining wings and body. It was far above me; but, of course, a great distance below the summit of the peak. Here was a forcible illustration of the change that had come about in the thirty-four years I had been mountain-climbing. When I first began the splendid sport, even the automobile was unknown, and only a few dreamers thought that man would ever fly. But now the sight of man-made wings soaring athwart the sky was so common as scarcely to call for passing notice. I myself had known the thrills of aerial flight.

As I was toiling up the hillside just below Horse Camp, two young men passed me on their way to climb the mountain. It was half-past two when I arrived.

What a change there had been since the year before! Instead of a wilderness camp-ground here was now the Sierra Club's Alpine Lodge, built from the native stone, with a great fireplace in one end, comfort apparent in every detail. In place of snow to melt for water, there were pipes with faucets from which to draw the cool liquid from a spring above. It was a true mountain home to which the weary climber was welcome at all times. And there was a host, to extend the hospitality of the Club to all who might come that way, in the person of J. M. Olberman of Sisson, caretaker of the lodge. I found Mr. Olberman to be not only a man of genial hospitality, but, also, something of an easy-mark, for, before the afternoon was over, I had inveigled him into doing the cooking and letting me eat with him.

The great mountain now so close at hand had a familiar look; but I could see there was much less snow on the lower part than there had been in June of the year before.

I slept in the shade for two or three hours during the afternoon. A pack-train had come up with the effects of a party of fourteen men and women who were intending to make the ascent next day. This had been an off day for climbers. Only one party was on the mountain. This was made up of W. L. Richardson, of Porterville, California, his two sons, Hilton, aged seventeen, and Billy, aged eleven, and his daughter Helen, aged nine. The father and the older boy made the entire climb successfully; but Billy and Helen went only as far as Thumb Rock. Here they pluckily remained alone until their father and brother returned from the summit.

The day waned in silence. The sun dropped toward the western sky-line with the promise of a perfect morrow. The warm balm of summer was in the air, the redolence of the primeval forest pervaded the vast solitude, and the mighty forces of nature seemed at rest. There was nothing to give portent of the things that were at hand.

As the solemn shades of night fell upon the great peak, a special train passed along the valley at its base bearing a doomed President. On this peaceful evening, Warren G. Harding was completing his last journey on earth. Unmindful of the tremendous scenes so near to him, he was being borne toward the city by the Golden Gate and to his final sleep, while History held her breath. In its calm majesty the mountain gave no sign. Time with his keen sickle swept onward in his changeless course, bearing upon the pinions of the fleeting hours the inscrutable mystery of human life. Could I have pierced the future's veil a few short weeks, I should have known that even then my own father's soul was preparing to wing its flight into the star-set depths of the Great Unknown.

The glorious moon rose in full radiance. A wonderful night it was, filled with the sublime beauty of God's age-long purpose. As the silvery glow flooded the dark forests and the white snow-fields above, the ineffable splendor of the heights was subdued from the brilliance of day to the gentle peace that comes with the hours of repose.

Just after dark nine young men arrived at the lodge from Sisson. They were intent upon a night-ascent of the mountain. I could not see the wisdom of such a plan, even though there would be moonlight the entire night, for I could see that they would reach the worst part of the climb long before daylight. But, of course, my advice was not asked, and I had no inclination to "butt in."

I spread out my sleeping-bag near Mr. Olberman's tent and went to bed at eight o'clock, intending to start at midnight. The two young men who had passed me just before reaching the lodge also planned to start at the same time, while the party of men and women who had come up with the pack-train expected to get away at one o'clock.

At half-past eleven I crawled from my sleeping-bag, having secured a few snatches of sleep. I ate nothing before starting, and a quarter of an hour before midnight was away. There was a tang of mountain snows in the air. The brilliant full moon swung in mid-sky. It was a silvery night and the great mountain loomed dimly and mysteriously through the weird light.

The knowledge of the mountain gained on my former ascent was now of great value to me. I had a good idea of the route I wished to take. After leaving the grassy slopes I came to the long moraines. Where we had traveled over firm snow the year before, I now found I must go over bare rocks, which made a rather tedious time of it. However, this tedium was greatly relieved by a contemplation of the weird beauty of the mysterious surroundings. It was intensely still, and the air was charged with the glow of moonbeams, while in the distance dimly loomed the mighty shape that I knew was one of earth's regal mountains. Slowly I passed up the great valley, the silence broken only by the ring of my ice-axe on the rocks.

The two young men had started a few minutes after I did. I could hear them as they climbed a sharp ascent on the opposite side of a deep gully, their voices coming in subdued tones and their hobnailed shoes clanging sharply upon the stony ground. I made no attempt to keep up with them, but silently let them pass on, as was their right by virtue of their youth and good physical condition, while I with my handicap was content to grind out the long hours, mathematically certain of ultimate success.

Upon the long moraines I found but occasional patches of snow. I kept a general direction up the great depression following the lines of least resistance. Never before had I taken a mountain so slowly, for never before had I been in such poor condition for climbing. I knew the immensity of Shasta and that I had before me one of the longest climbs in the United States. Probably a man who had been up against hard grinds less frequently than I might have over-done himself in the beginning and thus have thrown away his chance of success.

When I had been going an hour or more, I heard voices floating down through the eerie night, coming from some place in the mysterious distance, and then the ring of alpenstocks upon the rocks. Presently two ghostly forms appeared dimly in the moonlight. These soon resolved themselves into human beings, who proved, upon being hailed, to be two of the nine young men that had started up early in the evening. They were returning defeated at the very hour they should have been making their start upon the ascent.

At short intervals, two brilliant meteors flashed across the sky and disappeared behind the great black lava ridge that formed the wall of the depression on my right. Near at hand it was almost as light as day; but the light faded with distance; things not far away were but dimly seen, and there was the mystic charm of going into the unknown to possible adventures among the shadows of the dead volcano. The glorious moon, serene in its majestic right, swung triumphantly across the cloudless sky, the hordes of stars beyond paled by the greater brilliance of the nearer orb. Spread far below, the darker slumbering world reposed, stretching away to invisible infinity, bearing upon its bosom the thing we call Modern Civilization. The ancient, forested hills rose and fell in ceaseless numbers, and between the smoke-filled canyons lay, like bands of gray mystery. And high above gleamed the mountain's heavenly crown; and higher still the light-points of a thousand constellations, sun-stars shining in the immensity of endless space. How wondrous was the night! How charged with the immutable purpose of the ages! How big with things beyond the power of human understanding!

And I was alone in all this splendid isolation—alone, subdued, impressed with a sense of my own littleness!

But presently came the sound of other voices, the click of other alpenstocks upon the stones. More of the nine young men were returning—beaten. Throughout the night I continued to meet them by ones and twos—strangers suddenly appearing through the gloom from the mysterious world above and disappearing into the mysterious world below. Some inquired the way to Horse Camp; but all were intent upon getting down. Some were forced back upon the great steep slope below Thumb Rock; the foremost reached the Rock at about two o'clock and were there assailed by an icy wind that froze their enthusiasm and sapped their strength. Some did not return until after daylight; but of the nine that started the night before, only one reached the summit of the mountain.

Finally the moon began to pale in the sky and I knew that dawn was near. Slowly the silver light gave way to the gray of early morning. As this change took place, I reached the first snow-fields at the foot of the steepening slopes. The snow was rough and icy. In places it was piled in great humps, and it looked as though it had avalanched earlier in the season. I crossed from the moraine on to a small ice-filled depression, ascended a slight rise, and, at five o'clock, stopped on a rocky island at the foot of the great slope, to eat breakfast and watch the sun rise.

The moon was still high in the sky. The black night shadow was retreating across the mountains to the west, with queer, purple rays shooting from it to mark the unevenness of the earth. The mighty shadow of Shasta, stretching westward, was thrown upon this night-shadow in a weird chromatic blending. Away to the southwest, Castle Crags loomed in somber gray. The southern and the western skies were diffused with marvelous tints of purple and mellow gold, with exquisite tawny shadings creeping out like fingers of beauty. The high hills were dark with their rich mantles of evergreen, occasionally tipped with the ermine of snow-fields, while the depressions between were filled with silvery smoke-wreaths. The marvelous panorama grew into the full light of day, while I in my darkened corridor between lava walls watched it grow. It would still be hours before the sunlight burst into the great depression.

There was an abundance of deliciously fried chicken in my pack; but my appetite, as usual under such conditions, was on a strike. I ate only half a gizzard, half a liver, and one cracker. I ate nothing more that day. As a matter of fact, it was all I ate between the supper I had had with Mr. Olberman the night before and the breakfast I had with him the following morning—a period of about thirty-six hours.

As I "sunrised" and breakfasted, I saw the party of men and women that had come to Horse Camp with the pack-train filing up the long slope below. There were ten of them. They looked very picturesque as their long line slowly crept up over the snow in the subdued light of dawn. By the time I had finished my breakfast, the foremost were about even with me; and from there until I had nearly reached Thumb Rock I was near some of them all the time.

I spent hours on that tedious slope below Thumb Rock. The snow was terribly rough and icy; in places it was piled into fantastic heaps with big depressions between. It was down and up, down and up, over the slippery surface. Progress was of necessity slow—and there was always my handicap to consider. I decided to try the snow-field on the left-hand side of the Heart, as the snow looked to be smoother from near the end of the barrier onward. But the slope finally became so steep that, considering its hardness, I saw that I would have to cut a long line of steps in order to get up that way with any degree of safety. So I crossed directly over the Heart to the opposite side and worked up the usual route to the red cliffs of the barrier. Meanwhile the members of the other party were dropping out, a few at a time, and only one got farther than Thumb Rock.

Even though I traveled so slowly, I was rather surprised

to find that my endurance was apparently as good as ever. True, I noticed a marked shortage of breath; but frequent brief rests were sufficient to restore my equilibrium and send me on each time, every pull bringing me a little nearer the top.

The lower line of red cliffs was surmounted with little difficulty. I saw that most of the season's climbers were passing the barrier on the cornice by Thumb Rock; but I made up my mind to risk an attempt on the upper cliffs. A tongue of icy snow led well up into one of the gullies; but beyond was a perpendicular face of conglomerate, six or eight feet high, with protruding knobs that would do for precarious footholds and handholds. I saw that I should have to go up so rapidly as to give these holds no time to break loose under me. Having tossed my ice-axe up on to the level surface at the top, and thus, as it were, having burned my bridges behind me, I made a dash up the sheer wall. Some of the knobs gave threateningly beneath my weight; but I did not allow them time to complete the operation and in a few seconds I lay panting beside my ice-axe, waiting for my breath to catch up with me. It was eleven o'clock; the sun was shining brightly, and a chilly breeze was blowing.

The barrier was evidently formed by a comparatively recent flow from one of the big craters of the mountain, the rim of which remains intact as the cirque of McCloud Glacier. North of the barrier the black rim-cliffs stand firm and perpendicular above the snow-filled basin.

When I got to a point where I could look into the amphitheater, I was surprised to see far more snow than had been there in June the year before. The great cornice extended beyond both end-cliffs of the barrier nearly to Thumb Rock. The snow leaned well up against the overhanging rocks; but I knew beneath the treacherous covering there was a great chasm, between snow and crag, into which it would be a frightful thing to fall. Evidently most of the climbers were coming up into the niche between Thumb Rock and the barrier and then passing the latter obstruction by means of the cornice. A well-marked trail led along the snow-ridge showing that many feet had gone that way. Yet I knew that every one of these feet had passed directly over the gulf beneath, and it seemed to me it must be only a matter of time until the snow gave way beneath some one's weight and a tragedy result.

An expenditure of fifty or one hundred dollars at the barrier would make the ascent of Shasta almost absolutely safe, aside, of course, from the danger of rolling rocks which can never be completely avoided. A rope stretched down one of the short chimneys; a few iron bolts driven into the rocks for footholds and handholds; or a short trail would turn the trick.

I now turned summitward along the great upper ridge of the mountain. The way was mostly bare of snow and the traveling in volcanic scoria. I had gone but a short distance when I met H. E. Garner, a resident of Yreka, returning from the summit. He was the only one of the party of ten who reached the top. He said there was no one above us, as he was the last one to come back, so I felt that I should have the whole upper part of the big peak to myself.

Garner, like me, had climbed the cliffs of the barrier; but he was going down by way of the cornice. I waited to see him pass the obstruction.

When he got to the top of the upper line of cliffs, he took a look over the edge and then stepped out on to the snow, following the tracks of those who had gone before. All went well until he was directly below the overhanging crag at the end of the lower barrier. Then, suddenly, the snow gave way and he dropped through. He threw out his arms. Down to his waist he went, and hung suspended, with the lower part of his body dangling in the void. My heart jumped into my throat. At every instant I expected to see the snow break about the edges of the hole and the man disappear into the chasm beyond hope of rescue. Yet I was too far away to be of any help. The situation was a desperate one. It looked as though I was to be sole witness of a lonely mountain tragedy.

With his arms pressing downward on the snow, Garner slowly worked his way out of the hole, while I, far above, looked on in trembling, powerless to assist him. At last he crawled out on to the firm snow on his hands and knees and cautiously rose to his feet. A few steps then took him around the point of rock and I saw him no more. It was one of the closest shaves I have ever seen on a mountain.

Once more I turned toward the summit. But another surprise awaited me. I was still in sight of the cornice when I saw a man sitting on a rocky point above me. Since all were supposed to have left the summit ridge, I could not account for his presence. I soon came up to him, and we immediately scraped up an acquaintance. He was Earl Gerard, of Westwood, California. That morning he and his brother, Allan Gerard, of Fargo, North Dakota, had started up the mountain from Horse Camp. While still well down in the big depression, they separated, Earl starting up the great ridge on the left, while Allan followed the usual route. Earl had had a hard and adventurous time of it. He got in among spires and cliffs; he narrowly escaped being caught in two rock-slides; and he showed me where he had passed directly above big crevasses on perilously steep snow-slopes. He had taken chances that I should not have thought of taking, alone; yet he had come unscathed on to the summit ridge of the mountain, and now he did not know which way to go to reach the top. As he afterwards told me, if he had not met me, he would probably have gone on down without ever having reached the highest point.

While we were talking, another man appeared on the cornice at the end of the barrier. Gerard said this was undoubtedly his brother. As he passed, the newcomer looked rather dubiously into the hole in the snow that had been made by Garner. He got by the cliffs without accident and came on in our direction. Seeing that he would gradually overtake us, we did not wait for him, but started on toward the top.

During rests we discussed mountains and mountaineering. Gerard said he had climbed but one other mountain and that was one up in Washington, years ago when he was a "kid." I asked him what Washington peak he had climbed, and he answered, "Mount Stuart." So thus we met upon common ground.

In due time the other Gerard overtook us, and we went on together, they a little in advance, since neither had a handicap similar to mine. When we came to the level snowfield near the summit crags we found the snow in very bad condition. It was wet and soft and water was standing on it in many places. There was a well-defined trail through it, made by other climbers. It was a tedious job getting across, for we often sank in to our knees, or farther; but the distance was not so very great and we were soon at the foot of the summit pinnacle.

And there was no ice on the crags. The ridge of cliffs where first approached is almost sheer, and the rocks are more or less shattered, so most climbers find it the part of wisdom to approach this citadel from the rear where the talus slope reaches almost to the top. We clambered over a mass of huge boulders that had tumbled down from the sheer walls above. A short pull above these brought us on to the solid lava-cliffs along which we scrambled a few steps to the record-boxes. Just beyond, a rocky point jutting out marked the utmost altitude of Shasta. Aside from the sheeted ice upon the pinnacle which had balked us the year before, I had found the climbing conditions much more difficult than they had been in June of 1922.

But the last foot of the great mountain had now been overcome. It was five minutes past two o'clock, and I had leisure to view the immense panorama that lay spread below on every side. But like that of all summer panoramas that spread away from the observer on a mighty mountain peak, the outer fringe of this one was lost in the smoky distance, and the haze from forest fires obscured the farther glories of the scene. The ranges of northern California and of southern Oregon rolled away from this common center—monarch of them all—with stretches of farmlands lying like gray lakes in vast expanses of dark blue. Looking downward to the north we could see the broad top of Shastina, the great, twelve-thousand-foot cone that leans as if for support upon the mightier dome. Emerald lakes, set like gems in fields of snow, gave a trace of delicate beauty to the sterner features of the old volcano.

The Government once had a monument upon the highest point of Shasta; but it was destroyed by lightning, years ago. Only a couple of record-boxes now are there to show that man has been there before. We hurriedly glanced through the names in the books. Of the twenty-four who had tried the climb on this day, only seven of us reached the summit. None of those who failed got farther than Thumb Rock.

When we had long viewed the great scene below, we reluctantly bade good-by to the topmost spire and turned downward to see the wonder of Shasta. I had read much of the so-called boiling sulphur spring and I had a longing to look upon it with my own eyes. We soon found it. When we were a short distance down the talus slope, a little to the west of where we had come up, we heard a mighty gurgling roar and saw steam rising from farther down the slope.

This subterranean cataract appears to start well up the talus slope only a little lower than the highest point on the mountain. It rushes down nearly to the foot of the pinnacle and apparently turns and disappears along a depression between the main summit and another near-by peak just to the south. From the noise it makes, there must be a veritable river of it, and it is certainly forced upward through some internal chimney from a cauldron in the heart of the mountain. The whole thing would doubtless be invisible had not visitors pricked its outer covering. The underground channel is overlaid by several inches of what seems to be a blue clay. Wherever holes have been gouged in this by the points of alpenstocks or other sharp instruments, the boiling water bubbles through, making animated little springs from which the steam floats away. We saw several of these. The loose rocks on top are so hot that it is hardly possible to hold the hand on some of them, and the whole clay surface is uncomfortably warm.

I caught some of the boiling water in my cup and let it cool until I could drink it. To my surprise, the taste was agreeable—rather sour, resembling lemonade. I drank a considerable quantity and suffered no ill effects. Indeed, the rinds of many lemons lying about gave evidence that former visitors had here concocted a drink that probably is unique.

As I looked about upon this lonely scene, it was hard for me to realize that hundreds upon hundreds of human beings had been here before me. In fact, on the little flat just below where we sat were several rock enclosures that had been piled up for shelter by men who had had occasion to spend one or more nights at this place. Even in severe storm, it is possible for a man to survive, as the heat of the rocks above the boiling spring will keep one from freezing. More than one man whose name is a household word has passed the night in this remarkable location.

I had planned some on staying alone all night at the spring, should the weather continue favorable; but at three o'clock ominous-appearing clouds were beginning to gather near the mountain and it looked as though a storm were brewing. So I thought it best to get down.

My descent was made leisurely. The Gerards drew ahead of me. I passed the barrier by means of the gullies, having a rather slippery time of it on the icy snow. There was no sliding this day below Thumb Rock: the snow was far too rough. So I went right down the center of the Heart.

More people had come up from Sisson to climb the mountain. It is a curious thing to see how many men and women rush up to Horse Camp from this town, expecting to rush up the mountain and rush down again. Most of them fail in the higher rushes. Because of its proximity to the Southern Pacific Railway and the Pacific Highway, Shasta is probably the most favorably situated of any of our great peaks for this hectic mountaineering. When more individuals come to realize that such a tremendous dome is not to be taken on the jump, there will be more successful attempts to reach the top.

Shasta should receive more serious attention. It is worthy of better-regulated plans.

Next morning I visited the Alpine Lodge and delved briefly in the records there; but at seven-forty-five I bade my genial host, Olberman, good-bye, and started down through the great Shasta firs, intent upon catching the northbound train that was due to pass through Sisson just before noon. My third of a century of mountaineering was more than rounded out, and, if this should be my last journey to the ice-bound heights, I could not complain.

THE END

OTHER BOOKS FROM THE MOUNTAINEERS

50 Hikes in Mount Rainier National Park
101 Hikes in the North Cascades
102 Hikes in the Alpine Lakes, South Cascades and Olympics
103 Hikes in Southwestern British Columbia
109 Walks in B.C.'s Lower Mainland
Trips and Trails, 1: Family Camps, Short Hikes and View Roads around the North Cascades
Trips and Trails, 2: Family Camps, Short Hikes and View Roads in the Olympics, Mt. Rainier and South Cascades
Bicycling the Backroads Around Puget Sound
Bicycling the Backroads of Northwest Washington
Footsore 1: Walks and Hikes Around Puget Sound
Footsore 2: Walks and Hikes Around Puget Sound
Discover Southeast Alaska with Pack and Paddle
55 Ways to the Wilderness in Southcentral Alaska
Hikers' Map to the North Cascades: Routes and Rocks in the Mt. Challenger Quadrangle
Guide to Leavenworth Rock Climbing Areas
Cascade Alpine Guide: Climbing and High Routes, Columbia River to Stevens Pass
Cascade Alpine Guide: Climbing and High Routes, Stevens Pass to Rainy Pass
Climbers' Guide to the Olympic Mountains
Darrington and Index: Rock Climbing Guide
Snow Trails: Ski and Snowshoe Routes in the Cascades
Mountaineering: Freedom of the Hills
Medicine for Mountaineering
Mountaineering First Aid
Snowshoeing
The South Cascades: The Gifford Pinchot National Forest
Challenge of Mount Rainier
The Unknown Mountain
Fire and Ice: The Cascade Volcanoes
Across the Olympic Mountains: The Press Expedition
Men, Mules and Mountains: Lieutenant O'Neil's Olympic Expeditions
The Coffee Chased Us Up: Monte Cristo Memories
Challenge of the North Cascades
Bicycling Notes
Hiking Notes
Climbing Notes
Mountains of the World
Northwest Trees
The Ascent of Denali
Canoe Routes: Yukon Territory
Canoe Routes: British Columbia
Storm and Sorrow in the High Pamirs